Private International Law in the Czech Republic

Private International Law in the Czech Republic

Second Edition

Monika Pauknerová
Magdalena Pfeiffer

This book was originally published as a monograph in the International Encyclopaedia of Laws/Private International Law

General Editor: Roger Blanpain
Founding Editor: Frank Hendrickx
Volume Editor: Bea Verschraegen

Wolters Kluwer

Published by:
Kluwer Law International B.V.
PO Box 316
2400 AH Alphen aan den Rijn
The Netherlands
E-mail: international-sales@wolterskluwer.com
Website: lrus.wolterskluwer.com

Sold and distributed in North, Central and South America by:
Wolters Kluwer Legal & Regulatory U.S.
7201 McKinney Circle
Frederick, MD 21704
United States of America
Email: customer.service@wolterskluwer.com

Sold and distributed in all other countries by:
Air Business Subscriptions
Rockwood House
Haywards Heath
West Sussex
RH16 3DH
United Kingdom
Email: international-customerservice@wolterskluwer.com

Printed on acid-free paper

ISBN 978-94-035-1332-4

e-Book: ISBN 978-94-035-1372-0
web-PDF: ISBN 978-94-035-1401-7

This title is available on www.kluwerlawonline.com

Printed in the United Kingdom.

The Authors

Monika Pauknerová is the author of General Introduction, Part I and Part III of this monograph. She is Professor of Private International Law and International Commercial Law at the Faculty of Law, Charles University, Prague and Senior Research Fellow at the Institute of State and Law, Academy of Sciences, Prague. She graduated at the Charles University in 1975, completed her postgraduate studies at the Institute of State and Law of the Czechoslovak Academy of Sciences in Prague with the CSc. – *Candidatus Scientiarum* degree (thesis 'Liability of the carrier in the international carriage of goods conventions') in 1980. Since then she has been a research fellow at this Institute (now only part-time). Since 1993 she has been teaching Private International Law and International Commercial Law at the Charles University As an Associated Professor in 1996 (habilitation thesis 'Companies in private international law') and Full Professor since 2002. In 2009 she was awarded *Doctor Scientiarum* degree (DSc.), with the thesis 'European Private International Law', by the Academy of Sciences of the Czech Republic.

She is a well-known expert in Private International Law with almost two hundred publications (original papers and monographs). Since 1985 she is an arbitrator at the Arbitration Court in Prague. She is the Vice-President of the Czech Society for International Law. Since 2003 she has been the President of the Czech National Committee of the International Association of Legal Science (IALS) and a member of the International Committee of Comparative Law of the IALS. In 2003, she was elected as a member of the International Academy of Comparative Law, and since 2007 she has been the President of the Czech National Committee of this Academy. Since 2004 she has been a member of the prestigious European Group for Private International Law, and since 2014 a member of the Governing Council of UNIDROIT (re-elected in 2018); she is also a member of several editorial boards and learned societies.

The Authors

Magdalena Pfeiffer is the author of Part II of this monograph. She is Associate Professor of Private International Law and International Commercial Law at the Faculty of Law, Charles University in Prague. She graduated from the Philosophical Faculty of Charles University in 1990 and from the Law Faculty of Charles University in 2006. She joined the Law Faculty of Charles University as an internal PhD candidate in 2006 (PhD thesis: 'Habitual residence in Private International Law') and has been a Lecturer in Private International Law and International Trade Law since 2009. Following her habilitation ('Law applicable to cross-border succession relations'), she was appointed as Associate Professor in 2018. She is a member of the Czech Society for International Law.

Table of Contents

Table of Contents

List of Abbreviations

AA	The Act on Arbitral Proceedings and Enforcement of Arbitral Awards No. 216/1964 Coll. (Arbitration Act) (*Zákon o rozhodčím řízení a o výkonu rozhodčích nálezů*)
ABCH	Act on Bills of Exchange, Promissory Notes and Cheques No. 191/1950 Coll., as amended (*Zákon směnečný a šekový*)
ABGB	Allgemeines bürgerliches Gesetzbuch
Art.	Article
AUB	Acta Universitatis Brunensis
AUC	Acta Universitatis Carolinae
BA	Bankruptcy and Composition Act No. 328/1991 Coll., as amended (*Zákon o konkursu a vyrovnání*), repealed by the InsA
BCA	Business Corporations Act No. 90/2012 Coll., as amended (*Zákon o obchodních korporacích*)
CCP	The Code of Civil Procedure No. 99/1963 Coll., as amended (*Občanský* soudní řád)
CCPSC	The Code of Civil Procedure in Special Cases No. 292/2013 Coll.
CISG	Convention on Contracts for the International Sale of Goods
CivC	The Civil Code No. 89/2012 Coll., as amended (*Občanský zákoník*)
CivC 1964	The old Civil Code No. 40/1964 Coll., as amended, repealed by the CivC
CJEU	Court of Justice of the EU
Clunet	Journal du droit international
Coll.	Collection of Laws of the Czech (Czechoslovak) Republic (*Sbírka zákonů České republiky*)

List of Abbreviations

Coll. IT	Collection of International Treaties of the Czech Republic (*Sbírka mezinárodních smluv České republiky*)
ComC	The Commercial Code No. 513/1991 Coll., as amended (*Obchodní zákoník*), repealed by the CivC
COMI	Centre of Main Interests
Comm.	Communication (*Sdělení*)
ČMP	*Časopis pro mezinárodní právo* (International Law Review)
EC	European Community (Communities)
EEA	European Economic Area
EFTA	European Free Trade Association
EU	European Union
FA	Family Act No. 94/1963 Coll., as amended (*Zákon o rodině*), repealed by the CivC
IALS	International Association of Legal Science
InsA	Insolvency Act No. 182/2006 Coll., as amended (*Zákon o úpadku azpůsobech jeho řešení – insolvenční zákon*)
IPRax	Praxis des Internationalen Privat- und Verfahrensrechts
ITC	International Trade Code
Lugano Convention	Lugano Convention on jurisdiction and the recognition and enforcement of judgments in civil and commercial matters, OJ L 147, 10.6.2009, p. 5
para.	Paragraph
PIL	Private International Law
PILA, PIL Act 1963	The Act Concerning Private International Law and the Rules of Procedure Relating Thereto (Private International Law Act) No. 97/1963 Coll., as amended (*Zákon o mezinárodním právu soukromém a procesním)*
PIL Act	Act on Private International Law No. 91/2012 Coll., as amended (*Zákon o mezinárodním právu soukromém*)
R	Collection of Judicial Decisions and Opinions of the Supreme Court (of the Czech Republic) (*Sbírka soudních rozhodnutí a stanovisek*)

RabelsZ	Rabels Zeitschrift für ausländisches und internationales Privatrecht
Recueil	Recueil des cours, Académie de Droit international de la Haye
Rev. crit.	Revue critique de droit international privé
Rome Convention	Rome Convention on the Law Applicable to Contractual Obligations, OJ 2005 C 334, p. 1 (consolidated version)
Rsp.	Arbitral Award No. (the Arbitration Court attached to the Economic Chamber of the Czech Republic and Agricultural Chamber of the Czech Republic)
Sec.	Section (in Czech wording – §)
SMP	*Studie z mezinárodního práva* (Studies in International Law)
tlq	The Lawyer Quarterly, International Journal for Legal Research
YbPIL	Yearbook of Private International Law
Journal PIL	Journal of Private International Law

List of Abbreviations

General Introduction

§1. Historical Development

1. Private International Law (PIL) and Procedure in the Czech Republic has a long tradition stemming from the Vienna Draft of PIL of 1913.[1] Czech law belongs to the continental law system (the civil law system). The reception of Roman law occurred as early as at the beginning of the fourteenth century by adoption of *Ius regale montanorum* (elaborated between 1,300 and 1,305 at the request of the Czech King Wenceslaus II), and its importance spread throughout the Czech lands and was respected in all of Central Europe. However, under the Habsburg reign, the tradition of Czech law and Czech legal thinking was driven to the background and entirely deafened by the Austrian legal tradition – especially by the enactment of the General Civil Code (Allgemeines bürgerliches Gesetzbuch, hereinafter ABGB) in 1811, which was applied to all lands within the Austrian Empire. After the collapse of the Austro-Hungarian Empire, the Czechoslovak Republic was founded on 28 October 1918 as one of the successor states. In the Czech lands, that is Bohemia and Moravia, Austrian law was adopted by the so-called 'Reception Act'. From a comparative law aspect, Czech law belonged to the Austrian circle of continental law; Slovak law, its concept and institutions also belonged to continental law as based on Roman law.[2] The Czech science of PIL began to develop after the division of Charles University (founded in 1348 by Charles the IV, Czech King and Holy Roman Emperor), including its Law Faculty into separate Czech and German schools in 1882. At the beginning of this century, lectures on PIL were given by Prof. Jan Krčmář.[3] At the Faculty of Law of Masaryk University in Brno, Moravia, established in 1918, the leading academic was Prof. M.A. Zimmermann.[4]

1. *See* text in F. Mänhardt, *Die Kodifikation des österreichischen Internationalen Privatrechts*, Anhang III, Entwurf eines Gesetzes über Internationales Privatrecht (1914), 149–155, Schriften zum internationalen Recht, 10, Duncker&Humblot, Berlin 1978.
2. *See* V. Knapp, *Velké právní systémy, Úvod do srovnávací právní vědy* [*Great Legal Systems, Introduction to Comparative Law*] 118–120 (please stet all references to towns where the books were published! For example, Beck has publishing houses in all European countries. Moreover, in older books, you cannot google the location where the book was published. Beck 1st ed. 1996).
3. *See* J. Krčmář, *Úvod do mezinárodního práva soukromého* [*Introduction to Private International Law*] (Bursík & Kohout 1906).
4. *See* M.A. Zimmermann, *Mezinárodní právo soukromé* [*Private International Law*] (Právník 1933).

2. In the former Czechoslovakia, PIL was not regulated by a uniform act until 1948. In the Czech lands, in addition to the General Civil Code (ABGB) which contained only a few separate and brief provisions dealing with conflict of laws (*see* sections 4, 34–37, 300 ABGB), conflict rules were found in various special acts, for example in the Execution Order, and some areas remained without any legal regulation (e.g., Family Law, especially Matrimony and Divorce). In Slovakia, mostly customary law applied, so principles of PIL were formulated only by theory and case law. The consequence of this legal dualism led to the application of different rules with respect to the foreign element, or in terms of whether the issue was to be dealt within the Czech lands or in Slovakia, where different rules applied.

3. The initial draft of the PIL Act was prepared as far back as 1913 by the Ministry of Justice in Vienna, in particular by Jan Krčmář, Fryderyk Zoll and Gustav Walker. The Vienna Draft, widely recognized as an outstanding work,[5] greatly influenced not only the codification of Polish PIL in 1926 but also, even more noticeably, the Czechoslovak Private International Law Act of 1948.[6] The Vienna Draft was the primary basis for the elaboration of the governmental proposal of the Civil Code in the Czechoslovak Republic between the world wars (1920–1936). The preparatory works continued after 1945 (the sole Draft on PIL having been excerpted from the Civil Code Draft), and resulted in the adoption of the Act No. 41/1948 Coll., Concerning Private International and Interregional Law and the Legal Status of Aliens in the Sphere of Private Law, on 11 March 1948.

4. In 1948 when the first Act Concerning Private International and Interregional Law and the Legal Status of Aliens in the Sphere of Private Law[7] was adopted legal dualism in Czechoslovakia still existed, and its adoption is considered to be one of the first significant steps to overcome this dualism.[8] In 1950, a new Civil Code was adopted, which unified civil law in both parts of Czechoslovakia and repealed, *inter alia*, the Austrian Civil Code of 1811. This Act was a modern, detailed codification of conflict rules. However, it rather quickly became outdated in many respects, both in its contents and terminology, especially with the substantial changes since the Communist *coup d'état* in 1948 concerning policy, economics and law (nationalization, ownership changes, the state organization of foreign trade, etc.), as well as with the enactment of new uniform legal acts for all of Czechoslovakia.

5. A new, so-called 'socialist' Constitution was adopted in 1960. At this time, extensive codification works also began, which completely restructured the whole legal system. The Civil Code of 1950 was replaced by a group of new codes, namely the Civil Code, the Economic Code, and the International Trade Code (ITC). The

5. *See e.g.*, J. Kropholler, *Internationales Privatrecht* 71 (J.C.B. Mohr (Paul Siebeck) 3d ed. 1997).
6. *See* III A.N. Makarov, *Sources*, in IECL, *Private International Law*, Ch. 2, 5 (J.C.B. Mohr (Paul Siebeck)).
7. *See* E. Ledrer, *Nové zákony o nařízení* [*New Acts and Orders*] (Linhart 1948); F. Korkisch, *Das neue internationale Privatrecht der Tschechoslowakei* 410–450 with further references (RabelsZ 1952).
8. *See* Z. Kučera, *Třicet let československého mezinárodního práva soukromého* [*Thirty Years of Czechoslovak Private International Law*, in Czech] 54 (Acta Universitatis Carolinae iuridica 1975).

former system of private law was restructured and divided into three relatively separate regulations. This division was, of course, also relevant in a PIL sense. While the Civil Code[9] governed mutual property relations between individuals, and those between individuals and the so-called socialist organizations, the Economic Code[10] governed mutual economic relations arising from the regulation and management of the national economy on the basis of the central planning system between socialist organizations. The relationships between Czechoslovak enterprises for foreign trade and their commercial partners from abroad (international commercial connections, property relations in international commerce) were governed by the ITC.[11] If under the rules of PIL Czechoslovak law were to be applied, the ITC was applicable – in international commercial connections specified in detail in section 2 ITC (*see* section 3 ITC). The ITC contained classical provisions particularly concerning international commercial contracts. All these codes entered into force on 1 April 1964, together with the new PIL Act – 'The Act Concerning Private International Law and the Rules of Procedure Relating Thereto' (PIL Act 1963).[12]

6. The PIL Act 1963 formed part of the codification work of the mid-1960s. Despite the afore-mentioned substantial changes to the whole private law or, more exactly, the civil, economic and commercial law system in Czechoslovakia, PIL Act 1963 preserved many provisions of the preceding PIL Act of 1948, which served well and was adapted to the new system only within the necessary limits. In comparison with the preceding PIL Act of 1948, which merely included conflict rules and the legal status of aliens, the PIL Act 1963 consisted of two parts. The first part of the PIL Act 1963 covered provisions dealing with conflict of laws and the legal status of aliens, and the second part covered international civil procedural law. In my opinion, this combination with procedural rules, originally included within the Code of Civil Procedure (CCP), proved to be efficient. Arbitration proceedings in international commerce were covered by a special Act concerning arbitration in international trade and the enforcement of arbitral awards,[13] which, in addition to provisions concerning jurisdiction and procedure, provided for conflict rules on the admissibility of arbitration proceedings, requisites of an arbitration agreement, etc. Conflict rules concerning corporations, as well as some other relevant rules for commercial relations with an international element, were included by the ITC.

7. After the 'Velvet Revolution' of 1989 a new era in the political and economic life of Czechoslovakia began followed by fundamental changes to Czechoslovak legislation. The rule of law, transition to political pluralism and market economy were reflected in corresponding amendments to the Constitution. For PIL, the most important change was the removal of a hierarchy of different kinds of ownership. Equal protection was to be granted to all owners, and the expropriation or other forced limitation of property should have been allowed only if in common interest,

9. Act No. 40/1964 Coll., the Civil Code.
10. Act No. 109/1964 Coll., the Economic Code.
11. Act No. 101/1963 Coll., the International Trade Code.
12. Act No. 97/1963 Coll., the PIL Act.
13. Act No. 98/1963 Coll., Relating to Arbitration in International Trade and to the Enforcement of Arbitral Awards.

by the prescription of law or on the basis of the law, and in return for compensation. More generally, the protection of human rights was also introduced.

8. In 1990, radical economic reform began, which was accompanied by fundamental changes to the Czechoslovak system of civil, economic and commercial law. In the first stage, the three basic codes, that is the Civil Code, the Economic Code and the ITC, remained in force – the Economic Code being substantially amended to meet the most urgent requirements of the transition economy. In 1992, the Commercial Code[14] entered into force and repealed, *inter alia*, the Economic Code and the ITC. The Commercial Code replaced the ITC regulation also with respect to the provisions relevant to PIL aspects, especially in terms of conflict rules concerning corporations and/or companies and also regarding contractual relations in international trade. The Civil Code was substantially amended by the so-called Large Amendment.[15] The PIL Act 1963 was amended only partially as to the validity of the marriage of Czechoslovak citizens which took place abroad, and as to the changed structure of Czechoslovak judicial bodies.[16] PIL was also amended indirectly by the enactment of the Arbitration Act (AA),[17] which included a special part dealing with relations with foreign countries, laying down, *inter alia*, conflict of laws rules.

9. The Czech and Slovak Federative Republic dissolved in 1992. On 1 January 1993, two independent states, the Czech Republic and the Slovak Republic, came into being. In principle, both successor states entered into existing domestic law and binding international treaties, although not in an identical way. Further developments of the two legal systems, the systems of the Czech Republic and the Slovak Republic, are fully independent. As regards PIL regulation, while in Slovakia the PIL Act 1963, as amended, still applies, in Czechia a new PIL Act introducing a number of important changes was adopted in 2012 and entered into force in 2014.[18] In 2012, the process of the complete recodification of Czech private law was accomplished. New codes, which are closely linked to one another, have been adopted: Civil Code, No. 89/2012 Coll., Business Corporations Act, No. 90/2012 Coll., and PIL Act, No. 91/2012 Coll. The process of recodification was lengthy and difficult, accompanied by harsh intellectual discussions, primarily with respect to the new Civil Code and regarding the sources to be used and to find inspiration in.[19] Changes introduced by the new PIL Act are far from being as substantial and revolutionary as are those in the new Civil Code. The main reason for this difference is that conflict of law rules are considered neutral, and therefore more resistant with respect to the governing political and social system: the PIL Act 1963 was a standard European codification of PIL. The new PIL Act is primarily a reaction to the new Civil Code reflecting its new legal terminology and new legal concepts. But it also reflects

14. Act No. 513/1991 Coll., the Commercial Code.
15. Act No. 509/1991 Coll.
16. *See* Acts No. 234/1992 Coll., and No. 264/1992 Coll.
17. Act No. 216/1994 Coll., on Arbitral Proceedings and the Enforcement of Arbitral Awards.
18. Act No. 91/2012 Coll., on PIL.
19. In details *see* D. Elischer, O. Frinta & M. Pauknerová, *Recodification of Private Law in the Czech Republic*, in *The Scope and Structure of Civil Codes* 105–132 (J.C. Rivera ed., Springer 2013).

new trends in PIL and, e.g., replaces in most cases the connecting factor of nationality for that of habitual residence, in particular as regards personal, family and succession law. The intention of the legislature was to concentrate all rules related to PIL in one piece of legislation. The new PIL Act thus includes relevant conflict of law and international civil procedure rules concerning not only a general part, rules regarding persons, obligations, property, family and succession law, as well as civil procedure, but also conflict rules on bills of exchange, promissory notes, cheques and securities, rules on international insolvency, and on international arbitration. Rules on legal status of foreigners (alien law) that form traditional part of the Czech (formerly Czechoslovak) PIL are also included in the PIL Act. The changes are thus both structural and substantive.[20]

§2. International and Supranational Legal Framework

10. Pursuant to the Constitution of the Czech Republic,[21] the Czech Republic is a sovereign, unitary, democratic, and law-abiding state, founded upon the principles of respect for the rights and freedoms of the individual and citizen (Article 1). The power of the state can be exercised only in cases and within the limits described by law, and by the means set out by the law (Article 2(3)). The Charter of Fundamental Rights and Freedoms is a part of the constitutional order of the Czech Republic [22] (Article 3). Fundamental rights and freedoms enjoy protection of judicial bodies (Article 4). Promulgated treaties, to the ratification of which Parliament has given its consent and by which the Czech Republic is bound, form a part of the legal order; if a treaty provides something other than that which a statute provides, the treaty shall apply (Article 10). In other words, binding international treaties and conventions take precedence over the Czech domestic law.

11. The Czech Republic became a Member State of the European Union (EU) from 1 May 2004. This was the date on which the Treaty between EU Member States and the Czech Republic (along with other countries) concerning the accession of the Czech Republic (and other countries) to the EU entered into force; it was also the date on which the Act concerning the conditions of accession of the Czech Republic (and other countries) and the adjustments to the Treaties on which the EU was founded entered into force. The Act constitutes an integral part of the Accession Treaty and stipulates the requirements for the accession and modifications of other treaties invoked by the accession.[23] Amendments to Czech law were introduced in relation to the accession of the Czech Republic to the EU. One of the most important changes was the amendment to the Constitution of the Czech Republic

20. In details *see* in particular M. Pauknerová & M. Pfeiffer, *The New Act on Private International Law in the Czech Republic: Starting Points and Perspectives within the European Union*, 10 J. PIL, 205 (2014); and P. Uhlířová, *New Private International Law in the Czech Republic*, 16 YbPIL, 469 (2014/2015).
21. Constitutional Act No. 1/1993 Coll., The Constitution of the Czech Republic.
22. Constitutional Act No. 23/1991 Coll.
23. Act No. 44/2004 Coll. IT, and OJ of 23 Sep. 2003.

allowing for certain powers of the bodies of the Czech Republic to be transferred by treaty to an international organization or institution (Article 10a (1) of the Constitution).

12. Accordingly, the PIL Act contains a special provision on its relationship with both international conventions and EU law. According to the general clause (section 2) the PIL Act shall be applied within the limits of the rules of international conventions binding the Czech Republic and within the directly applicable provisions of the EU law. As a consequence, the new PIL Act focuses on, first, general legal issues, and, second, legal issues that are not covered by international conventions and EU law and, in procedural law, mainly on third-country relations.

§3. Nature and Scope

13. Czech private law, including PIL, is traditional continental law. The Civil Code is based on standard principles of the European continental legal tradition – particularly in Austrian and German context. PIL forms a part of the Czech legal system, it is a part of Czech domestic law. As far as the nature of Czech PIL is concerned, several opinions exist. Textbooks and monographs about PIL are based on the opinion that PIL is an independent, special branch of Czech domestic law.[24] Under the civilist tradition, PIL is part of civil law, as it is primarily concerned with civil law relations, and based upon civil law concepts.[25] The internationalist approach, under which PIL forms part of international law, is not contended in the current Czech legal literature.[26] In general, within private law, particular attention is paid to PIL. Courses in PIL are compulsory at the law faculties of all universities in the Czech Republic.

14. The PIL Act is rather broadly conceived as it comprises rules on conflict of laws, provisions on the legal status of aliens, as well as rules on international civil procedure. The mission of the new PIL Act 2012 was to concentrate all PIL rules into one piece of legislation. The existing material scope of the PIL Act has been extended, as some conflict rules and international civil procedure rules were taken over from other legal acts, for example rules on international company law that were originally included in the Commercial Code, which was repealed by the new Civil Code (now section 30 PIL Act), or rules on international arbitration that were taken

24. *See* Z. Kučera, et al. *Mezinárodní právo soukromé* [*Private International Law*] 35 with further references; P. Kalenský, *Trends of Private International Law* 158 (Academia Prague 1971); R. Bystrický, *Mezinárodní právo soukromé* [*Private International Law*], textbook, 21 (Orbis Prague 1958).

25. *See e.g.*, A. Kanda, *Caractéristiques et tendances de la réglementation juridique des relations commerciales internationales* (in Czech with French summary), Studie z mezinárodního práva [*Studies in International Law*], 204–206 (Academia Prague 1986); Krčmář, *supra*, 99.

26. *See e.g.*, O. Kunz, *Některé otázky mezinárodního práva soukromého v novější právní nauce socialistických zemí* [*Questions of Private International Law in the Recent Legal Science of Socialist States*], *Právník* (Lawyer), 104 (1977).

over from the Arbitration Act (now sections 117–122 PIL Act), etc. In civil procedure, the jurisdiction of Czech courts is based on a sufficiently close link between the forum and the considered case: this typically concerns relationships with subjects from third countries which are not covered by the EU legislation.

15. The scope of PIL includes:

(a) conflict rules, which are the nucleus of PIL;
(b) the so-called direct rules of substantive law, i.e., uniform substantive law rules, the sources of which are mostly international conventions; these rules are directly applicable to relations with an international element, that is they shall be used directly, without the previous application of conflict rules;
(c) rules governing the legal status of aliens; and
(d) rules of international civil procedure law.

16. The PIL Act not only follows the tradition established by its predecessor the PIL Act 1963 but also reflects the new concepts brought in by the new Czech Civil Code. At the same time the PIL Act takes into consideration the development and tendencies in PIL on legislations in other states, as well as the required compatibility of the Czech system with the EU legislation. The new PIL Act encompasses 125 sections as compared to seventy sections of the former PIL Act 1963, which means that it is almost double in size. It is divided into eight chapters. Chapters 1–3 (sections 1–28) contain provisions regarding general issues of PIL. Chapter 4 is the most comprehensive chapter (sections 29–101); it entails jurisdiction, conflict rules, provisions regarding recognition and enforcement of foreign decisions in respect to individual kinds of relations (legal capacity, agency, limitation, family matters, registered partnership, rights in rem, succession, obligations, labour law, unilateral legal acts, set-off, non-contractual obligations arising out of violations of privacy and rights relating to personality, including defamation). Chapter 5 (sections 101–110) contains provisions regarding legal assistance to aliens, Chapter 6 (sections 111–116) includes provisions in regard to insolvency, Chapter 7 relates to arbitration matters (sections 117–122). The last chapter, Chapter 8 (sections 123–125), consists of transitional and final provisions.

17. A number of provisions in the PIL Act is devoted to general issues of PIL. These issues have so far been dealt with in the Czech doctrine or case law only, with no stipulation in the former PIL Act 1963, except for *renvoi* and public order reservation. New provisions regarding general issues such as overriding mandatory rules (sections 3 and 25), evasion of law (section 5), qualification or characterization (section 20), incidental or preliminary questions (section 22), determination and application of foreign law (section 23) have now become part of the new legislation. The first three chapters of the PIL Act (sections 1–28) deal with general issues of PIL, subdivided further into general issues of international civil procedure and general issues of conflict of laws. The Czech PIL Act includes not only conflict rules but also provisions regulating international civil procedure and arbitration: mainly jurisdiction rules and provisions on the recognition and enforcement of foreign decisions and foreign arbitral awards, as well as provisions on legal assistance.

§4. CHARACTERISTICS OF CZECH PIL

18. Special characteristics of Czech PIL, as outlined in the preceding paragraphs, may be summarized as follows:

(i) Czech Law is exclusively written law. As regards PIL, special legal regulation, the Act on PIL was adopted in 2012 (*see supra*). PIL regulation has a relatively long tradition in the Czech Republic when compared with other countries. Special characteristics of Czech PIL stem from the characteristics of the Czech law in general.

(ii) The legal regulation of PIL in the Czech Republic is comprehensive and relatively detailed. The PIL Act includes not only conflict rules but also provisions concerning the legal status of aliens and rules on international civil procedure law. Such a legal concept, combining both conflict rules and procedural rules, has been considered as an advanced approach, based on the fact that questions of the conflict of laws and procedure are closely linked, particularly in legal practice. A judge, dealing with a case which includes a 'foreign element', must first consider the question of the jurisdiction of Czech courts. He can find both jurisdiction and conflict rules in one legal regulation, which deals with private law relations having an international element. From this point of view including conflict rules and procedural rules in one act seems to be appropriate. Similar concept of PIL acts has been adopted in Switzerland, Italy, or Belgium, and it is also the concept of some Hague Conventions and EU Regulations.

(iii) PIL is mostly considered as either an independent branch of Czech domestic law or a special part of Czech civil law.

(iv) The general principles of PIL in the Czech Republic have been defined as follows:
   - the principle of the equality of all legal systems: no discrimination of the law of another country is allowed:
   - the principle of conflicts justice, i.e., an equitable solution with regard to conflict of laws, corresponding to the spatially or locally closest connection;
   - the principle of the reasonable settlement of legal relations, traditionally based on the characteristic performance relevancy and habitual residence of the performer; and
   - the principle of the priority of binding international treaties and priority of EU law over the domestic law.

(e) The Czech Republic is, as a result of the dissolution of the Czech and Slovak federation in 1993, a unitary state with only one legal system. If Czech law is the applicable law in a particular case, the question of legal areas shall not arise.

(f) It should be stressed that the Czech language is the mother tongue of 10 million people, and from this point of view it is very important that the Czech

Republic is a contracting party to the European Convention concerning Information on Foreign Law of 1968, and to the Additional Protocol to this Convention of 1978.[27]

§5. Domestic Authorities Involved, Interpretation and Application of PIL

19. Domestic authorities applying PIL are courts, notaries and some non-judicial authorities, mostly registry offices and some regional and district administrative authorities. The Czech Republic has traditionally been participating in the Hague Conference on PIL, as well as in other institutions unifying private law, such as the UNCITRAL, Council of Europe, etc. Judicial bodies had acquired experience with cases with international element long before the accession of the Czech Republic to the EU. This tradition and experience are reflected in the new PIL Act, which, as already mentioned, expressly states the priority of promulgated international treaties and directly applicable provisions of the EU law over its provisions.

20. Important interpretative role is played by the case law of the Supreme Court and the Supreme Administrative Court, upper courts, and the Constitutional Court. Effective assistance is provided by the International Civil Department of the Ministry of Justice and the Internal Judicial Network for cooperation in civil and commercial matters, which is a platform for judges and other experts specialized in cross-border cases.

21. The principle of equality of all legal systems is related to the principles of the treatment of foreign law in litigation before Czech courts and other authorities. These principles may be subdivided as follows: (a) The duty to apply foreign law: if a conflict of laws rule determines the law of another country as applicable, the foreign law must be applied (section 23 PIL Act). This principle stands with respect to application of conflict rules contained in the domestic law, binding international conventions and EU law. The principle of reciprocity in the recognition of foreign laws no longer applies. (b) Foreign law applies as a law and not as a fact which needs to be proved. (c) The principle *Iura novit curia* refers to Czech domestic law (section 121 of the CCP).[28] The judicial organ is obliged to take all necessary measures to ascertain the provisions of foreign law; it may request the opinion of the Ministry of Justice (*see* section 23 PIL Act). It is drawn from the wording of the PIL Act that such opinions are not binding on courts as the judges should be independent. (d) Foreign law should be applied in the same manner as in the country of its origin, that is, the judge or arbitrator should take into account not only the wording of such foreign provisions but also the broader legal framework as well as the judicature (*see* expressly section 23 PIL Act).

27. *See* Communication No. 221/1998 Coll. – both documents entered into force in the Czech Republic on 25 Sep. 1998.
28. Act No. 99/1963 Coll., Civil Procedure Code, as amended.

22. The principle of equality of all legal systems does not apply absolutely. Some exceptional cases exist under which the *lex fori* shall apply instead of the otherwise applicable foreign law (on the basis of the respective conflict rule). This is especially the case of the overriding mandatory rules ('rules of necessary application'), which are to be taken into account regardless of the governing law. Such rules belong mostly to domestic law (*lex fori,* section 3 PIL Act), and rather exceptionally, also overriding mandatory rules of a foreign state might be taken into account (section 25 PIL Act). Exceptionally, if provisions of an otherwise applicable foreign law (i.e., applicable pursuant to conflict rules) do not apply due to public policy reservation (section 4 PIL Act), the *lex fori* provisions are applied instead. Foreign law might also be replaced by the *lex fori* if the law, quite exceptionally, provides for it. For instance, if under conflict rules on adoption a foreign law which does not permit adoption, or does so under extremely difficult conditions, would have to be applied, Czech law shall be applied instead provided the adopter or at least one of the adopting spouses or the adoptee is habitually resident in the Czech Republic (cf. section 61 PIL Act). Finally, it should be remarked that the *lex fori* would apply also if the provisions of an applicable foreign law could not be ascertained by the court in reasonable time (section 23 PIL Act).

23. Interpretation of Czech PIL is based on general private law principles; however specific features linked with the international element of the respective legal relations have to be taken into consideration. In addition to the general principles, the principles governing other areas closely connected with PIL, namely alien law and international civil procedure law, are also relevant:

- The principle of the equal treatment of aliens in the sphere of personal and property rights guaranteeing them the same status as Czech citizens, irrespective of sex, race and national origin (section 26 PIL Act).
- The principle of non-interference in the jurisdiction of foreign judicial bodies: Czech judicial bodies interfere only in those situations which have some relationship – personal or material – to the Czech Republic (*see* sections 6–19 PIL Act).
- In proceedings before Czech courts, all parties shall have equal status in claiming their rights (section 8 PIL Act).
- Unlike in PIL, in international civil procedure law the *lex fori* shall apply in principle, with some exceptions: Czech courts shall act in accordance with Czech procedural rules (section 8 PIL Act).

24. If we consider the principles of PIL, the very question of conflict of laws becomes relevant only if a foreign or, an international or a cross-border element exists (section 1 PIL Act). The question of applicable law is relevant only if there is contact with some legal system other than that of the *forum* state. Such contact with a foreign state should have certain intensity – there should be a relevant foreign element (the so-called relevant contact, *see infra*). The assessment of its intensity is left to the judge or the arbitrator.

Part I. General Principles (Choice of Law Technique)

Chapter 1. Sources of PIL

§1. PUBLIC INTERNATIONAL LAW

25. PIL is considered a branch of domestic law; it does not constitute part of public international law. The question of whether in the Czech Republic public international law is a source of PIL is complicated in itself. Sources of Czech PIL are of either domestic or European or international origin. Fundamental sources of public international law are international treaties and international customs; other sources are only subsidiary means for the determination of rules of law.[29]

26. International treaties binding on the Czech Republic are considered a source of law. Pursuant to section 2 PIL Act, this Act shall be applied within the limits of the provisions of promulgated international treaties by which the Czech Republic is bound and directly applicable provisions of the EU law. In other words, the provisions of international treaties binding on the Czech Republic take precedence over the Act, or, more precisely, provisions of the PIL Act are applied only if such a treaty does not provide otherwise. Similar provisions are contained in section 47 AA.[30] In general, the publication of such a treaty in the Collection of International Treaties (Coll. IT) is considered a prerequisite for its application as a necessary requirement of legality, irrespective of the fact whether or not such a prerequisite is included in a particular provision.[31] The preferential application of international treaties is laid down in the amended Article 10 of the Constitution, under which promulgated treaties, to the ratification of which Parliament has given its consent and by which the

29. *See* Č. Čepelka & P. Šturma, *Mezinárodní právo veřejné* [*Public International Law*, in Czech] 96 (C.H. Beck 2008), referring to Art. 38(1) of the Statute of the International Court of Justice.

30. *See e.g.*, s. 47 AA: 'The provisions of this Act shall apply, unless an international treaty binding on the Czech Republic, and which is published in the Collection of Laws, provides otherwise.'

31. *See* Z. Kučera & L. Tichý, *Zákon o mezinárodním právu soukromém a procesním. Komentář* [*Act on Private International Law and Rules of Procedure Relating Thereto, Commentary*, in Czech] (Prague 1989) (hereinafter Kučera/Tichý, *Komentář*) 31; in details *see* M. Pauknerová, *Otázka klauzulí o přednostní aplikaci mezinárodních smluv* [*The Issue of Clauses on the Preferential Application of International Treaties*, in Czech with an English summary], in *O vztahu ústavního a vnitrostátního práva* [*The Relationship Between Constitutional and International Law*] 73 (AUC Iuridica 1997).

Czech Republic is bound, form a part of the legal order; if a treaty provides something other than that which a statute provides, the treaty shall apply. Another solution has been adopted with regard to intellectual property issues. The Copyright Act, for instance, states that the provisions of this act shall apply to the works of foreign nationals in accordance with international conventions, or in the absence thereof, when reciprocity is assured (*see* section 107(2) of the Copyright Act). Obviously, this wording is a consequence of the principle of territoriality, which is a characteristic feature of the protection of intellectual property rights in general (for details *infra* Part II Chapter 4Paragraph 288 et seq.)).

27. Czech constitutional law, as amended by the Constitutional Act No. 395/2001 Coll., is based on the principle that the Czech Republic shall observe its obligations resulting from international law (*see* Article 1(2) of the Constitution, as amended). The relationship between international treaties and domestic law anchored in the Constitution corresponds with the moderated monistic scheme (interlinkage of national and international law).[32] This represents a significant change indicating the general preference in application of all ratified international treaties which are officially promulgated; that is, published in the Collection of International Treaties of the Czech Republic (till 2000 in the Collection of Laws of the Czech Republic). In view of this, PIL is closely connected with public international law, especially if in a particular case the relevant source of law is an international treaty. Specific clause on the preferential application of international treaties is also contained in the Act No. 61/2000 Coll., on Maritime Navigation, according to which provisions of this Act shall apply, provided that an international treaty, which is binding on the Czech Republic, or generally recognized rules of international law, does not stipulate otherwise (*see* section 82(1) of the Act).

28. The Czech Republic participates in a number of international treaties, both multilateral and bilateral. Apart from treaties of a public law nature, Czech Republic is a contracting party to international conventions in the area of private law, such as conventions adopted by the Hague Conference on PIL, conventions on the international sale of goods, international transport, intellectual property, as well as conventions concerning international procedure law, especially international arbitration. An important role is played by a number of bilateral treaties, e.g., on legal assistance or promotion and the reciprocal protection of investments (BITs).

29. International treaties and conventions concerning PIL, to which the Czech Republic is a party, may be divided as follows:[33]

Choice of Law Conventions

(i) Convention on the Law Applicable to Traffic Accidents, The Hague 1971.

---

32. *See* Č. Čepelka & P. Šturma, *supra*, 199 with further references.
33. Obviously, such a division is only schematic, as international treaties or conventions sometimes include both substantive and conflict rules, some of them, as, for example, many international transport conventions, also include rules on jurisdiction.

(ii) Convention Concerning the International Administration of the Estates of Deceased Persons, The Hague 1973.
(iii) Convention on the Law Applicable to Contractual Obligations, Rome 1980.
(iv) Protocol on the Law Applicable to Maintenance Obligations, The Hague 2007.

Substantive Law Conventions

(i) The International Sale of Goods:
- United Nations Convention on Contracts for the International Sale of Goods (CISG), Vienna 1980.
- Convention on the Limitation Period in the International Sale of Goods, New York 1974, as amended by the Additional Protocol, Vienna 1980.

(ii) International Transport:
- Convention Concerning International Carriage by Rail (COTIF), Berne 1980, as amended by the Protocol, Vilnius 1999.
- Convention on the Contract for the International Carriage of Goods by Road (CMR), Geneva 1956.
- Convention for the Unification of Certain Rules Relating to International Carriage by Air, Warsaw 1929, as amended by the Protocol, The Hague 1955.
- Convention Supplementary to the Warsaw Convention for the Unification of Certain Rules Relating to International Carriage by Air Performed by a Person Other than the Contracting Carrier, Guadalajara 1961.
- Convention for the Unification of Certain Rules for International Carriage by Air, Montreal 1999.
- United Nations Convention on the Carriage of Goods by Sea, Hamburg 1978.
- Convention on the Contract for International Carriage of Passengers and Luggage by Road (CVR), Geneva 1973.
- Convention on the Contract for the Carriage of Goods by Inland Waterways (CMNI), Budapest 2001.

(iii) Protection of Intellectual and Industrial Property Rights:
- International Convention for the Protection of Industrial Property, Paris 1883, revised at The Hague 1925, London 1934, Lisbon 1958, and Stockholm 1967, and amended in 1979.
- Madrid Agreement Concerning the International Registration of Marks, Madrid 1891, revised at Brussels 1900, Washington 1911, The Hague 1925, London 1934, Nice 1957, and Stockholm 1967, and amended in 1979 and the Protocol Relating Thereto, 1989.
- Madrid Agreement for the Repression of False or Deceptive Indications of Source on Goods, Madrid 1891, revised at Washington 1911, The Hague 1925, London 1934 and Lisbon 1958, and supplemented by the Additional Act of Stockholm 1967.
- Nice Agreement Concerning the International Classification of Goods and Services for the Purposes of the Registration of Marks, Nice 1957, revised at Stockholm 1967 and at Geneva 1977, and amended in 1979.

- Lisbon Agreement for the Protection of Appellations of Origin and Their International Registration, Lisbon 1958, revised at Stockholm 1967, and amended in 1979.
- Locarno Agreement Establishing an International Classification for Industrial Designs, Locarno 1968, amended in 1979.
- Berne Convention for the Protection of Literary and Artistic Works, Berne 1886, revised at Berlin 1908, Rome 1928, Brussels 1948, Stockholm 1967, Paris 1971, and 1979.
- Universal Copyright Convention, Geneva 1952, revised at Paris 1971.
- Rome Convention for the Protection of Performers, Producers of Phonograms and Broadcasting Organizations, Rome 1961.
- Patent Cooperation Treaty, Washington 1970, amended in 1979 and modified in 1984.
- Strasbourg Agreement Concerning International Patent Classification, Strasbourg 1971, amended in 1979.
- Budapest Union on the International Recognition of the Deposit of Microorganisms for the Purposes of Patent Procedure, Budapest 1977, modified in 1980.
- International Convention for the Protection of New Varieties of Plants, 1961, revised at Geneva 1972, 1978, and 1991.

(iv) Family Law (including choice of law rules and procedural rules):

- European Convention on the Adoption of Children, Strasbourg 1967.
- European Convention on the Legal Status of Children Born Out of Wedlock, Strasbourg 1975.
- Convention on Rights of a Child, New York 1989.
- Convention on Protection of Children and Cooperation in Respect of Intercountry Adoption, The Hague 1993.
- European Convention on the Exercise of Children's Rights, Strasbourg 1996.
- Convention on Jurisdiction, Applicable Law, Recognition, Enforcement and Cooperation in respect of Parental Responsibility and Measures for Protection of Children, the Hague 1996.
- Convention on the International Protection of Adults, The Hague 2000.
- Convention on Contact concerning Children, Strasbourg 2003.
- Convention on the International Recovery of Child Support and Other Forms of Family Maintenance, the Hague 2007.
- Protocol on the Law Applicable to Maintenance Obligations, The Hague 2007.

Procedural Law Conventions

(i) Convention Relating to Civil Procedure, The Hague 1905.

(ii) Convention on Civil Procedure, The Hague 1954.

(iii) Convention on the Enforcement of Maintenance Obligations Abroad, New York 1956.

(iv) Convention on the Recognition and Enforcement of Decisions Relating to Maintenance Obligation in Respect of Children, The Hague 1958.
(v) Convention Abolishing the Requirement of Legalization for Foreign Public Documents, The Hague 1961.
(vi) Convention on the Service Abroad of Judicial and Extrajudicial Documents in Civil or Commercial Matters, The Hague 1965.
(vii) European Agreement on the Transmission of Applications for Legal Aid, Strasbourg 1967.
(viii) European Convention on Information on Foreign Law, London 1968, as amended by the Additional Protocol, Strasbourg 1978.
(ix) European Convention on the Abolition of the Legalization of Documents Executed by Diplomatic Agents or Consular Officers, London 1968.
(x) Convention on the Taking of Evidence Abroad in Civil or Commercial Matters, The Hague 1970.
(xi) Convention on the Recognition of Divorces and Legal Separations, The Hague 1970.
(xii) Convention on the Recognition and Enforcement of Decisions Relating to Maintenance Obligations, The Hague 1973.
(xiii) Convention on International Access to Justice, The Hague 1980.
(xiv) Convention on the Civil Aspects of International Child Abduction, The Hague 1980.
(xv) European Convention on Recognition and Enforcement of Decisions Concerning Custody of Children and on Restoration of Custody of Children, Luxembourg 1980.
(xvi) Convention on the International Protection of Adults, The Hague 2000.
(xvii) Convention on Choice of Court Agreements, The Hague, 2005.
(xviii) Convention on Jurisdiction and Recognition and Enforcement of Judgments in Civil and Commercial Matters, Lugano 2007.

Conventions on Arbitration

(i) Protocol on Arbitrator Clauses, Geneva 1923.
(ii) Convention on Enforceability of Foreign Arbitral Awards, Geneva 1927.
(iii) Convention on the Recognition and Enforcement of Foreign Arbitral Awards, New York 1958.
(iv) European Convention on International Commercial Arbitration, Geneva 1961.
(v) Convention on the Settlement of Investment Disputes between States and Nationals of Other States, Washington 1965.

Trade-Related Treaties and Agreements

(i) Agreement Establishing the World Trade Organization (the WTO Agreement), Marrakesh 1994.

(ii) The Europe Agreement Establishing an Association between the European Communities and their Member States and the Czech Republic, Luxembourg 1993.
(iii) Treaty on EU and Treaty on the Functioning of the EU, OJ C 83 2010.
(iv) Charter of Fundamental Rights of the EU, OJ C 83 2010.
(v) Treaty establishing the European Atomic Energy Community, OJ C 84 2010.

Bilateral Treaties

(i) Treaties on mutual legal assistance, recognition and enforcement of foreign decisions, and jurisdiction.
(ii) Treaties on promotion and reciprocal protection of investments (BIT).
(iii) Treaties on special issues, as for example transport, industrial property, etc.

30. The second source of public international law is international customary law. The influence of international customary law upon PIL is undoubtedly less direct. Pursuant to Article 1 of the Constitution the Czech Republic is a law-abiding state and shall observe its obligations resulting from international law. Therefore, according to some opinions, international customary law may be applied in international civil procedure, as, for example, rules on jurisdictional immunities or rules on protection of aliens, or on protection of human rights (*see infra* §6).

§2. Supranational Law

31. Czech Republic is a Member State of the EU since 1 May 2004 and is fully subject to the EU legislation. Rules of European PIL can be found primarily in the secondary legislation – *see* an outline of the most important Regulations in the area of PIL; a number of Directives have been implemented into the Czech national (autonomous) law. However, EU primary law is also relevant as it stipulates certain principles significant for the interpretation of conflict of law and procedural rules, such as the principle of non-discrimination on the grounds of nationality, the principle of free movement of persons, goods, services, capital and the freedom of establishment. EU law takes preference over the Czech autonomous law in its application.

§3. National Law

32. Czech law is an exclusively written law, consisting of statutes or laws (legal acts, including constitutional acts), governmental ordinances and decrees (legal regulations of ministries, other central administrative bodies and of the Czech National Bank). The official collection of these legal acts and other statutes is contained in the Collection of Laws of the Czech Republic (Coll.). Laws and decrees are cited by their number and year of publication. In the Collection of Laws important awards of the Constitutional Court and some other communications and notifications are also published (if the law provides so). Until 2000, international treaties and conventions binding on the Czech Republic were also published in the Collection of Laws. Since 2000, under the new Act No. 309/1999 Coll., on the Collection of Laws and the Collection of International Treaties (Coll. IT), international treaties and conventions have been published in the Coll. IT by means of a communication of the Ministry of Foreign Affairs with detailed information concerning when a treaty or convention was signed, approved, ratified and entered into force on the part of the Czech Republic, as well as information about withdrawals or other relevant facts concerning any such treaty. Until 1999, the publication of the wording of international treaties or conventions was only in Czech; since 2000, based on the new above-mentioned legislation, international treaties are published in the wording relevant for its interpretation under international law together with a translation into Czech language, unless the Czech text of an international treaty is authentic.[34]

33. The fundamental source of Czech PIL is Act No. 91/2012 Coll., as amended, on PIL Act. This new, modern act contains all provisions relevant for PIL, including those that were formerly contained in special acts, as conflict rules on bills of exchange and cheques (formerly included in Act No. 191/1950 Coll., on Bills of Exchange, Promissory Notes and Cheques), rules on international company law (formerly included in the Commercial Code No. 513/1991 Coll., which was repealed by the new Civil Code), rules on international arbitration (formerly included in the Arbitration Act No. 216/1994 Coll.), and rules on certain matters related to international insolvency proceedings that are not covered by the Insolvency Regulation. Fundamental principles are anchored in the Constitution of the Czech Republic (Constitutional Act No. 1/1993 Coll.) and in the Charter of Fundamental Rights and Freedoms (Constitutional Act No. 23/1991 Coll.). These principles, such as the equality of sex, race, religion, political or other convictions, etc. become relevant especially when public policy (ordre public) reservation is applied, as they concern the social and governmental systems that must unexceptionally be observed (section 4 PIL Act).

§4. Case Law

34. In Czech law, case law is not a source of law. It is necessary, however, to distinguish case law which is not binding as such from the factual law-making operation of the judicature; that is, court decisions and arbitral awards. The Collection of judgments and resolutions of the Constitutional Court and the Collection of

34. *See also* the Act No. 545/1992 Coll., on the Collection of Laws, which was repealed by the Act No. 309/1999 Coll. The new Act entered into force on 1 Jan. 2000; legal acts, awards of the Constitutional Court and international treaties published in the Collection of laws and being in force at the day of the entry of the new Act in force, shall be considered to be published in conformity with this Act (*see* s. 14 of the Act No. 309/1999 Coll.).

judicial decisions and opinions of the Supreme Court contain selected court decisions of the Constitutional Court and the Supreme Court of the Czech Republic. Selected decisions of the Supreme Court, upper courts, as well as decisions of the Constitutional Court and of the Supreme Administrative Court, are available on the internet (www.nsoud.cz, www.usoud.cz, www.nssoud.cz). Although decisions of the courts are not source of law, decisions of the Constitutional Court are an exception to this as enforceable decisions of the Constitutional Court are binding to all authorities and persons (Article 89 of the Constitution). However, in practice, particularly the decisions of the Supreme Court have a significant weight. Apart from national decisions, the decisions of the Court of Justice of the EU (CJEU) and of the International Court of Human Rights are also relevant and cited as interpretation sources of PIL. Besides, pursuant to section 13 of the Civil Code anyone seeking legal protection may reasonably expect that his legal case will be decided similarly to another legal case that has already been decided and coincides in essential aspects with his legal case; where the legal case has been decided differently, anyone seeking legal protection has the right to a persuasive explanation of the reasons for such a variance.

§5. Doctrine

35. The doctrine as such is not a source of law. Especially in the era before 1990, the role of the doctrine and its influence upon the application and interpretation of law had been very limited. Nowadays court decisions – especially those of the Constitutional Court and the Supreme Court – often cite arguments and opinions expressed in commentaries, as well as those in legal literature.[35] Besides, the PIL Act is based on a professorial draft: it is (in particular in the general part) based on the textbook of the late Prof. *Zdeněk Kučera*,[36] the leading personality in the field of the Czech PIL and one of the main drafters of this Act. Currently, the arguments of courts are often justified by reference either to his now updated textbook or to the commentaries to PIL Act. Argumentation of courts based on opinions expressed in legal literature have undoubtedly become an increasing trend.

§6. Customary Law

36. Customary law has only limited importance within Czech law, as Czech law is exclusively written law. Customary law does not exist as a parallel system to written law in purely domestic law. In relations with an international element the situation is more complex. Certain significance of customary law derives from Article 1 of the Constitution, under which the Czech Republic is a law-abiding state.

35. Such was the radical change of the concept of jurisdictional immunity of states – decision of the Supreme Court No. 21 Cdo 2215/2007, *see* M. Pauknerová, *Jurisdictional Immunity of States and Brussels I Regulation – Recent Development in the Czech Republic*, 9 Eur. Legal Forum, 241 (2009).

36. *See* Z. Kučera, *Mezinárodní právo soukromé* [*Private International Law*], (7th ed. Brno-Pilsen 2009), cited as Kučera, *Mezinárodní právo soukromé (2009).*

37. First, it is necessary to distinguish between custom and usage. It is recognized in general that customary law must be followed continuously (*usus longaevus*) and must be reasonable in nature (*opinio iuris*). Only under these two conditions may a custom be treated as a source of law. In this respect, some international customary rules may be applied especially in international civil procedure, as for example the principle *actor sequitur forum rei*, the principle of immunity of a state; *denegatio iustitiae* with respect to an alien is to be looked upon as internationally unlawful conduct, etc.

38. In the opinion of some authors, customary rules may be applied especially where there are gaps in laws; in particular, this is the case of international procedure law. It is impossible to assume a simplified attitude in legal practice towards such gaps stating that a judicial authority shall not be liable to deal with questions not expressly governed in an act, whereas it must be examined whether a solution cannot be deduced from rules or principles of international law.[37] Under section 7 PIL Act, foreign states enjoy immunity from jurisdiction of Czech courts as regards proceedings arising out of the state's acts and actions undertaken while exercising their state, governmental or other public powers and functions. Immunity from the jurisdiction of Czech courts does not apply to other acts, actions or cases, to the extent in which general international law or international agreements allow institute proceedings against a state before the courts of another state. The term 'general international law' means rules of international customary law by which the Czech Republic is bound towards the states who are not party to relevant international treaties and that apply also to questions not regulated by such treaties.[38]

39. Unlike custom, usage is not considered a source of law, because it lacks *opinio iuris*, which is a substantial element of a custom. In domestic law, the role of usage is expressly regulated by the Civil Code: In legal transactions with an entrepreneur, account is taken to the trade usage prevalent in general or in particular field, unless excluded by the agreement of the parties or by law. Unless stipulated otherwise, the trade usage takes precedence over those provisions that are not of a mandatory nature; otherwise, the entrepreneur can invoke a trade usage if he provides that the other party should have known the particular usage and agreed to the procedure in conformity with such usage (section 558(2) CivC). As the predominant majority of contract law provisions in the Civil Code are of a non-mandatory nature, the business practices shall be applicable, unless the parties stipulate otherwise. The Civil Code reflects some international standards of regulations of contractual obligations, in particular those included in the CISG, in the UNIDROIT Principles of International Commercial Contracts, or in the Principles of European Contract Law.[39]

---

37. *See* V. Steiner, *Občanské právo procesní v teorii a praxi* [*Law of Civil Procedure in Theory and Practice*] 28 (Prague 1975); *see also* 92 O. Eller, *Sources and Principles of Czechoslovak International Law*, in *Miscellany of Papers in International Law*, AUB, 133 (Masarykova univerzita 1991).
38. *See*, accordingly, Kučera & Tichý, *Komentář*, 263.
39. *See* critically P. Janečková in N. Rozehnalová, K. Drličková & J. Valdhans, *Nový občanský zákoník pohledem mezinárodních obchodních transakcí* 63 (Masarykova univerzita 2014).

Chapter 2. Determination of the Applicable Law

§1. Conflict of Law Rules

I. Types of Conflict of Law Rules

40. In Czech theory of PIL, conflict rules are rules which only determine the applicable or governing law and do not contain substantive regulation. Conflict rules are understood to be either one-sided or two-sided (all-sided, multi-sided). Two-sided conflict rules, also called total conflict rules, state which law is applicable to the given situation, which may be either foreign law or domestic law. One-sided conflict rules, also called partial conflict rules, indicate that only domestic law, the law of the *forum* (the *lex fori*) is applicable.

The Czech PIL Act, as a modern codification of PIL, contains an overwhelming majority of two-sided conflict rules, for example section 69(1) PIL Act, pursuant to which rights in rem in immovable property as well as in tangible, movable property shall be governed by the law of the place where such property is located. The governing law may be not only the law of the *forum* but also a foreign law, other than that of the forum. One-sided conflict rules are rather exceptional, for example pursuant to section 49(1) PIL Act, the personal relations between spouses shall be governed by the law of the state in which they are both citizens. Should they be citizens of different states, such relations shall be governed by the law of the state in which both spouses are habitually resident, otherwise by the Czech law (the third rule in this hierarchy is a one-sided conflict rule). Another example of one-sided conflict rules is the rule applicable to arbitration agreements, under which an admissibility of an arbitration agreement shall be assessed according to the Czech law (*see* section 117(1) PIL Act).

41. Conflict of law rules are either mandatory or non-mandatory. Non-mandatory conflict rules allow the participants of legal relations to exclude their application and to choose the law of another state as applicable. Mandatory conflict rules cannot be derogated from by participants of legal relations, there is no possibility to choose another applicable law. In the autonomous Czech PIL Act, mandatory rules are, for example, the conflict of law rules on rights in rem (section 69 PIL Act), or rules stipulating the law applicable to the status of natural persons (section 29 PIL Act) and legal entities (section 30 PIL Act). Non-mandatory rules are typically rules on the law applicable to contracts. As for the issues not falling into the scope of directly applicable provisions of the EU law and international treaties, contracts shall be governed by the law of the state with which the contract is most closely connected, unless the parties have chosen the applicable law (*see* section 87(1) PIL Act). A conflict rule may consist of a basic rule and a supplementary rule. Basic rule is the general rule, e.g., section 29(1) PIL Act: legal capacity shall be governed by the law of the state in which a person is habitually resident. Supplementary rule is intended to preserve the validity of an act which would be invalid under the basic rule, e.g., section 29(2) PIL Act: unless otherwise stipulated by this Act, it shall be sufficient when a natural person undertaking a legal act has legal capacity under the law applicable at the place where the legal act is undertaken.

42. Conflict rules have a specific structure. In the Czech theory of PIL, a conflict rule is divided into two parts: a referring section (or 'testing part') and a connecting section. The referring section, or testing part, is defined as a scope of legal issues or questions and/or the category of such issues to which a conflict rule applies; in other words, it defines its scope of application. For example, pursuant to a conflict rule in section 48(1) PIL Act, the capacity of a person to celebrate marriage shall be governed by the law of the state in which the person is a citizen; the referring section is 'the capacity of a person to celebrate marriage'. The connecting section determines the law, which shall apply to a particular legal issue with the scope of the referring section of such a conflict rule; in other words, it contains the respective link with the applicable law. In the given example, the connecting section is the statement, 'shall be governed by the law of the state in which the person is a citizen'. In the connecting section, connecting factors or points of contact are used. In the given example, the connecting factor is the citizenship of the respective person.

II. Connecting Factors

43. In Czech autonomous law, the most important connecting factors or points of contact are habitual residence as regards natural persons, and the place of incorporation as regards legal persons. Supplementary connecting factors include nationality. The notion 'domicile' in its original meaning within Common law does not appear in Czech law.[40] In the law of obligations, the dominating connecting factor is the intention of the parties (*lex electa*), as a supplementary connecting factor of the closest connection is applied, combined with the habitual residence or the seat of a party whose performance seems to be characteristic. Some other classical factors, such as the location of the act and the location of a thing (*lex actus* and *lex rei sitae)*, apply in a current and habitual sense; that is, the *lex loci actus* especially in legal acts, and the *lex rei sitae* in rights in rem. The new PIL Act brought significant changes with respect to connecting factors, there is a clear shift from the nationality-connecting factor to that of habitual residence. There have also been developments in alternative and cascade connecting factors both in conflict rules and in procedure. The cascade of connecting factors increases legal certainty, e.g., in case of conflict rules in matrimonial matters: the personal relations between spouses are subject to the law of the state in which they are both citizens. If they are citizens of different states, these relations are subject to the law of the state in which both spouses have their habitual residence, failing that to Czech law (section 49(1) PIL Act). Alternative connecting factors give the court a higher degree of flexibility in its decision-making, e.g., in the case of determining applicable law in matters of securities where there is a choice of different connecting factors to be applied based on the nature of the security in question (section 82 PIL Act).[41] Another example

40. However, the translations of the Czech terminology into English are not consequential and sometimes the Czech term '*bydliště*' (residence) is translated as domicile.

41. Section 82 PIL Act stipulates according to the nature of the security as applicable law *lex societatis, lex causae, lex loci actus, lex domicilii* or *lex electa*.

may be the determination of a law applicable to formal validity of a contract or other legal act: such act shall be valid as to its form provided the form complies with the law of the state (a) governing the contract or other legal act and a legal relation established thereby, (b) in which one of the actors expressed its will, (c) in which one of the actors has habitual residence or seat, or (d) in which an immovable property concerned by the legal act is located (section 42(1) PIL Act). Under this provision, alternative connecting factors should ensure the formal validity of acts.

III. Time Factors

44. Time factors may be relevant under various viewpoints. Setting the time of localization of the connecting factor increases legal certainty and predictability. In Czech autonomous law, the time factor is relevant when ascertaining the relevant nationality (section 28 PIL Act), when determining the law applicable to divorce (section 50 PIL Act), parentage (section 54 PIL Act), rights of unmarried mothers (section 59 PIL Act), adoption (section 62 PIL Act), rights in rem (sections 70 and 72 PIL Act), securities (section 83 PIL Act) and obligations (sections 87, 90 and 91 PIL Act).

IV. *Dépeçage*

45. In general, the choice of the law applicable to a contractual obligation may relate to the whole contract or only to a part thereof (the so-called subjective *dépeçage*, *see* Article 3 Rome I Regulation). The parties may subject different parts of the contract to different laws. Czech doctrine allows 'a choice of several legal orders'. It is also permitted to designate the law governing only a part of the contract.[42] *Dépeçage*, that was possible already under the former legislation, is expressly admitted by the Czech PIL Act. Pursuant to section 87(1) PIL Act contracts shall be governed by the law of the state with which the contract is the most closely connected, unless the parties have chosen the applicable law. The choice of law shall be made expressly or shall be undoubtedly demonstrated by the terms of the contracts or the circumstances of the case. The parties may choose different laws for different parts of the contract, provided that these parts are sufficiently severable.[43]

46. Special provision on *dépeçage* is included in conflict rules on trust funds or similar institutions. Under section 73(1) PIL Act a trust fund shall be governed by a law chosen by the settlor provided the chosen law regulates the fund or the provisions of that law may be otherwise applied thereto. Provided a certain element of the fund may be separated from the other fund elements, the applicable law may be determined separately thereto (section 73(3) PIL Act).

42. Kučera, Pauknerová, Růžička, *Mezinárodní právo soukromé*, 2015, 131.
43. *See* s. 9 of the old PIL Act of 1963 and Kučera & Tichý, *Komentář*, 98.

V. Legal Consequences

47. The legal consequence of the application of a conflict rule is the determination of applicable law. In case of two-sided conflict rules, the applicable law is determined on the basis of connecting factors, objectively stipulated criteria. The applicable law is selected irrespective of the outcome of the particular case, that is, without regard to the substantive provisions of the law in question. Foreign governing law established in such a way shall only exceptionally not be applied, for example some provisions of a foreign law might be excluded for reasons of public policy or it might be replaced by the *lex fori* for reasons that such foreign law cannot be ascertained.

48. In some cases, the court may take into consideration not only the conflict of laws aspect, that is the law of which state seems to be more closely connected to the particular issue, but also the aspect of substantive law, that is the substantive outcome of an applicable law coming into question. Undoubtedly, such a consideration is possible only if the law expressly provides for it. In the Czech autonomous PIL, for example, the determination of parentage shall be governed by the law of the state whose citizenship the child acquired by birth. Should it be in the interest of the child, the law of the state in which the mother was habitually resident at the time of the conception of the child shall apply. Should the child be habitually resident in the Czech Republic and should it be in the interest of the child, the Czech law shall apply (section 54 PIL Act). Another example may be found in section 50 PIL Act: Divorce shall be governed by the law of the state governing personal relations of the spouses at the time the divorce proceedings were initiated. Should it be necessary to apply foreign law which does not permit divorce or does permit it only under extremely difficult conditions, Czech law shall be applicable provided at least one of the spouses is a citizen of the Czech Republic or at least one of the spouses is habitually resident in the Czech Republic.

§2. Relevant Contact and Evasion of the Law

49. PIL as such comes into play only when the legal issue has a cross-border dimension. A foreign element may be a fact, an event or a transaction. In principle it concerns persons, either natural or legal, that have some relations with abroad (foreign nationality, foreign law of incorporation, residence abroad, etc.), property located abroad, performance of a relevant act in another country, etc. The introductory provision of the PIL Act stipulates fields of legal relations with a cross-border element included in its scope (section 1 PIL Act). Not every foreign or cross-border element is considered 'relevant' enough to trigger the application of PIL rules (of either Union, or international, or domestic origin). The 'relevant foreign element' must have certain intensity.

50. In contrary, in some cases, the fact that a person concerned lives on the territory of the Czech Republic may be considered as such a relevant link with the

Czech Republic that the *lex fori* applies. E.g., generally, the determination of parentage shall be governed by the law of the state whose citizenship the child acquired by birth, but should the child be habitually resident in the Czech Republic and should it be in the child's interest, parentage shall be determined under Czech law (section 54 PIL Act). Another example is in the conflict rule for adoption in section 61 PIL Act: Should foreign law apply which does not allow adoption or admits it only under extremely onerous circumstances, the Czech law shall apply provided the adopter or at least one of the adopting spouses or the adoptee is habitually resident in the Czech Republic.

51. In certain cases, the place where the act was performed (the *lex loci actus*) might also be considered a relevant link which can overturn the otherwise applicable foreign law. Supplementary or subsidiary conflict rules preserve the validity of an act if it was performed in conformity with local law, that is in conformity with the law of the state where the act occurred, despite the fact that pursuant to the applicable law, determined by the basic conflict rule, such an act would not be valid. For example, pursuant to section 29 PIL Act, the legal capacity of a person shall be governed by the law of the state in which a person is habitually resident. However, unless otherwise stipulated, it shall be sufficient when a natural person undertaking a legal act has legal capacity under the law applicable at the place where the legal act is undertaken. The *lex loci actus* principle applies also in other cases (*see infra*).

52. The requirement of a relevant link may partially eliminate the evasion of the law. Evasion of the law takes place when persons, in order to avoid the application of the normally applicable legal system, act to artificially create connecting factors pointing to some other legal system for the purpose of evading the law which would be otherwise applicable under the respective conflict rules, e. g. an artificially established residence in some state. The assessment of circumstances of a case should therefore always be done based on the link that is relevant and corresponds to the localization of the particular legal relation. *See infra* Chapter 3 §9.

§3. Choice of Law

53. Czech PIL Act enables in line with the principle of party autonomy in conflict of laws the choice of applicable law mainly in the law of obligations but also, in conformity with the general trend, in some other areas. In general, the possibility for choice of law in the new Act has been strengthened.[44] Choice of law is permitted in contracts (sections 87 and 119 PIL Act), in non-contractual obligations (section 101 PIL Act), in unilateral acts (section 90 PIL Act), security of obligation (section 91 PIL Act), set-off (section 92 PIL Act), trusts (section 73 PIL Act), securities (section 82 PIL Act) and investment instruments (section 83 PIL Act). Choice of law is also allowed in case of agreed matrimonial property regime (section 49(4) PIL Act). Unlike the EU law, the PIL Act does not allow choice of law to divorce (compare sections 50(1) and 49(1) PIL Act and Article 5 Rome III). European PIL

44. P. Uhlířová, *New Private International Law in the Czech Republic*, YbPIL, 478.

makes it possible to select the applicable law for contractual obligations (Rome I), non-contractual obligations (Rome II), divorce and legal separation (Rome III), succession (Succession Regulation), maintenance obligations (Hague Maintenance Protocol) and matrimonial property regime (Matrimonial Property Regimes Regulation), as well as for the property consequences of registered partnerships (Partnerships Regimes Regulation). For details *see infra.*

54. Within the Czech autonomous PIL, the choice of governing law applicable to contractual obligations is unlimited – it is possible for the parties to choose any law in force, irrespective of whether there is a relevant link between the selected law and the respective case. The admissibility of a choice of law and its validity shall be determined by the law, which would govern it if the contract were valid (*see* Article 8 Rome Convention, Article 10 Rome I).[45] In other cases, the choice may be limited, e.g. in an agreement on matrimonial property regime the spouses may choose either the law of the state in which one of the spouses is a citizen or in which one of the spouses is habitually resident, or the law of the state in which an immovable property is located, should the matter concern the immovable property, or the Czech law (section 49(4) PIL Act).[46] The choice of governing law cannot prevent the application of overriding mandatory rules, which enforce their application without regard to the otherwise applicable law, especially of those forming part of the *lex fori* (*see infra*):

- *Contracts*: In the Czech autonomous PIL, contracts shall be governed by the law of the state with which the contract is the most closely connected, unless the parties have chosen the applicable law. The choice of law shall be made expressly or shall be undoubtedly demonstrated by the terms of the contract or the circumstances of the case (section 87(1) PIL Act). Choice of law may be concluded not only in written form but also in oral form; the implied choice of the applicable law is permitted under the conditions of this provision.
- *Arbitration agreements*: The principle of the unlimited choice of governing law also applies in arbitral proceedings. Pursuant to section 119 PIL Act, a law applicable to a dispute shall be the law chosen by the parties. If the parties have not chosen such law, it shall be determined by the arbitrators in accordance with the provisions of this Act. Should the parties expressly mandate the arbitrators thereto, the arbitrators may decide the dispute in accordance with the principles of justice.
- *Unilateral legal acts, security of obligation, and set-off:* Unlimited choice of law is also allowed in the provision on unilateral legal acts (section 90 PIL Act). Unilateral legal acts are, for example, a public offer (section 1780 CivC) or a public tender (section 1772 CivC), or the notification of a bank to a beneficiary of the opening of a letter of credit to his benefit (section 2683 CivC). Pursuant to section 91 PIL Act, a security of obligation shall be governed by the same law as the secured obligation, with some exceptions – one of the exceptions being that a

45. This rule based on European PIL applies in general.
46. This provision is superseded by the Regulation 2016/1103 applicable to the matrimonial property regime after 29 Jan. 2019.

party who provided the security by means of a unilateral expression of intent chooses the application of another law. A statutory lien over claims and other rights shall be governed by the same law as the claim or other right over which the statutory lien was established, unless the parties choose the application of another law. Similarly, set-off shall be governed by the same law as the claim against which the right to set-off is asserted. The parties by means of an agreement may choose the application of a different law (section 92 PIL Act).

- *Certain non-contractual obligations:* Non-contractual obligations arising out of violations of privacy and rights relating to personality, including defamation, shall be governed by the law of the state in which the violation occurred. Nevertheless, the affected (injured) person may choose the law of the state in which (a) the affected person has habitual residence or seat, (b) the violation initiator (perpetrator) has habitual residence or seat, or (c) the result of a violating conduct appeared (manifested itself) provided the violation agent could predict it (section 101 PIL Act). This provision is supplementary to Rome II Regulation which expressly excludes these obligations from its scope (Article 1(2) g) Rome II).
- *Trusts:* A trust fund or a similar institution shall be governed by a law chosen by the settlor provided the chosen law regulates the fund or the provisions of that law may be otherwise applied thereto (section 73(1) PIL Act). The provisions on trusts were inspired by the Hague Convention on the Law Applicable to Trusts and on their Recognition[47] of 1985, which is not binding for the Czech Republic.
- *Securities:* Questions whether a security is validly issued, whether there are rights associated with it in such a manner that they cannot be exercised after the issuance of a security through all the term of its validity without the security concerned, and what rights and what legal effects are connected thereto, shall be governed according to the nature of the security by, *inter alia*, the law determined in a security provided the nature of the security admits it (*see* section 82 e) PIL Act).
- *Investment instruments:* A choice of law in investment instruments is admitted only exceptionally. A statutory lien over a security shall be governed by the law applicable in place of habitual residence or a seat of a lien creditor in a decisive time period, unless the parties choose another law. Notwithstanding this provision, handling book-entry or immobilized securities or other securities entered in a depository or handling a depository-entered right which acts as a book-entry security shall be governed by the law of the state in which the entry is undertaken; *renvoi* shall be excluded. A choice of law shall be admissible only if it concerns a law of a state in which the entity administering the depository has its seat or branch at the time of the choice of law and administering a depository belongs among usual activities of such an entity (in details *see* section 83 PIL Act).
- *Matrimonial property regime*: The choice of the applicable law is limited. Concerning an agreement on matrimonial property regime, the spouses may agree upon that their property regimes shall be governed either by the law of the state

47. Available at: http://www.hcch.net/index_en.php?act=conventions.text&cid=59. (accessed 10 Feb. 2014).

in which one of the spouses is a citizen or in which one of the spouses is habitually resident, or by the law of the state in which an immovable property is located, should the matter concern the immovable property, or by the Czech law (*see* section 49(4) PIL Act, primarily based on the law applicable to the property regimes of spouses at the time of the agreement negotiation). This provision is superseded by the Matrimonial Property Regimes Regulation, applicable only to spouses who marry or who specify the law applicable to the matrimonial property regime after 29 January 2019. Under Article 22, the spouses or future spouses may agree to designate, or to change, the law applicable to their matrimonial property regime, provided that that law is either the law of the State where the spouses or future spouses, or one of them, is habitually resident at the time the agreement is concluded; or the law of a State of nationality of either spouse or future spouse at the time the agreement is concluded.

§4. Objective Connecting Factor

I. Principle of the Closest Connection

55. The principle of the closest connection is important in particular in EU PIL; it has been the leading connecting factor under Article 4 of the Rome Convention as the law applicable in the absence of choice: the contract shall be governed by the law of the country with which it is most closely connected. Despite the fact that it had been often criticized for enabling a broad application of the principle of proximity at the expense of predictability and legal certainty, its influence can be traced in the current Czech legislation. In the Rome I Regulation the principle of the closest connection has become just a subsidiary rule whose application has only a limited importance (*see* Article 4(4) Rome I). The principle of proximity has been preserved in escape clauses which allow derogation from a basic rule when a particular legal situation shows a closer connection to a different law.[48]

56. In autonomous Czech PIL, the principle of the closest connection is expressly formulated in section 87(1) PIL Act, under which contracts shall be governed by the law of the state with which the contract is most closely connected, unless the parties have chosen the applicable law. As directly applicable provisions of the EU law and international treaties take precedence, its application is limited to the issues excluded from the scope of the relevant EU Regulations and international treaties, unless these laws and treaties allow the application of this Act. Under section 73(2) PIL Act on trusts, in the absence of choice of the applicable law, the trust shall be governed by the law of the state with which it has the closest connection. When determining such a law, a consideration shall be paid in particular to (a) a place from which the fund is administered, (b) a place in which the property the fund consists of is predominantly located, (c) a place of a seat or habitual residence

48. For details *see* M. Pauknerová, *Escape Clauses and Legal Certainty in Private International Law*, Yb PIL, 62.

of the trustee, (d) the purposes intended by the creation of the fund as well as to the places where these purposes are to be achieved.

57. In the Czech theory of PIL, the closest connection is not considered as a connecting factor. It only reflects the generally formulated link between a legal relation and applicable law, as e.g., 'contracts shall be governed by the law of the state with which the contract is the most closely connected'. In such formulations, the connecting factor is not expressed; it is hidden because in application of such a conflict rule it is necessary, on the basis of one or more relevant facts (which as such could be conflict rules alone), to assess which of them leads to application of a legal order meeting the requirement set by the conflict rule. Such a conflict rule may formulate a principle which is specified by further conflict rules.[49] Compare section 73(2) PIL Act.

II. Nationality

58. A person's status may be tested by his or her nationality. Under the former Czech autonomous PIL, nationality was one of the most important connecting factors. Obviously, it corresponded to the trends of the time when the former PIL Act was adopted (1963). In the current PIL Act, the connecting factor of nationality has been mostly replaced by that of habitual residence, and thus even matters that have traditionally always been governed by the *lex patriae* are now governed by the law of the state of habitual residence of the person in question, legal capacity of natural persons (section 29 PIL Act) being the most prominent example. Currently, the nationality-connecting factor still applies in conflict rules on bills of exchange and checks that are formulated in conformity with the Geneva Conventions,[50] and in family law (where habitual residence and lex *fori* also apply).

59. Section 28 PIL Act contains a special conflict of laws rule on multiple or indeterminate citizenship (nationality) to solve possible conflicts. Pursuant to section 28(1) PIL Act, if at the decisive time, a person is a Czech citizen and another state also considers this person to be its citizen, Czech citizenship prevails. Czech citizenship is regulated by Act on the Citizenship of the Czech Republic.[51] Pursuant to section 28(2) PIL Act, if someone is in the decisive time period a citizen of several foreign states, the last acquired nationality shall be decisive provided, considering the person's life situation, the relation of such a person to another state in which he or she is a citizen shall not substantially prevail; in such a case the nationality of that (latter) state shall be decisive. A person who in the decisive time period is not a citizen of any state or whose nationality cannot be determined shall be

49. Kučera, Pauknerová, Růžička, *Mezinárodní právo soukromé*, 2015, 116.

50. Convention Providing a Uniform Law for Bills of Exchange and Promissory Notes of 1930 and Convention Providing a Uniform Law for Cheques of 1931. These conventions were signed by Czechoslovakia but not ratified; however, most of their rules were incorporated into the Czech (and Slovak) law.

51. Act No. 186/2013 Coll., on the Citizenship of the Czech Republic.

regarded as a citizen of the state in the territory of which he or she has habitual residence in the decisive time period, and if it cannot be determined, in the territory of which he or she resides. If even that cannot be determined, for the purposes of the PIL Act it shall be proceeded as if he or she was a citizen of the Czech Republic (section 28(3) PIL Act). If someone is an applicant for granting international protection, an asylum seeker or a beneficiary of subsidiary protection or is homeless under another law or international agreement, the personal status of such a person shall be governed by provisions of international agreements stipulating the legal status of refugees and the legal status of stateless persons (section 28(4) PIL Act).[52]

60. The connecting factor of nationality is to be found in conflict rules on bills of exchange and cheques and in the area of family law. In some conflict rules in the PIL Act nationality is a precondition for the *lex fori* being applied instead of foreign law.

Name

– A change of the name of a natural person shall be governed by the law of the state in which the person is a citizen. However, such a person may invoke an application of the law of the state in the territory in which he or she has habitual residence (section 29(3) PIL Act). This newly codified provision is based on the nationality principle, admitting with respect to the territory where the person lives that the factor of habitual residence may be invoked.

Bills of exchange and cheque capacity

– In conformity with Geneva conventions, the capacity of a person to obligations (to be legally bound) under bills of exchange or cheques shall be governed by the law of the state in which he or she is a citizen. Should that law claim another state's law is applicable, the law of the other state shall apply (*see* section 31 PIL Act).

Relations between spouses

– The capacity of a person to celebrate marriage as well as the conditions for its validity shall be governed by the law of the state in which the person is a citizen (section 48(1) PIL Act).
– Personal relations of spouses shall be governed by the law of the state in which they are both citizens. Should they be citizens of different states, such relations shall be governed by the law of the state in which both spouses are habitually

52. *See* in particular the Act on asylum No. 325/1999 Coll., the Act on temporary protection of aliens No. 221/2003 Coll., Convention relating to the Status of Refugees of 1951, Convention relating to the Status of Stateless Persons of 1954, Convention on the Reduction of Statelessness of 1961, and Convention on the International Protection of Adults of 2000.

resident, failing that by the Czech law (section 49(1) PIL Act). In the cascade of connecting factors in this conflict of laws rule the common nationality of the couple is the primary connecting factor.

- Property regimes of spouses shall be governed by the law of the state in which both spouses are habitually resident; failing that by the law of the state in which both spouses are citizens; failing that by the Czech law (section 49(3) PIL Act).
- In an agreement on matrimonial property regime, the spouses may agree upon that their property regimes shall be governed either by the law of the state in which one of the spouses is a citizen or in which one of the spouses is habitually resident, or by the law of the state in which an immovable property is located, should the matter concern the immovable property, or by the Czech law (*see* section 49(4) PIL Act).
- Divorce shall be governed by the law of the state governing personal relations of spouses at the time of the proceedings' institution. Should it be necessary to apply foreign law which does not allow divorce or admits it only under extremely onerous circumstances, the Czech law shall apply provided at least one of the spouses is a citizen of the Czech Republic or at least one of the spouses is habitually resident in the Czech Republic (section 50(1) and (2) PIL Act).

Relations between parents and children and some other relations

- Establishing and contesting parentage shall be governed by the law of the state, the nationality in which the child acquired by birth. If the child acquired by birth more than one nationality, the Czech law shall apply[53] (section 54(1) PIL Act).
- Claims of a mother towards her child's father to whom she is not married shall be governed by the law of the state in which the mother is habitually resident at the time of the child's birth. The mother may invoke the application of the law of the state in which she is a citizen at the time of the child's birth. Claims of an unmarried pregnant woman shall be governed by the law of the state in which she is habitually resident at the time of filing the application, unless she invokes the application of the law of the state in which she is a citizen at the time of filing the application. Should a child's mother who is a foreigner be habitually resident in the Czech Republic at the time of the child's birth and should a child's father be a citizen of the Czech Republic, the rights of the child's mother shall be governed by the Czech law (section 59 PIL Act). This provision is probably completely superseded by the Hague maintenance protocol.[54]
- Adoption shall be subject to conditions stipulated by the law of the state the citizen of which is the adoptee as well as of the state the citizen of which is the adopter. Should the adopting spouses have different nationalities, the conditions stipulated by the laws of both spouses determined according to their nationalities

53. The exceptions concern the situation when the child habitually resides in the Czech Republic. In such a case, parentage may be determined under Czech law, if this is in the child's interest [*see* s. 54(2) PIL Act].

54. M. Zavadilová, In Pauknerová, Rozehnalová, Zavadilová, *Zákon o mezinárodním právu soukromém. Komentář*, 410.

as well as by the law of the state the citizen of which is the adoptee shall be complied with (section 61 PIL Act). [55] The effects of adoption shall be governed by the law of the state the citizens of which are all parties at the time of adoption, otherwise by the law of the state in which all parties are habitually resident at the time of adoption, otherwise by the law of the state the citizen of which is the adoptee (section 62(1) PIL Act).

III. Residence

61. In Czech civil law, the term 'domicile' (as in Czech '*bydliště*') means the place where a natural person is staying with the intention to stay permanently. The Civil Code defines domicile as the place where an individual stays with the intention to live there permanently, subject to changes in circumstances; such intention may be evident from his declarations or from the circumstances of the case. If an individual states as his domicile other place than where he or she is in fact domiciled, anyone may also invoke his actual place of domicile. No one may claim to have his actual domicile elsewhere against anyone who, in good faith, invokes the actual domicile (section 80(1) CivC). The Czech alien law in the Act on Residence of Aliens on the Territory of the Czech Republic[56] applies the notion of 'residence' (*pobyt*) and differentiates between the 'temporary residence'[57] (sections 16 et seq.) and the 'permanent residence with a residence permit' (sections 65 et seq.). These notions are important for the Czech substantive law of aliens. Further, the Civil Code in its general provisions uses the notion 'domicile' (in Czech '*bydliště*') to distinguish foreign persons from Czech persons: As for natural persons, a foreign person shall be understood for the purposes of this Code to be a natural person domiciled outside the territory of the Czech Republic.[58] An analogous provision is contained in the Trades Licensing Act: An individual who has his residential address outside the territory of the Czech Republic is a 'foreign person'. For the purposes of this Act a domicile in the territory of the Czech Republic means permanent residence.[59]

62. In conflict of laws regulation, the terminology is different. The notion of 'habitual residence' (in Czech '*obvyklý pobyt*') was introduced into the Czech

55. Under the hardship clause included in s. 61(3) PIL Act, should it be necessary to apply foreign law under the paras 1 and 2 which does not allow adoption or admits it only under extremely onerous circumstances, the Czech law shall apply provided the adopter or at least one of the adopting spouses or the adoptee is habitually resident in the Czech Republic.
56. Act No. 326/1999 Coll., on Residence of Aliens on the Territory of the Czech Republic.
57. The temporary residence is further differentiated to be either the 'temporary residence on the territory of the Czech Republic on the basis of a short-term visa' or of a long-term visa'.
58. *See* s. 3024(1) CivC.
59. *See* s. 5(2) of the Trades Licensing Act No. 455/1991 Coll., as amended, referring to the Act on the residence of foreigners on the territory of the Czech Republic.

autonomous law with the new PIL Act in 2012.[60] In line with the European PIL and Hague Conventions, habitual residence has become the most frequently applied connecting factor and jurisdiction ground in the new PIL Act: It is applied more than sixty times. As already mentioned, the frequency of habitual residence corresponds to the gradually increasing diversion from the traditional connecting factor of nationality in continental legislation. Even matters that have traditionally always been governed by *lex patriae* are now governed by the law of the state of habitual residence of the person in question. Section 20(4) PIL Act explicitly stipulates that connecting factors used in national conflict rules shall be interpreted in accordance with Czech law. However, respecting the widely adopted factual nature of the notion of habitual residence, a legal definition has not been drafted and the Explanatory Report[61] on the PIL Act refers to its interpretation in the framework of case law of the CJEU.[62] The place of habitual residence must always be determined according to concrete factual circumstances of each case and the decision on habitual residence is not necessarily an easy and simple one. Especially in the field of succession law, the determination of habitual residence may have substantial impact on the outcomes.[63]

A. *Domicile*

63. As already mentioned, domicile is not applied as a connecting factor in Czech autonomous conflict of laws rules.

B. *Habitual Residence* (obvyklý pobyt)

64. Legal personality and legal capacity

- Legal personality and legal capacity shall be governed by the law of the state in which a person is habitually resident. This provision represents one of the most striking changes in the PIL Act. Habitual residence is also a supplementary connecting factor in the conflict rule on a name of a natural person. A change of the name of a natural person shall be governed by the law of the state in which the person is a citizen. However, such a person may invoke an application of the law of the state in the territory of which he or she has habitual residence (section 29 PIL Act).

60. The connecting factor of habitual residence appeared in the old PIL Act in only one case, in a conflict of laws rule regarding promissory notes in s. 11a, which implemented the Directive 2002/65/EC of the European Parliament and of the Council of 23 Sep. 2002 concerning the distance marketing of consumer financial services.
61. Explanatory Report on the 2012 PIL Act (in Czech), 13.
62. E.g. Case C-523/07 *A* [2009] ECR I-02805; Case C-497/10 PPU *Barbara Mercredi v Richard Chaffe* [2010] ECR I-14309. *See* M. Pfeiffer, *Pojem obvyklého pobytu v mezinárodním právu soukromém* (Leges 2014).
63. *See* Pfeiffer in Pauknerová, Pfeiffer, *The New Act on PIL in the Czech Republic: Starting points and Perspectives Within the European Union*, J. PIL, 222.

- Habitual residence is also applied in the conflict rule on restriction of legal capacity and guardianship. Under section 34 PIL Act, the conditions for an establishment and termination of guardianship and conditions for restriction of legal capacity as well as for incapacitation shall be governed by the law of the state in which the ward has habitual residence. An obligation to accept and exercise guardianship shall be governed by the law of the state in which the guardian is habitually resident (section 35 PIL Act).

Agency

- Habitual residence of the principal is one of the alternatively stipulated connecting factors for the effects of a legal act undertaken by an agent. Moreover, a legal relation between the agent and a third party established as a result of exceeding the authority, as well as a legal relation between a person acting on behalf of another person without a due authority and a third party, shall be governed by the law applicable in place where the agent or the person acting on behalf of another person without a due authority has a seat or habitual residence (*see* section 44 PIL Act).
- The effects of acts on the basis of a proxy (*prokura* in Czech) for the principal shall be governed by the law of the state in which a person granting the proxy has a seat or habitual residence (*see* section 45 PIL Act).

Relations of spouses

- In the cascade of connecting factors in the conflict of laws rule on matrimonial property regimes, the common habitual residence of the spouses is the primary connecting factor, while in the conflict rule on personal relations of spouses this connecting factor applies only if the application of the connecting factor of common nationality fails: Property regimes of spouses shall be governed by the law of the state in which both spouses are habitually resident; failing that by the law of the state in which both spouses are citizens; failing that by Czech law. Personal relations of spouses shall be governed by the law of the state in which they are both citizens. Should they be citizens of different states, such relations shall be governed by the law of the state in which both spouses are habitually resident, failing that by the Czech law. The conflict rule on personal relations of spouses applies also to divorce. In an agreement on matrimonial property regime the spouses may agree upon that their property regimes shall be governed either by the law of the state in which one of the spouses is a citizen or in which one of the spouses is habitually resident, or by the law of the state in which an immovable property is located, should the matter concern the immovable property, or by the Czech law (*see* sections 49 and 50 PIL Act).

Parentage

- Establishing and contesting parentage shall be governed by the law of the state the nationality of which the child acquired by birth. Should it be in the interest of the child, the law of the state in which the mother was habitually resident at the time of the conception of the child shall apply. Should the child be habitually resident in the Czech Republic and should it be in the interest of the child, the Czech law shall apply to establish and contest parentage (*see* section 54 PIL Act).

Rights of unmarried mothers

- Claims of a child's mother against the father to whom she is not married shall be governed by the law of the state in which the mother is habitually resident at the time of the child's birth. Claims of an unmarried pregnant woman shall be governed by the law of the state in which she is habitually resident at the time of filing the application, unless she invokes the application of the law of the state in which she is a citizen at the time of filing the application. Should a child's mother who is a foreigner be habitually resident in the Czech Republic at the time of the child's birth and should a child's father be a citizen of the Czech Republic, the rights of the child's mother shall be governed by the Czech law (*see* section 59 PIL Act).

Adoption

- In the conflict rule on adoption habitual residence is a supplementary connecting factor. Should it be necessary under section 61(1–2) PIL Act to apply foreign law which does not allow adoption or admits it only under extremely onerous circumstances, the Czech law shall apply provided the adopter or at least one of the adopting spouses or the adoptee is habitually resident in the Czech Republic. The effects of adoption shall be governed by the law of the state the citizens of which are all parties at the time of adoption, otherwise by the law of the state in which all parties are habitually resident at the time of adoption, otherwise by the law of the state the citizen of which is the adoptee.

Certain non-contractual obligations

- The PIL Act contains conflict of laws rule on non-contractual obligations arising out of violations of privacy and rights relating to personality, including defamation that are excluded from the scope of application of the Rome II Regulation. The affected (injured) person may choose the law of the state in which (a) the affected person has habitual residence or seat, or (b) the violation initiator (perpetrator) has habitual residence or seat (section 101 PIL Act). If no choice of law is performed the law of the state in which the violation occurred applies.

European PIL

– In European PIL, habitual residence is one of the most important connecting factors applied in conflict of laws rule on contractual and non-contractual obligations (Rome I and Rome II), succession (Succession Regulation), maintenance (Hague Protocol on Law Applicable to Maintenance Obligations) and on matrimonial property regime and property consequences of registered partnership (Matrimonial Property Regime Regulation and Property Consequences of Registered Partnership Regulation).

C. Temporary Residence (přechodný pobyt)

65. As already mentioned, this notion is used only in the substantive law of aliens (section 16 of the Act on Residence of Aliens on the Territory of the Czech Republic).

IV. Law of the Incorporation and the Registered Office (Seat) of Legal Persons

66. Czech conflict rules concerning legal persons are contained in section 30 PIL Act. Legal personality and legal capacity of an entity other than a natural person shall be governed by the law of the state under which it was established (incorporated). This law shall also govern a trading name or a name and internal relations of such an entity, the relations between such an entity and its partners or members, mutual relations of its partners or members, a responsibility of its partners or members for liabilities of such an entity, a person responsible for acting on behalf of such an entity, as well as its winding up (section 30(1) PIL Act). Czech company law is based on the incorporation principle: The law, under which the entity was founded, shall apply regardless of whether or not such an entity also has its actual seat in the state of incorporation. Czech law permits the transfer of the statutory seat of a foreign legal person to the Czech Republic as well as the transfer of the seat of a Czech legal person abroad, provided the legal requirements are fulfilled.

67. The incorporation principle is modified by the real seat principle. There are two exceptions to the incorporation principle in the PIL Act: the law applicable to the capacity of a legal person to act and the possibility of cross-border transfer of the seat. Under section 30(2) PIL Act, for an entity other than a natural person to be bound by its regular acts it shall be sufficient when such an entity has such capacity under the law applicable at the place where the legal act was undertaken. Pursuant to section 30(3) PIL Act, a legal entity domiciled in the Czech Republic may be established only under the Czech law. This shall not affect the possibility to transfer a seat of a legal entity domiciled abroad and incorporated under the law of a foreign state to the Czech Republic, provided it is allowed by an international treaty, a directly applicable provision of the EU law or other legislation. Detailed provisions on the transfer of the seat are contained in the Civil Code (sections 138–143 CivC) and in sections 384a–384p of the Transformations Act.[64] Both acts require applicable law to change after the transfer of the seat of a legal person to the Czech Republic: after transferring its registered office to the Czech Republic, internal legal relations within the legal person shall be governed by the laws of the Czech Republic. The liability of its members and the members of its bodies for the debts of the legal person incurred after the effective date of the transfer of the registered office to the Czech Republic shall also be governed by the legal order of the Czech Republic (*see* section 138(3) CivC). In our opinion, this provision modifies the incorporation principle in favour of the real seat principle as it requires that the law applicable to legal personality and legal capacity of a legal person changes after the transfer.[65]

68. The notion of a statutory seat of a legal person plays a significant role in the definition of foreign and Czech legal person in Czech alien law. For the purposes of the Civil Code, a foreign legal person shall be understood to be an entity with its seat (registered office) outside the territory of the Czech Republic (section 3024 CivC). Similarly, under the Trades Licensing Act, a foreign person is a legal entity which has its registered office (seat) outside the territory of the Czech Republic; a legal entity whose registered office (seat) is situated on the territory of the Czech Republic is considered a Czech person (section 5(2) of the Trades Licensing Act).

69. Czech substantive law is based on the concept of a statutory seat. If a legal person is subject to registration in a public register, it is sufficient if the forming juridical act specifies the name of the municipality where the registered office of the legal person is located; however, in the application for registration in the public register, the legal person shall indicate the full address of its registered office. Anyone may invoke the real seat of a legal person. A legal person may not claim to have its seat elsewhere against anyone who invokes the registered office entered in a public register (sections 136(2) and 137 CivC). Czech commercial companies must be registered in the commercial register.[66]

70. As for conflict of laws, the seat factor has only secondary importance in the determination of the personal statute of legal entities; in the law of obligations, habitual residence of legal persons may correspond with their seat.

V. *Lex loci delicti*

71. The *locus delicti*, the place where the delict was committed, is a classical connecting factor which is applied in the Czech PIL only in one provision (section

64. Act No. 125/2008 Coll., substantially amended in 2011, on the Transformation of Business Corporations and Cooperatives (Transformations Act).
65. *See* in details M. Pauknerová & J. Brodec Czech Republic, in *The Private International Law of Companies in the European Union* 340–365 (C. Gerner-Beuerle et al., eds., C.H. Beck 2019).
66. *See* Act No. 304/2013 Coll., on Public Registers of Legal and Natural Persons.

101 PIL Act, *see infra*), complementing the Rome II Regulation on the law applicable to non-contractual obligations. Formerly, the principle of the *lex loci delicti* was the basic solution for non-contractual obligations in virtually all EU Member States, but the practical application of the principle where the component factors of the case were spread over several countries varied which engendered uncertainty as to the applicable law.[67] The former Czech PIL Act was no exception. Pursuant to its section 15 liability claims (unless a consequence of breach of obligations arising from contracts and other legal acts) shall be governed by the law of the place where the damage occurred or the place where the event on which the claim is based took place. The former Czech PIL Act provided for two alternative connecting factors in torts: the law of the place where the damage occurred (*lex loci damni infecti*) and the law of the place where the event on which the claim is based took place (*lex loci delicti commissi*). These connecting factors may not be pointing to the law of the same state; for example, in unfair competition conduct the effects of such conduct may occur in another state. The choice between the two connecting factors was up to the court.[68] The legal uncertainty connected with such a formulation of the conflict rule was undesirable and was one of the reasons in favour of the second connecting factor for non-contractual obligations: A connection with the country where the direct damage occurred (*lex loci damni*) strikes a fair balance between the interests of the person claimed to be liable and the person sustaining the damage. The applicable law should be determined on the basis of where the damage occurs, regardless of the country in which the indirect consequences could occur.[69] For these reasons, as the general rule in the Rome II Regulation was selected the *lex loci damni:* 'Unless otherwise provided for in this Regulation, the law applicable to a non-contractual obligation arising out of a tort/delict shall be the law of the country in which the damage occurs irrespective of the country in which the event giving rise to the damage occurred and irrespective of the country or countries in which the indirect consequences of that event occur' (Article 4(1) Rome II). The *lex loci delicti* principle has only a supplementary function in special provisions of the Rome II Regulation.

72. The *lex loci delicti* principle is laid down as a supplementary connecting factor in Article 7 Rome II on the law applicable to environmental damage, under which the law applicable to a non-contractual obligation arising out of environmental damage or damage sustained by persons or property as a result of such damage shall be the law determined pursuant to Article 4(1), unless the person seeking compensation for damage chooses to base his or her claim on the law of the country in which the event giving rise to the damage occurred. In other words, the victim has a right to choose the law of the place of conduct (*lex loci delicti*) which will replace the law of the place of injury.

73. Pursuant to Article 8 Rome II, as for the infringement of intellectual property rights, firstly, the law applicable to a non-contractual obligation arising from an

67. *See* Recital 15 of the Preamble to the Rome II Regulation.
68. *See* Kučera & Tichý, *Komentář*, 133.
69. *See* Recitals 16 and 17 of the Preamble to the Rome II Regulation.

infringement of an intellectual property right shall be the law of the country for which protection is claimed. The principle of *lex loci delicti* applies as the second connecting factor: In the case of a non-contractual obligation arising from an infringement of a unitary Community intellectual property right, the law applicable shall, for any question that is not governed by the relevant Union instrument, be the law of the country in which the act of infringement was committed.

74. The Rome II Regulation excludes from its scope non-contractual obligations arising out of violations of privacy and rights relating to personality, including defamation (*see* Article 1(2) g Rome II). As a consequence, the Czech PIL Act provides for a special conflict rule in section 101 on 'Certain Non-Contractual Obligations'. Under this section, non-contractual obligations arising out of violations of privacy and rights relating to personality, including defamation, shall be governed by the law of the state in which the violation occurred. Nevertheless, the affected (injured) person may choose the law of the state in which (a) the affected person has habitual residence or seat, (b) the violation initiator (perpetrator) has habitual residence or seat, or (c) the result of a violating conduct appeared (manifested itself) provided the violation agent could predict it. The *lex loci delicti* is thus the primarily applicable law unless the injured person selects another law.[70]

VI. *Lex Rei (Cartae) Sitae*

75. In the autonomous Czech law, the place where the property is located is the most important connecting factor in the sphere of rights in rem. However, in relations between contracting parties, as far as movables are concerned, this principle is replaced in a particular case (section 70(2) PIL Act) by the proper law of contract. The location of property is also applied as an alternative connecting factor in conflict rules on the formal validity of legal acts, agency, matrimonial matters and trusts (sections 42, 44, 49, 73 PIL Act).

Rights relating to real and movable property in general

- Rights in rem in immovable property as well as in tangible movable property shall be governed, unless otherwise stipulated by the PIL Act or other (Czech) law, by the law of the place where the property is located. The same law shall also apply to determine whether a property is immovable or movable. Under section 498 of the Civil Code, immovable things are tracts of land and underground structures with a separate intended purpose, as well as in rem rights therein and rights declared by a statute to be immovable things. If another legal regulation provides that a certain thing is not a component part of a tract of land, and if it cannot be transferred from place to place without violating its substance, such a thing is also an immovable thing. All other things, whether of a corporeal or

70. For details *see* J. Valdhans, In Pauknerová, Rozehnalová, Zavadilová, *Zákon o mezinárodním právu soukromém. Komentář*, 652.

incorporeal nature, are movable. The general conflict rule determines *lex rei sitae* as the law applicable to both movables and immovables.
- Property rights to vessels and aircrafts registered in a public register, their creation as well as their extinguishment shall be governed by the law of the state that administers the respective register.

Movables: the establishment and termination of the rights to movables

- The creation and extinguishment of rights in rem in tangible movable properties shall be governed by the law of the place where the property was located at the time of occurrence of an event giving rise to the creation or extinguishment of the right (section 70(1) PIL Act). This provision addresses the so-called 'mobile conflicts'.
- The creation and extinguishment of an ownership right in tangible movable properties that are being transferred on the basis of a contract shall be governed by the law governing the contract which forms the basis for the creation and extinguishment of the ownership right (section 70(2) PIL Act). The governing law is the proper law of contract (*lex causae*). This provision, that was missing in the former PIL Act is an exception to the general application of the *lex rei sitae*.
- If a legal act which shall form the basis for the creation and extinguishment of rights in rem to tangible movable properties was undertaken in a time period after the commencement of a carriage of such a property and for the duration of the carriage, such a creation and extinguishment shall be governed by the law of the place from which the property was sent. However, if the creation and extinguishment of rights in rem in these properties occur by means of disposition of a security which must be submitted in order to give the property out and dispose of it, the law of the place where the security is located at the time of the disposal shall be applied (section 70(3) PIL Act). With regard to transported goods (*res in transitu*) the connecting factor of the *situs* at the moment of a particular transaction is not considered suitable; therefore, in Czech law the decision was made to link the governing law to the place from which the goods were dispatched (*lex loci expeditionis*). As for securities which should be submitted in order to release the property and dispose of it, the law of the location of the security at the time of the disposal (*lex situs cartae*) shall apply.

Immovables: entries in public register

- Provisions on registration (records) in public books and similar registers applicable in place where the immovable property or movable property is located shall apply also when the legal title for creation, extinguishment, limitation or transfer of the registered right is governed by a different legal order (section 71 PIL Act). Regarding entry in public register *lex rei sitae* shall be applicable even if rights in rem are governed by another law (the law of the habitual residence or nationality of the decedent (*see* Articles 21 and 22 of the Succession Regulation) or a proper law of contract (*see* Article 3 Rome I)).

Movables: acquisitive prescription

– Pursuant to section 72 PIL Act, prescription shall be governed by the law applicable in place where the property was at the beginning of the course of the prescription period. A person entitled from prescription may, however, invoke the law of the state in the territory of which prescription took place provided from the time when the property entered the state all prescription prerequisites stipulated by the law of that state have been met. Generally, the *lex rei sitae* applies; the supplementary conflict rule in the second sentence of this section resolves the particular 'mobile conflict'.

Contracts concerning immovables

– Contracts concerning immovables, as other contracts in general, may be governed by any law selected by the contracting parties, the choice of law being unlimited (*see* Article 3 Rome I). In the absence of a choice of law, contract relating to a right in rem in immovable property or to a tenancy of immovable property shall be governed by the law of the country where the property is located – *lex rei sitae* (*see* Article 4(1) (c) Rome I).

Lex situs cartae

– Pursuant to section 83 PIL Act, unless stipulated otherwise by law, a right to a security shall be governed by the law applicable in place where the security is located, while a transfer of a right to a security shall be governed by the law applicable in place where the security is located at the time of its disposition, that is, the applicable law in both cases is the *lex situs cartae*. This connecting factor shall also apply with respect to a statutory lien over a security: Should a security which must be submitted in order to give out and handle properties be concerned, the law applicable in place where the security is located in the decisive time period shall be applied. Notwithstanding these provisions, handling book-entry or immobilized securities or other securities entered in a depository or handling a depository-entered right which acts as a book-entry security shall be governed by the law of the state in which the entry is undertaken (section 83 PIL Act).
– As already mentioned in connection with movables and mobile conflicts, the *lex situs cartae* also applies as concerns *res in transitu*. If the creation and extinguishment of rights in rem to such property occur by means of disposition of a security which must be submitted in order to release the property out and dispose of it, the law of the place where the security is located at the time of the disposal shall be applied (section 70(3) PIL Act).

Trusts

- The *situs* principle is also a supplementary criterion for the assessment of the closest connection as concerns trusts or similar institutions: Should a law not be chosen or should it not be possible to apply, the trust fund shall be governed by the law of the state with which it has the closest connection. When determining such a law, a consideration shall be paid *inter alia* to a place in which the property the fund consists of is predominantly located (*see* section 73(2) b PIL Act).

§5. Changes in the Connecting Factors; Changes in the Lex Causae

76. In general, changes in the connecting factors lead to changes in the relevant link to a particular legal system, resulting in a change in the applicable law (the *lex causae*). Most of the connecting factors may change – e.g., the place where a property is located (except for immovables), the nationality of a person, its habitual residence, etc. In such a case, the question of which particular time frame should be considered relevant for the afore-mentioned link must be resolved. Unless an express localization of a connecting factor with regard to a specific time is laid down in the conflict rule or some related provisions, the so-called mobile conflicts can emerge. Czech autonomous law resolves potential mobile conflicts in several provisions of the PIL Act.

Nationality and habitual residence

- Mobile conflicts may emerge as a result of changes of nationality or habitual residence. In the general rules on multiple or indeterminate nationality (section 28 PIL Act) nationality is being assessed to 'the decisive time period'. In other provisions where nationality or habitual residence is applied as a connecting factor, the PIL Act stipulates expressly the moment which is relevant for its assessment

Matrimonial property regime

- Pursuant to section 49(4) PIL Act, an agreement on matrimonial property regime shall be governed by the law applicable to the property regimes of spouses at the time of the agreement negotiation.

Divorce

- The abolishment of marriage through divorce shall be governed by the law of the state governing personal relations of spouses at the time of the proceedings' institution (section 50 PIL Act), the law governing personal relations of spouse is contained in section 49(1) PIL Act.

Parentage

- Establishing and contesting parentage shall be governed by the law of the state the nationality of which the child acquired by birth (section 54 PIL Act).

Rights of unmarried mothers

- Pursuant to section 59 PIL Act, claims of a child's mother against the father to whom she is not married shall be governed by the law of the state in which the mother is habitually resident at the time of the child's birth. The mother may invoke the application of the law of the state in which she is a citizen at the time of the child's birth. Claims of an unmarried pregnant woman shall be governed by the law of the state in which she is habitually resident at the time of filing the application, unless she invokes the application of the law of the state in which she is a citizen at the time of filing the application. Should a child's mother who is a foreigner be habitually resident in the Czech Republic at the time of the child's birth and should a child's father be a citizen of the Czech Republic, the rights of the child's mother shall be governed by the Czech law.

Adoption

- The effects of adoption shall be governed by the law of the state the citizens of which are all parties at the time of adoption, otherwise by the law of the state in which all parties are habitually resident at the time of adoption, otherwise by the law of the state the citizen of which is the adoptee (section 62 PIL Act).

Movables: the lex rei sitae

- In sections 70 and 72 PIL Act the connecting factor of the location of the property can change in time with respect to movable assets.
- Pursuant to section 70 PIL Act, the creation and extinguishment of rights in rem in tangible movable properties shall be governed by the law of the place where the property was located at the time of occurrence of an event giving rise to the creation or extinguishment of the right. If a legal act which shall form the basis for the creation and extinguishment of rights in rem to tangible movable properties was undertaken in a time period after the commencement of a carriage of such a property and for the duration of the carriage, such a creation and extinguishment shall be governed by the law of the place from which the property was sent. However, if the creation and extinguishment of rights in rem in these properties occur by means of disposition of a security which must be submitted in order to give (release) the property out and dispose of it, the law of the place where the security is located at the time of the disposal shall be applied.
- Acquisitive prescription shall be governed by the law applicable in place where the property was at the beginning of the course of the prescription period. A person entitled from acquisitive prescription may, however, invoke the law of the state in the territory of which acquisitive prescription took place provided from

the time when the property entered the state all acquisitive prescription prerequisites stipulated by the law of that state have been met (section 72 PIL Act).

Securities

- Unless stipulated otherwise by law, a transfer of a right to a security shall be governed by the law applicable in place where the security is located at the time of its disposition. A statutory lien over a security shall be governed by the law applicable in place of habitual residence or a seat of a lien creditor in a decisive time period unless the parties choose another law. Should a security which must be submitted in order to give out and handle properties be concerned, the law applicable in place where the security is located in the decisive time period shall be applied. Notwithstanding these provisions, handling book-entry or immobilized securities or other securities entered in a depository or handling a depository-entered right which acts as a book-entry security shall be governed by the law of the state in which the entry is undertaken. A choice of law shall be admissible only if it concerns a law of a state in which the entity administering the depository has its seat or branch at the time of the choice of law and administering a depository belongs among usual activities of such an entity (section 83 PIL Act).

Obligations

- Article 19(3) Rome I lays down that for the purposes of determining the habitual residence the relevant point in time shall be the time of the conclusion of the contract. This rule may also be applicable for other conflict rules on contractual obligations, outside the scope of Rome I, as e.g., for securities of obligation.
- Pursuant to section 90 PIL Act, legal relations arising from unilateral legal acts shall be governed by the law of the state in which the person undertaking the unilateral legal act had habitual residence or seat at the time when the legal act was undertaken, unless the person has chosen the application of a different law.
- As concerns alteration of an obligation, a transfer of rights and obligations by operation of law shall be governed by the law applicable to cases for which the law stipulates such a transfer, unless it follows otherwise from the nature of the matter. The right and the obligation are governed by the same law as before the transfer (section 91(3) PIL Act).

77. In some conflict rules, the PIL Act does not provide for the exact determination of the relevant point in time for the determination of the link to the applicable law. In these cases, should there be a mobile conflict; the judge decides which is the relevant point in time in a particular case. For example, in personal and property relations between spouses, the law of common nationality or the law of common habitual residence of spouses should be applied (*see* cascades of connecting factors in section 49(1) and (3) PIL Act). In some cases, it might be necessary to evaluate such relations and decide the case under the law determined on the basis of the nationality or the habitual residence of the spouses, which might have changed in the meantime, and it may be rather complicated to unequivocally determine the decisive time frame. Any change of the connecting factor should not prejudice the rights of third persons.[71]

§6. Combination of Connecting Factors

78. A legal relationship may consist of individual components which might be assessed under various conflict rules applying different connecting factors which might result in a mosaic of applicable laws. In case of a contract:

- the law of the habitual residence of a natural person and/or the law of the incorporation of a legal person is the law governing the capacity to act and conclude such a contract (sections 29 and 30 PIL Act);
- the *lex electa* determined by the parties or the law of the habitual residence (seat) of a contracting party whose performance is characteristic or has the closest relation to such a contract (Article 4 Rome I, section 87 PIL Act) is the proper law of contract (Article 3 Rome I, section 87 PIL Act);
- the *lex causae* or the *lex loci conclusionis contractus* (and/or some other factors might also be taken into consideration) is applicable as to the form of such a contract (Article 11 Rome I).

79. Within the Czech autonomous conflict of laws, continental law by tradition in this respect, combination of connecting factors may be classified as: cumulative connecting factors, compound connecting factors, alternative connecting factors, cascade and supplementary connecting factors.

- *Cumulative connecting factors*: In exceptional situations, two legal systems should be applied simultaneously to one particular issue. For example, as regards the capacity to perform a legal act, which establishes a particular relationship, the requirements prescribed by the legal systems of both of the participants in such a relationship should be met. In Czech law, as for the conclusion of marriage, the legal capacity of a person to conclude marriage, as well as the conditions of the validity of such a marriage shall be governed by the law of the state whose citizenship such a person possesses (section 48 PIL Act). Obviously, if such persons have different nationalities, the conditions set for the conclusion of marriage of the states of both persons should be met. Another example and maybe a better one (as in the first example the connecting factor is nationality but it can lead to different laws which as such shall be cumulated) is adoption. Under section 61 PIL Act, adoption shall be subject to conditions stipulated by the law of the state the citizen of which is the adoptee as well as of the state the citizen of which is

71. Kučera & Tichý, *Komentář*, 162.

the adopter. Should the adopting spouses have different nationalities, the conditions stipulated by the laws of both spouses determined according to their nationalities as well as by the law of the state the citizen of which is the adoptee shall be complied with.

- *Compound connecting factors*: Czech law of purely domestic origin does not provide for complicated compound connecting factors; that is, provisions requiring that more than one connecting factor should be simultaneously taken into consideration. Examples may be found in some Hague conventions on PIL. For example, Article 4 of the Hague Convention on the Law Applicable to Product Liability of 1973 states that the applicable law is the law of the place where the damage took place if this is also the place of the domicile of the damaged party. Consequently, two connecting factors are relevant and both of them have to be located in the same state. Similar provisions are contained in the Hague Convention on the Law Applicable to Traffic Accidents 1971, which is binding for the Czech Republic (Decree No. 130/1976 Coll.). Under Article 4 of this Convention, *inter alia*, where only one vehicle is involved in the accident and it is registered in a state other than that where the accident occurred, the internal law of the state of registration is applicable to determine liability towards a victim who is outside the vehicle at the place of the accident and whose habitual residence is in the state of registration.
- *Alternative connecting factors*: In conflict rules with alternative connecting factors only one of them may apply. The assessment is performed either by the court, as e.g., in the conflict rule on the law applicable to securities in section 82 PIL Act, or by the parties provided the conflict rule allows a limited choice of law and offers a number of connecting factors to choose from. Pursuant to section 82 PIL Act whether a security is validly issued, whether there are rights associated with it in such a manner that they cannot be exercised after the issuance of a security through all the term of its validity without the security concerned, and what rights and what legal effects are connected thereto, shall be governed according to the nature of the security by (a) the law governing the legal capacity and internal relations of a legal entity which issued the security, (b) the law governing the legal relation for which an issuance of a security is stipulated, (c) the law applicable in place where the security was issued, (d) the law of the state in which an entity issuing the security has a seat or habitual residence, unless the nature of the security corresponds to an application of another law, or (e) the law determined in a security provided the nature of the security admits it. The decision between the connecting factors (except for letter (e)) is not made by the parties to the proceedings, but by the court which shall assess the security in question. Another example may be rules applicable to the matrimonial property regime. An agreement on matrimonial property regime shall be governed by the law applicable to the property regimes of spouses at the time of the agreement negotiation. Concerning an agreement on matrimonial property regime, the spouses may also agree upon that their property regimes shall be governed either by the law of the state in which one of the spouses is a citizen or in which one of the spouses is habitually resident, or by the law of the state in which an immovable property is located, should the matter concern the immovable property, or by the Czech law (section 49(4) Act).

- *Cascade*: Unlike alternative connecting factors, in a cascade of connecting factors they step in one after another. This tiered system, sometimes called a ladder, is based on the fact that the following connecting factor applies only when the application of the preceding connecting factor fails. The cascade increases legal security regarding a particular connecting factor which will be applied where several connecting factors are stipulated. For example, under section 49(1) PIL Act, personal relations of spouses shall be governed by the law of the state of their common nationality. Should they be nationals of different states, such relations shall be governed by the law of the state in which both spouses are habitually resident, failing that by the Czech law. There is legal security and predictability that the court will first apply the law of the common nationality of the spouses even where the spouses have also a common habitual residence (in another country) and that the Czech law will only be applied provided the spouses have neither common nationality nor common habitual residence. The cascade of connecting factors has been introduced to the conflict rules of the autonomous Czech law by the current PIL Act in 2012.[72]
- *Supplementary connecting factors*: In some conflict rules the general connecting factor is supplemented by a subsidiary connecting factor in favour of the validity of a legal act or relation. For example, legal capacity of a natural person shall be governed by the law of the habitual residence; however, unless otherwise stipulated, it shall be sufficient when a natural person undertaking a legal act has legal capacity under the law applicable at the place where the legal act is undertaken (*see* section 29 PIL Act). With regard to this provision, the connecting factor of habitual residence is supplemented by the place where the act was undertaken to preserve the validity of such a legal act.

---

72. *See* Kučera, Pauknerová, Růžička, *Mezinárodní právo soukromé*, 121.

Chapter 3. Basic Terms

§1. Characterization (Classification)

80. Characterization is usually defined as a process of subsuming legal categories or legal questions raised by a factual situation, formulated in accordance with one legal system, under one of several conflict rules applicable in the *forum* state. The judge has to allocate a legal question concerning particular facts of the case at issue to the referring section of a certain conflict rule (*see supra* Part I Chapter 2 §1) which is applicable before Czech courts or other authorities, i.e., conflict rules of the Czech law or EU law, or conflict rules included in an international convention. Classification of the same legal question may vary from country to country; however, the legal categories used in the referring sections of conflict rules of the Czech PIL Act naturally correspond, above all, to the Czech legal system. Although in some cases, legal categories used in referring sections of the conflict rules of PIL Act are formulated in such a general way that enables the subsumption of legal concepts that are unknown to the Czech legal system.

81. In general, the problem of characterization which is based on differences between the rules of *legis fori* and the rules of the potentially applicable foreign law arises in two situations.

First, when there are differences in the systematic order of domestic law and foreign law. Under Czech law, escheat (*bona vacantia*) is a concept systematically assigned under the law of succession (*see* section 1634 CivC), while, for example, under English law is an institution of the law applicable to real rights (rights in rem). Under Czech law, prescription and set-off are categories of substantive law (with special conflict rules in sections 46 and 92 PIL Act and Articles 12 and 17 Rome I), while under English law these categories are part of procedural law. In contract law, difficulties might arise when it comes to the characterization of, e.g., an employment contract and a work contract; the difference may have important consequences as the employee, unlike the performer, enjoys special protection (*see* Article 8 Rome I). Secondly, when there is in the foreign law a legal category unknown in domestic law. For example, Czech law does not recognize legal institutions, such as legitimacy, *walayat* or same-sex marriage.

82. Czech PIL contains special provisions on the characterization problem. Pursuant to the basic rule in section 20(1) PIL Act, *lex fori* shall be applied when assessing the legal relationship or legal question for the purpose of its subsumption under the scope of a conflict of laws rule. Besides, under section 20(2) PIL Act, the so-called functional classification may also be taken into account. If legal provisions from different laws could be applied to a legal relationship or legal question, it is also possible to take into account the function which these provisions fulfil within the law to which they belong. The purpose of this rule is to prevent a mechanical application of the *lex fori* classification. In cases where the applicable law has been designated for the basic legal relationship, the assessment of legal relationships or questions accessory to the basic relationship is also usually based on this law (section 20(3) PIL Act).

83. Under section 20(4) PIL Act the facts used in conflict of laws rules of this Act for designating the applicable law (the connecting factors) shall be assessed in accordance with Czech law. The PIL Act anticipates cases in which legal categories and institutions of foreign law unknown in Czech law may appear. E.g., section 67 PIL Act provides for 'a registered partnership or a similar partnership', or section 73 PIL Act mentions 'a trust fund or similar institution'. The wording opens the application of such conflict rules also to concepts that are not part of the Czech law. Special provision is contained in section 69(1) PIL Act: Rights in rem in immovable properties as well as in tangible movable properties shall be governed by the law of the place where the property is located. The same law shall also apply to determine whether a property is immovable or movable.

84. In practice, the courts will mostly characterize the pertinent legal question by the *lex fori* and apply national (domestic) principles of law to allocate such legal question to a particular conflict rule. However, it is not excluded that it would be necessary to proceed in a particular way, in accordance with special provisions of section 20 PIL Act.

85. The doctrine of Czech PIL has always stressed the necessity of individual approach with respect to the analysis of a given issue. Prof. Zdeněk Kučera, author of this provision, distinguishes in his textbook *Private International Law* three types of situations.

First, the issue can be as a whole attributed only to one law on the basis of the relevant conflict rule, with no other conflict rules coming into consideration (in situations with relatively independent legal regulation). In such cases, the subsumption of the issue under a legal category in the conflict rule shall be done according to the *forum* law. By means of the conflict rules, the legislator tends to cover all possible situations of private law relations with foreign element, reflecting his idea of the just, fair, and correct treatment of these situations. The characterization is done in the same manner in all cases with a foreign element of a given class, with the same result, and leads to the subsumption of the given class of cases under the same conflict rule. The second type of situation results from the fact that the solution of the issue requires the application of more than one law on the basis of different conflict rules, governing different components of the case, mutually dependent (interdependent situations). In these situations, the respective components are functionally connected, as, for example, the regulation of capacity and form concerning the requirements for the testament. Where the joint application of the rules extracted from two applicable laws would lead to absurd or intolerable results, the characterization *lege fori* should have priority over the functional characterization that is based on the function of legal rules in social and legal life. The third type of situation comes up after the applicable law governing the given case has been determined according to the relevant conflict rule, and it is necessary to determine the applicable law to another question that is not separate enough, but forms part of the basic situation, and a special conflict rule should correspond to it. The problem of characterization arises after the applicable law for the main question has been determined (characterization in successive stage). Firstly, the conflict rule for the basic situation is to be selected based on the *lex fori* classification; the following classification is based preferably on the applicable foreign law, on the lex *causae*.[73]

86. In some cases, uniform rules on characterization may be found in international agreements and conventions binding on the Czech Republic. For example, Article 6 paragraph 2 of the Treaty on the Elimination of Double Taxation between the Czech Republic and the Slovak Republic (No. 100/2003 Coll.) states that the question whether a property is to be considered as movable or immovable shall be governed by the law of the state on the territory of which it is located. Unfortunately, such provisions in international conventions are only exceptional.

87. Applying the EU law, the use of the classification rules under the PIL Act may be limited by the principle of autonomous interpretation of the terms contained therein.[74] Autonomous interpretation by the CJEU means that the terms used in EU law have their proper meaning, independent of national laws of the states concerned.[75]

88. If the subsumption under any conflict rule fails, e.g., no guideline is found to assess a legal concept completely unknown to the Czech law, an ad hoc solution may be applied.[76] In such a case, we could consider application of the provision on exceptional and subsidiary determination of applicable law. Under section 24(2) PIL Act should it not be possible to determine, under other provisions of this Act, the law applicable to a certain relation or question falling into the scope of this Act, the law which is in the closest connection to them shall be applied unless the parties have chosen or have otherwise identified the application of a certain law.

§2. Preliminary Question

89. The treatment of preliminary question in PIL may cause some difficulties if the conflict rule of the *forum* relating to the matter refers to a foreign law. For example, a claim to share in the estate of a deceased person may depend upon the validity of the marriage to a deceased person or upon the validity of an adoption. In such a case, the preliminary question can be treated in two different ways. Either the conflict rules of *lex causae* or the conflict rules of *lex fori* are applied.

90. In practice, this problem becomes relevant only if the conflict rules *legis fori* and those *legis causae* lead to different laws and possibly different substantive answers to the preliminary question. Czech PIL Act contains explicit and clear rules. Pursuant to section 22(1) PIL Act, the provisions of this Act shall apply to determine the law applicable to the preliminary question. Should the Czech courts not

73. *See* Z. Kučera, *Mezinárodní právo soukromé*, 7th ed. (2009), *supra*, 145–155; Z. Kučera, *The Problem of Classification* in *Miscellany of Papers in International Law* 99–118 (Masarykova univerzita v Brně, Brno 1991).
74. Uhlířová, *supra*, 479.
75. ECJ, Case 29-76 *LTU Eurocontrol.*
76. M. Pauknerová, In Kučera Z., *Mezinárodní právo soukromé* (2015), *supra*, 151.

have jurisdiction to decide upon the preliminary question if it was considered in a separate case, the conflict of law provision of the law governing the main question shall apply to determine the applicable law provided such a question is governed by a foreign law.

91. This solution corresponds with the Czech doctrine of PIL, which had preferred the *lex fori* approach (the so-called independent connection). The reasoning behind this approach was the interest to achieve internal harmony of the decision-making of the Czech courts as such legal questions should always be decided under the same applicable law, be they main or only preliminary, especially in personal status matters. Therefore, the *lex causae* approach may only be applied when the preliminary question has no relation to the Czech Republic. In such cases Czech courts would not have jurisdiction to decide upon the preliminary question if it was considered in a separate case and the conflict rule *legis causae*, of a foreign law, may be applied.[77]

92. If a preliminary question had already been granted a final judgment by a competent Czech public authority or a court or by an authority of a foreign state the judgment of which fulfils conditions for recognition in the Czech Republic, such a judgment shall be binding for the court (section 22(2) PIL Act). Under the Czech autonomous civil procedure rules, the court may consider questions which are within the decision-making competence of another authority (except for decisions that a crime or an administrative delict was committed and who committed it and decisions about the personal status of a particular person) unless a competent authority had already issued a decision regarding such a question (section 135 CCP). If there is no such court decision, be it a decision of a Czech court or a decision of a foreign court, which meets the conditions for the recognition of such a decision by Czech courts, the Czech court which has jurisdiction to decide the main question is obliged to resolve the preliminary question, too.

93. Additional rules linked to preliminary questions are to be found in EU law. For example, under Recital 41 of the Preamble to the Succession Regulation, for the purposes of the application of the Regulation, the determination of the nationality or the multiple nationalities of a person should be resolved as a preliminary question. The issue of considering a person as a national of a State falls outside the scope of this Regulation and is subject to national law, including, where applicable, international conventions, in full observance of the general principles of the EU.

§3. Substance and Procedure

94. The PIL Act belongs to modern codifications of PIL which contain choice of law rules, international civil procedure rules, as well as rules of alien law. The rules

77. *See* in details Kučera, *Mezinárodní právo soukromé* (2009), *supra*, 165–168.

of alien law are substantive rules, directly applicable to persons who are not citizens of the Czech Republic or have a seat outside the territory of the Czech Republic (foreigners and foreign legal entities, *see* section 26 PIL Act). This concentration of all three kinds of rules in one piece of legislation proved to be efficient; it is a traditional solution contained already in former PIL Act 1963. This solution was adopted in some recent national PIL Acts, EU Regulations and modern Hague Conventions.

95. The system of the PIL Act is structured as follows: Part One: General Provisions, Part Two: General Provisions of Procedural International Law, Part Three: General Provisions of PIL, Part Four: Provisions Concerning Individual Types of Private-Law Relations (mostly including jurisdiction, applicable law, and recognition and enforcement of judgments in particular field), Part Five: Judicial Cooperation in Relations with Foreign States, Part Six: Insolvency Proceedings, Part Seven: Arbitration and Recognition and Enforcement of Foreign Arbitral Awards, and Part Eight: Transitional and Final Provisions. This structure is logical but sometimes rather complicated as many issues are partly covered by the EU law and/or international conventions which enjoy preferential application over the PIL Act provisions.

§4. *Renvoi*

96. In general, *renvoi* is a situation when the conflict rule of the forum determines foreign law as applicable and the conflict rule of the applicable law refers back to the application of *lex fori* (back reference, *renvoi*, remission), or refers to the application of the law of a third state (further reference, transmission). Czech law takes a favourable position towards *renvoi.* Section 21(1) PIL Act states that where the provisions of this Act stipulate the application of foreign law the provisions of which refer back to the Czech law, the substantive law provisions of the Czech law shall apply. Where the provisions of foreign law refer to the law of another foreign state, the substantive law provisions of that law shall apply, should it be applied under its conflict of law provisions; otherwise, the substantive law provisions of the Czech law shall apply. It should be noted that this formulation – referring to substantive law provisions – avoids a vicious circle of endless references from one law to another.

97. This *renvoi* provision differs from its counterpart in the former PIL Act 1963 which conditioned the acceptance of *renvoi* by a 'reasonable and just settlement of the relations involved' (*see* section 35 PIL Act 1963). This vague and general formulation left the judge sufficient space for the consideration of the matter involved. The new formulation of section 21(1) PIL Act is clear and leads to predictable results – evidently, in majority of cases, the *lex fori* will apply.

98. Under section 21(2) PIL Act, *renvoi* is excluded in contractual obligations and labour-law relations. It is also excluded in case of choice of law unless agreed otherwise by the parties. Unless the manifested will of the contracting parties indicates otherwise, the conflict rules of the selected law shall be ignored.

99. There is a special provision on choice of law in arbitration proceedings in section 119 PIL Act stipulating that a law applicable to a dispute shall be the law chosen by the parties. If the parties have not chosen such law, it shall be determined by the arbitrators in accordance with the provisions of this Act. The conflict of law provisions of the applicable law shall be taken into consideration only provided it follows from the choice of law made by the parties.

100. *Renvoi* is expressly admitted in the law applicable to bills of exchange and cheques. Under section 31(1) PIL Act, the capacity of a person to obligations under bills of exchange or cheques shall be governed by the law of the state in which he or she is a citizen. Should that law claim another state's law is applicable, the law of the other state applies. Admission of *renvoi* in this field is a classical solution in line with the Geneva conventions on bills of exchange and cheques the provisions of which were implemented into the Czech (formerly Czechoslovak) law.

101. In European conflict rules on obligations and family law, *renvoi* is expressly excluded (*see* Article 15 Rome Convention, Article 20 Rome I, Article 24 Rome II, Article 11 Rome III, Article 32 Regulation on matrimonial property regimes). The only exception so far is the limited admission of *renvoi* in Article 14 of the Succession Regulation as in succession matters *renvoi* has been traditionally accepted.

§5. General Choice of Law Rule/Special Choice of Law Rule

102. Historically, the former PIL Act was enacted in 1963 and entered into force in 1964. This fact is important when considering the characteristic features of the conflict rules included in Czech autonomous law. At that time, most of the conflict rules were of a general nature with very few special conflict rules only. Therefore, the former PIL Act contains mostly general conflict rules. In a number of cases, special conflict rules were missing, as e.g., conflict rules on licensing contract, suretyship, product liability, unfair competition, etc. The general nature of conflict rules in the former PIL Act also mirrored the rather general substantive rules of the former socialist legislation.

103. Currently, the situation is different. The new PIL Act had to respect the fact that at the time of its adoption several very important EU regulations were applicable, in particular Rome I and Rome II which contain both general and special conflict rules in the law of contractual and extra-contractual obligations. After the adoption of the PIL Act in 2012, other EU regulations entered into force, namely the Succession Regulation, Regulation on Matrimonial Property Regime and Regulation on Registered Partnership Regime which include both general and special conflict rules. These regulations take precedence over the conflict rules contained in the PIL Act, in conformity with the intertemporal provisions of the regulations.

104. The general conflict rule on contractual obligations in section 87(1) PIL Act is therefore a supplementary rule with respect to the material scope of the Rome I Regulation (Article 1 Rome I). There are special conflict rules concerning contractual obligations which are not explicitly covered by the scope of the Rome I, as e.g., conflict rules on unilateral legal acts in sections 90 and 91 PIL Act.[78] Other special conflict rules for contracts transpose rules contained in directives, as e.g., law governing the timeshare contracts (section 87(4) PIL Act). In the field of extra-contractual obligations, Rome II contains both general and special conflict rules. The PIL Act contains only one special rule on law applicable to non-contractual obligations arising out of violations of privacy and rights relating to personality, including defamation (section 101 PIL Act) which is explicitly excluded from the material scope of Rome II (cf. Article 1(2) g) Rome II).

105. In areas not covered by EU law or international conventions, PIL Act lays down both general and special conflict rules. This concerns law of persons (sections 29 and 30 PIL Act), law applicable to bills of exchange and cheques (sections 31–32, 43 and 93–100 PIL Act), capacity limitation and guardianship (sections 33–38 PIL Act), legal acts (sections 41–43 PIL Act), agency, proxy and limitation (sections 44–46 PIL Act). In family law, autonomous rules on marital regimes apply (sections 48–50 PIL Act),including general and special conflict rules which are partly covered by the Matrimonial Property Regimes Regulation taking priority. Parent-child regimes, including parentage, maintenance, custody and care of minors and rights of unmarried mothers are governed by autonomous conflict rules (sections 54, 56, and 59 PIL Act); however, special rules of the Hague Maintenance Protocol and the Hague Convention on Children's Protection shall take preference. There are autonomous special conflict rules on adoption in sections 61–62 PIL Act. Section 67(2) PIL Act, which contains special rules on registered partnership and similar regimes, is partly overlapped by the Registered Partnership Regulation. Sections 69–73 and 80 PIL Act contain both general and special rules on the law applicable on rights in rem. As for the rules on succession (sections 76–78 PIL Act), in most cases the Succession Regulation prevails (*see infra* Part II Chapter 6). Special conflict rules for securities and investment instruments are laid down in sections 82–83 PIL Act. Special conflict rules apply in arbitration (sections 117 and 119 PIL Act).

106. The probably most general conflict rule in the Czech PIL Act is the rule in section 24(1) on exceptional determination of applicable law. In exceptional cases it shall be possible to decline from the application of a conflict rule under this Act provided it seems inappropriate and contrary to a reasonable and fair arrangement of the participants' relations, following a due and reasoned assessment of all circumstances of the case. Under these conditions and provided the rights of third persons are not prejudiced, the law the application of which corresponds to such an

78. *See* M. Pauknerová, *Law Applicable to Unilateral Juridical Acts and Uniform Conflict-of-Law Rules*, J. Comp. Law, Association for Comparative legal Studies, Wallington, UK, 115–126 (2011).

arrangement shall be applied. In other words, a general rule is based on a reasonable assessment of all circumstances of the case. The wording calls for very strict and narrow interpretation.

§6. Assimilation

107. Assimilation or adaptation is a method used if different aspects of a case are governed by different legal systems and the operation of different laws leads to apparently unusual or unacceptable results creating injustice or hardship. Assimilation is a process that shall redress the balance of solutions by means of adapting the applicable law or laws in an unusual situation. For example, the proper law of contract, either the law selected by the contracting parties (Article 3 Rome I) or the otherwise applicable proper law determined under Article 4 Rome I shall also be applicable with respect to the changes, security and consequences of breaches of obligations unless the parties provide otherwise (*see* Article 12 Rome I). As concerns the security of obligations, under section 91 PIL Act a security of obligation shall be governed by the same law as the secured obligation, unless a right in rem is concerned or it follows otherwise from law or nature of the matter or the parties or a party who provided the security by means of a unilateral expression of intent chooses the application of another law. In the case of a suretyship where several guarantors cover an obligation, the suretyship of each of them may be governed by a different law. Such laws may resolve the question of the mutual relations of the guarantors in a different way and thus lead to unacceptable consequences.

108. Assimilation may be carried out either at the level of substantive law or at the level of conflict rules. With the former approach substantive rules of the applicable laws which come in question are assimilated resulting in an acceptable solution; with the latter approach conflict rules are adjusted so that a law that offers a reasonable solution is determined. Czech legal theory favours the former of these two solutions – assimilation at the level of substantive rules.[79]

109. The Succession Regulation anticipates the possibility of assimilation/adaptation of rights in rem. Pursuant to Article 31, where a person invokes a right in rem to which he is entitled under the law applicable to the succession and the law of the Member State in which the right is invoked does not know the right in rem in question, that right shall, if necessary and to the extent possible, be adapted to the closest equivalent right in rem under the law of that State, taking into account the aims and the interests pursued by the specific right in rem and the effects attached to it.

110. Special rules on adaptation of rights in rem are provided in the Matrimonial Property Regimes Regulation. Under Article 29, where a person invokes a right in rem to which he/she is entitled under the law applicable to the matrimonial property regime and the law of the Member State in which the right is invoked does not

79. *See* Z. Kučera, *Mezinárodní právo soukromé*, 2009, *supra*, 185.

know the right in rem in question, that right shall, if necessary and to the extent possible, be adapted to the closest equivalent right under the law of that State, taking into account the aims and the interests pursued by the specific right in rem and the effects attached to it.

111. In general, in order to resolve unacceptable results due to the operation of conflict rules by means of assimilation or adaptation of the applicable laws which come into question, the principle of a reasonable settlement of the respective legal relation (*see* section 24(1) PIL Act) should always be preferred to interpretations built up merely by the *lex fori*. In our opinion, it is impossible to codify general rules that resolve disharmonic results of different provisions.

§7. Ordre Public (Public Policy)

112. The reservation of public order (public policy) gives courts the opportunity of refusing the application of a provision or provisions of the governing foreign law when the outcome of the application would be manifestly incompatible with the fundamental principles of the Czech political, social and legal systems. The reservation of public policy is used only exceptionally – a foreign rule which would otherwise be applicable will not take effect if contrary to Czech public policy. Public policy reservation is directed towards the effects of the application of a foreign rule, not against a rule as such because such an approach would interfere with the sovereignty of a foreign state. Reservation of public order is also one of the grounds for non-recognition or non-enforcement of foreign judgments or arbitral awards.

113. Under section 4 PIL Act, provisions of a foreign law which is to be applied pursuant to the provisions of this Act shall not be applied if the effects of such application are manifestly incompatible with the public policy. For the same reasons it shall not be possible to recognize foreign judgments, foreign court settlements, foreign notarial acts and other public documents (authentic instruments), foreign arbitral awards, to undertake a procedural act based on a request from abroad (from foreign authorities), or to recognize a legal relation or an event which originated abroad or under a foreign law.

114. The public policy reservation is triggered when the effects of application of the foreign governing law are contrary to the provisions that represent fundamental principles of the Czech public order, particularly those which are included in the Charter of Fundamental Rights and Freedoms, thereby forming a part of the constitutional order of the Czech Republic,[80] in particular the fundamental (overriding mandatory) rules of Czech law, such as the equality of races or sex, or the regulations relating to children (*see also* R 26/87, pp 491–492). However, divergent provisions on the period of limitation in the applicable foreign law should not trigger

80. *See* Constitutional Act No. 1/1993 Coll., Constitution of the Czech Republic, and No. 2/1993 Coll., instituting the Charter of Fundamental Rights and Freedoms as a part of the constitutional order of the Czech Republic.

the application of public policy reservation (*see* Collection of Decisions of the Supreme Court of the Czech Republic, No. 132/1965).

115. Pursuant to the Czech autonomous PIL the public policy reservation concept corresponds in principle to the public policy concept under the European conflict of laws (*see* in particular Article 21 Rome I, Article 26 Rome II, Article 35 of the Succession Regulation, Article 31 of the Matrimonial Property Regimes Regulation, etc.). According to these rules, the application of a provision of the law of any country specified by these instruments may be refused only if such application is manifestly incompatible with the public policy (*ordre public*) of the forum. The same applies to international conventions. Pursuant to Article 22 of the Hague Convention on the Protection of Children, the application of the law designated by the provisions of this convention can be refused only if this application would be manifestly contrary to public policy, taking into account the best interests of the child.

116. According to the doctrine of the Czech PIL, public policy should only be invoked in exceptional circumstances, depending on the intensity of a particular relationship to the *forum* state. The closer a relationship is to the *forum* state, the greater the danger of undesirable consequences. Thus, for example, should a Czech court probate the estate of an alien – for example an Iranian – located in the Czech Republic, the applicable law concerning the legal relations of the heirs will be the Iranian law according to the habitual residence of the decedent. A preliminary question arises as to the validity of a polygamous marriage of the decedent because there are two of the decedent's spouses in Iran who assert to be heirs. In such a case, there would be no reason to deny the application of the respective provisions of the Iranian Civil Code, even if based on the principle of polygamy which would otherwise be contrary to the fundamental principles of Czech family law. The relation of this case to the *forum* state is not intensive enough.[81]

117. The gap in the applicable law as a consequence of the public policy should be substituted by the *lex fori,* if necessary. In some cases, when a rule of a foreign law has been set aside, the gap does not have to be filled. Under some laws, for example, interracial marriages are prohibited and it is obvious that the Czech authorities would simply refuse to apply such provisions of foreign law.

118. The relevant moment for the assessment of the effects of the application of a foreign law, the consequences of which are contrary to the fundamental principles of Czech public order, is when the court decides.

119. Reservation of public order is also applied in international procedural law. As mentioned above, a foreign decision is neither recognized nor enforced if contrary to the Czech public order (section 4 PIL Act, second sentence). The same applies to foreign arbitral awards; when contrary to the Czech public order, they are neither recognized nor enforced in the territory of the Czech Republic (section 121 d) PIL Act).

---

81. *See* Z. Kučera, *Mezinárodní právo soukromé*, 2009, *supra*, 195–196.

120. Ordre public reservation is a standard ground for refusal of recognition and enforcement of foreign judgments contained in EU law and international conventions. Pursuant to Article 45(1) a) of the Brussels I Recast, on the application of any interested party, the recognition of a judgment shall be refused if such recognition is manifestly contrary to public policy (ordre public) in the Member State addressed. *See also* Article 22 Brussels II*bis*, Article 24 of the Maintenance Regulation, Article 40 of the Succession Regulation, Article 31 of the Matrimonial Property Regimes Regulation, etc. Special rule is included in Article 33 of the Insolvency Regulation: Any Member State may refuse to recognize insolvency proceedings opened in another Member State or to enforce a judgment handed down in the context of such proceedings where the effects of such recognition or enforcement would be manifestly contrary to that State's public policy, in particular its fundamental principles or the constitutional rights and liberties of the individual. Public policy reservation is also contained in international conventions, e.g., in Article 23(2) lit. d of the Hague Convention on Protection of Children.

§8. Overriding Mandatory Rules

121. Pursuant to the Czech PIL theory overriding mandatory rules or imperative rules[82] – are usually defined as mandatory substantive rules which have to be taken into account in international cases, irrespective of the law governing the particular case. Overriding mandatory rules are not rules that form part of PIL, as they are mostly rules of public law. However, these rules may have important legal consequences for cross-border private law relations. Overriding mandatory rules are defined in Article 9(1) Rome I as provisions, the respect for which is regarded as crucial by a country for safeguarding its public interests, such as its political, social or economic organization, to such an extent that they are applicable to any situation falling within their scope, irrespective of the law otherwise applicable to the contract. Similarly, according to the Matrimonial Property Regimes Regulation, overriding mandatory provisions are provisions, the respect for which is regarded as crucial by a Member State for safeguarding its public interests, such as its political, social or economic organization, to such an extent that they are applicable to any situation falling within their scope, irrespective of the law otherwise applicable to the matrimonial property regime pursuant to this Regulation (Article 30(2) of the Regulation).

122. Internal mandatory rules, unlike overriding mandatory rules or mandatory rules in international cases, cannot be contracted out by the parties in the framework of one legal system; however, such rules may be contracted out by the choice of another law by the parties (*see* Article 3 Rome I and Article 3 Rome Convention permitting an unlimited choice of law for obligations). For example, under section

82. *See*, *inter alia*, Z. Kučera, *Mezinárodní právo soukromé*, 2009, *supra*, 235 et seq.; M. Pauknerová, *Mandatory Rules and Public Policy in International Contract Law*, ERA Forum 11, 29 et seq. (2010); and M. Pauknerová, 'Overriding Mandatory Rules and Czech Law', *Czech Yearbook of International Law* (2010): 81 et seq. with further references.

2175 CivC, by purchasing an enterprise, the buyer shall acquire everything that pertains to the enterprise as a whole. Even where the parties exclude an individual item from the purchase whereby the whole does not lose its nature of an enterprise, it is considered as a purchase of an enterprise. Rules on validity of legal acts, discharge of obligations, recognition of obligations, or rules on public offer or public tender are other examples of mandatory provisions in Czech CivC (*see* section 1(2) CivC, pursuant to which, unless expressly prohibited by a statute, persons can stipulate rights and duties by way of exclusion from a statute; stipulations contrary to good morals, public order or the law concerning the status of persons, including the right to protection of personality rights, are prohibited). However, in an international contact such provisions may be excluded by a choice of another applicable law.

123. Overriding mandatory rules cannot be contracted out by the parties by a choice of another law. These rules are imperative (mandatory) as they claim to be taken into account immediately, regardless of the governing law. They are mostly rules of public law: e.g., foreign exchange rate regulations, export/import restrictions, protection of employees in labour-law relations, residency permits, etc. Another example are provisions of the Act on Foreign Trade with Military Material[83] that require for the exportation of military material both a general licence and a permit for every particular transaction issued by Czech authorities (*see* sections 7–22 of the Act). Without the licence and the permit, a sales contract would be invalid. Overriding mandatory provisions are also to be found, e.g., in section 89 of the Employment Act,[84] pursuant to which a labour contract with an alien (either a foreign national or a person without nationality) is concluded provided such persons have been granted both residence and work permit.[85] If the place of the performance of the work were located on the territory of the Czech Republic, Czech courts would, in the absence of such permits, consider a labour contract invalid whatever the applicable law to the contract might be. The application of overriding mandatory rules that are part of the *lex fori* is generally recognized in European PIL codifications. *See* Article 9(2) Rome I, Article 7(2) Rome Convention, and Article 16 Rome II.

124. The Czech PIL Act contains a similar provision on overriding mandatory rules in section 3, pursuant to which provisions of the PIL Act shall not prevent the application of such provisions of the Czech legal order which are, within the limits of their subject matter, always applicable regardless of which law governs the legal relations that are affected by the application of such provisions.

125. Problems may appear when the Czech court shall take into consideration overriding mandatory rules of another legal system than those of the *forum*. The

83. Act on Foreign Trade with Military Material no. 38/1994 Coll., as amended.
84. Employment Act No. 435/2004 Coll., as amended.
85. Citizens of other EU Member States and their family members shall have the same status in the legal relations regulated by this Act as citizens of the Czech Republic, unless otherwise stated by this Act. *See* s. 3(2) of the Employment Act.

Czech PIL Act has a special provision on the application of foreign overriding mandatory rules. Upon request of a party, overriding mandatory provisions of a foreign law apply irrespective of governing law provided the rights and obligations concerned have a sufficiently significant connection to the other state and it is fair given the nature of these provisions, their purpose or consequences (implications) which their application or non-application would have on the parties. The party invoking such provisions shall prove the validity and content of these rules (section 25 PIL Act). This provision leaves sufficient space to the judge for assessment of all relevant circumstances of the case. It is applicable only to cases that are not covered by uniform rules: either EU regulations or international conventions which precede over the Czech law (section 2 PIL Act).

126. The rules on application of foreign overriding mandatory rules that form part of the governing law (foreign *lex causae*) are contained in section 23(1) PIL Act, in connection with rules on application of foreign law. Pursuant to this provision, the foreign law, which is to be applied under the provisions of this Act, shall be applied regardless of its systematic classification or its public nature, provided it is not contrary to the overriding mandatory provisions of the Czech law.

127. As for international treaties and conventions, reference to overriding mandatory provisions may be found, e.g., in Article VIII, section 2(b) of the Bretton Woods Agreement on International Monetary Fund of 1944, or Article 7 of the Hague Convention on the Law Applicable to Traffic Accidents of 1971.

128. Under EU regulations, pursuant to the Rome I Regulation, effect may be given to the overriding mandatory provisions of the law of the country where the obligations arising out of the contract have to be or have been performed, insofar as those overriding mandatory provisions render the performance of the contract unlawful. In considering whether to give effect to those provisions, regard shall be had to their nature and purpose and to the consequences of their application or non-application (Article 9(3) Rome I). Provisions of the Rome Convention, which partly inspired the Czech treatment of overriding mandatory rules, may still be relevant. Under Article 7(1) Rome Convention, when applying the law of a country, effect may be given to the mandatory rules of the law of another country with which the situation has a close connection, if and insofar as, under the law of the latter country, those rules must be applied whatever the law applicable to the contract. In considering whether to give effect to these mandatory rules, regard shall be had to their nature and purpose and to the consequences of their application or non-application.

129. The Succession Regulation contains a special rule in Article 30 on the application of special rules imposing restrictions concerning or affecting the succession in respect of certain assets. Under this provision, where the law of the State in which certain immovable property, certain enterprises or other special categories of assets are located contains special rules which, for economic, family or social considerations, impose restrictions concerning or affecting the succession in respect of those assets, those special rules shall apply to the succession in so far as, under the law of that State, they are applicable irrespective of the law applicable to the succession (*see also* Recital 54 of the Preamble to the Regulation).

130. A question arose before the Arbitration Court attached to the Economic Chamber of the Czech Republic and Agricultural Chamber of the Czech Republic in Prague whether or not an imperative foreign trade regulation of Hungary, which was neither the applicable law nor the law of the *forum* state, should be taken into account. The parties to the arbitral proceedings were a company with a head office in the Czech Republic on the one hand, and a company with its head office in Austria on the other. The governing law of the mandate contract at stake, which allegedly contravened the Hungarian law, was the Czech law. The arbitrators arrived at the conclusion that, in principle, they do not *a Priori* refuse to take into account such imperative regulations of a foreign state whose law is not the applicable law to the concrete relation. They stated that Czech law does not explicitly deal with this question; however, it is possible to find out the actual state in the development of legal theory and practice by comparing other legal regulations, even though they were not binding for the Czech Republic, for example Article 16 of the Hague Convention on the Law Applicable to Agency of 1978, or Article 16(2) of the Hague Convention on the Law Applicable to Trusts and on Their Recognition of 1985, or Article 7(1) of the Rome Convention of 1980. Also, in proceedings in the Czech Republic, it is possible, in principle, to take into account viewpoints of the same character as formulated in Article 7(1) Rome Convention. However, in this particular case, the defendant did not come up, despite repeated requests by the arbitrators, with copies of the respective Hungarian regulations. It is not the duty of arbitrators to know these regulations, as the principle *iura novit curia* relates only to domestic law (*see* section 53(1) PIL Act 1963). The duty to ascertain the provisions of foreign law relates only to the law applicable on the basis of a domestic conflict rule. However, in the given case, Hungarian law was not the applicable law. The arbitrators therefore were not obliged to ascertain the existence and know the contents of these regulations. If a party to the proceedings had invoked particular public law regulations of Hungarian law, it would have been up to him or her to prove its existence and wording, which the defendant did not do.[86] In other words, the duty to ascertain the existence and contents of a foreign law relates only to a foreign law set by the domestic conflict rule and not to the law of a third state which enforces its application, whatever is the law applicable to the contract. The afore-mentioned decision thus admitted the principle of the applicability of foreign imperative rules, even if in the end the foreign public law was not applied.

131. This decision partly inspired the formulation of section 25 of the Czech PIL Act that applies in areas not covered by international conventions or EU regulations, i.e., in particular in law of persons, rights in rem, and some parts of family law.

86. Arbitral Award No. 78/92 of 22 Mar. 1995. *See* M. Pauknerová, *Eingriffsnormen im tschechischen Internationalen Privatrecht*, in *Festschrift für Hans Jürgen Sonnenberger* 575 et seq. (Verlag Beck 2004).

§9. EVASION OF THE LAW

132. Evasion of the law takes place when persons, in order to avoid the applicable law, artificially create relevant connecting factors in other states for evading the law which would otherwise be applicable. In Czech autonomous PIL, the evasion concerns mandatory conflict rules. Therefore, it does not come into consideration in the Czech conflict law of obligations where an unlimited choice of law by the parties is permitted (*see* section 87(1) PIL Act and Article 3 Rome I which takes precedence over the autonomous rules). Evasion of the law may take place only where no choice of law is admitted or where a limited choice of law is admitted, e.g., regarding an agreement on matrimonial property regime where the choice of law is limited to nationality, habitual residence, location of an immovable property, or the *lex fori* (*see* section 49(4) PIL Act).

133. Czech PIL includes an explicit provision on evasion of law. Under section 5 PIL Act, facts created or pretended by a deliberate act with an intention to eliminate the application of such provisions of this Act which cannot be derogated from by an agreement, or to apply them differently than if such created or pretended facts did not exist, shall be disregarded. This concept applies in relation both to conflict of law and to jurisdiction rules.

134. Under section 580(1) CivC, a juridical act is (among others) invalid if it is contrary to good morals or contrary to a statute, if so required by the sense and purpose of a statute. Pursuant to this provision, a legal act shall be invalid if its contents or purpose contradicts or circumvents the law, under further conditions of the Civil Code, in particular, if such an act is contrary to public order.[87] In view of this, if an act circumvents the law – that is, an act has been performed *in fraudem legis* – such an act shall be invalid. The Civil Code differentiates between an apparent contradiction which establishes absolute nullity, and a contradiction to good morals or to statute which will be taken into consideration only upon a motion (relative nullity).[88]

135. In conflict of laws, evasion of law is treated differently. The artificially created connecting factor is irrelevant, and the judge treats the case as if the parties had not fabricated any artificial connecting factor and applies the substantive law otherwise applicable under regular conflict rules. This substantive law, as the governing law of the case (*lex causae*), shall also hold whether or not such acts were invalid and/or no matter what the consequences of such an act are. In international civil procedure, evasion of law means intentional creation of conditions for the establishment of jurisdiction of a court of certain state. Nowadays, when choice of applicable law and prorogation of a court are often permitted, evasion of law in PIL is rather exceptional.

---

87. In details *see* M. Pauknerová, in Pauknerová/Rozehnalová/Zavadilová, *Zákon o mezinárodním právu soukromém. Komentář*, 2013, at 50.
88. *Ibid.*, with further references.

136. Divorce cases were the most frequent cases of evasion of the law in the past, and Czech legal regulation seems to be relatively satisfactory in this respect. The applicable law to divorce is the law of the state whose citizens the spouses were at the time the divorce proceedings were initiated; if they are citizens of two different states, the law of the state in which both spouses are habitually resident applies, failing that, the Czech law applies (sections 49 and 50 PIL Act). Under section 50(2) PIL Act, should it be necessary to apply foreign law which does not allow divorce or admits it only under extremely onerous circumstances, Czech law shall apply provided at least one of the spouses is a citizen of the Czech Republic or at least one of the spouses is habitually resident in the Czech Republic. This provision should be assessed in connection with the jurisdiction rules (*see* in particular Articles 3–7 Brussels II*bis* Regulation). Under the Czech autonomous law, section 47 PIL Act on jurisdiction in family matters stipulates that unless an international treaty or a directly applicable provision of the EU law provides otherwise, Czech courts have jurisdiction for proceedings on divorce if one of the spouses is a citizen of the Czech Republic or if the defendant has habitual residence in the Czech Republic. If the spouses are foreigners and the defendant is not habitually resident in the Czech Republic or in another Member State of the EU, nor is a citizen of a Member State of the EU and is not domiciled in the United Kingdom or in Ireland, the Czech courts shall have jurisdiction in these matters provided (a) both spouses were habitually resident in the Czech Republic and the plaintiff still has habitual residence in the Czech Republic, (b) the plaintiff has habitual residence in the Czech Republic and the second spouse joined the application, or (c) the plaintiff has habitual residence in the Czech Republic and has had such habitual residence for at least one year prior to filing the action. Each particular case shall always depend upon the assessment of the respective court.

137. The evasion of law cases (if any, *see* section 5 PIL Act) will mostly be resolved with reference to a public order reservation.

§10. Reference to the Law of States with Multiple Legal orders

138. Czech Republic is a unitary state; however, historically, former Czechoslovakia was divided into Czech lands and Slovakia with different legal systems that were unified in 1950 (31 December 1950). Under the section 54 of the PIL Act 1948, the interregional PIL was applied also in the Czechoslovak territory.

139. Pursuant to the current PIL Act, should a legal order of a state with more than one legal system or with different provisions for individual groups of persons apply, the law of such state shall determine the application of relevant legal provisions (section 23(4) PIL Act). It is necessary to differentiate whether the connecting factor refers to a particular place within the state (residence, seat, place where the contract was concluded, place where the damage occurred), or refers to a state as a whole (nationality). In the first case the interregional law of the area where the place is located will apply. In the second case, in addition to the affiliation of a person to a particular place, his/her domicile, last habitual residence etc. could also be taken into consideration.

140. Under Article 22(1) Rome I and Article 25(1) Rome II, where a State comprises several territorial units, each of which has its own rules of law in respect of obligations, each territorial unit shall be considered as a country for identifying the law applicable under the Regulation. A Member State where different territorial units have their own rules of law in respect of obligations shall not be required to apply this Regulation to conflicts solely between the laws of such units.

141. Similar rules are to be found in international conventions, e.g., the Hague convention on the law applicable to traffic accidents. Under Article 12 of the Convention, every territorial entity forming part of a State having a non-unified legal system shall be considered as a State when it has its own legal system, in respect of civil non-contractual liability arising from traffic accidents. It means that the law applicable in such a territorial entity will be applied, without regard to interregional rules of such state.

142. However, under the Succession Regulation, where the law specified by this Regulation is that of a State which comprises several territorial units, each of which has its own rules of law in respect of succession, the internal conflict of laws rules of that State shall determine the relevant territorial unit whose rules of law are to apply. In the absence of such internal conflict of laws rules: (a) any reference to the law of the State referred to shall, for the purposes of determining the law applicable pursuant to provisions referring to the habitual residence of the deceased, be construed as referring to the law of the territorial unit in which the deceased had his habitual residence at the time of death; (b) any reference to the law of the State referred to shall, for the purposes of determining the law applicable pursuant to provisions referring to the nationality of the deceased, be construed as referring to the law of the territorial unit with which the deceased had the closest connection; (c) any reference to the law of the State referred to shall, for the purposes of determining the law applicable pursuant to any other provisions referring to other elements as connecting factors, be construed as referring to the law of the territorial unit in which the relevant element is located (for details *see* Article 36 of the Succession Regulation).

143. As for interpersonal collisions, in some states different substantive rules apply to particular groups of persons (according to religion, European or another origin, etc.). Under section 23(4) PIL Act should a legal order of a state with more than one legal system or with different provisions for individual groups of persons apply, the law of such state shall determine the application of relevant legal provisions. Under Article 37 of the Succession Regulation, in relation to a State which has two or more systems of law or sets of rules applicable to different categories of persons in respect of succession, any reference to the law of that State shall be construed as referring to the system of law or set of rules determined by the rules in force in that State. In the absence of such rules, the system of law or the set of rules with which the deceased had the closest connection shall apply.

144. In cases of interpersonal collisions, it is necessary to examine whether the effects of application of a foreign law are not contrary to public order.

Part II. Conflict of Law Rules

Chapter 1. Persons

§1. Natural Persons

145. Legal capacity of natural persons is an ability to amend rights and obligations. It has to be differentiated from legal personality, the ability to hold and to exercise rights and duties, which is a prerequisite to legal capacity. Pursuant to section 15(1) of the CivC legal personality is the capacity to have rights and duties within the legal order. Legal personality is attained upon birth (section 23 CivC); however, Czech law follows the *nasciturus* fiction extending legal personality to unborn foetus if born alive and if it is in its interest (section 25 CivC).

146. Legal personality dies with the person (section 23 CivC). If death cannot be determined in the prescribed manner, the court, even of its own motion, shall declare the individual dead if the individual was involved in such an event that his death, given the circumstances, seems certain. In its decision, the court establishes the date of death (section 26(2) CivC). The declaration of death or of absence before a Czech court is always governed by Czech law (section 39(3) PIL Act). Czech courts have exclusive jurisdiction to declare Czech nationals dead or absent (section 39(1) PIL Act). Czech courts also have jurisdiction to declare foreigners dead or absent; however, legal effects of such a declaration are limited as it has legal consequences only for Czech nationals (the place of their habitual residence is irrelevant) and for persons who are habitually resident and the property is situated on the territory of Czech Republic (section 39(2) PIL Act).

147. Full legal capacity of natural persons is acquired upon reaching the age of majority, which is eighteen years (section 30(1) CivC). Before reaching the age of majority, full legal capacity can be acquired by entering into marriage or by being granted full legal capacity by court (section 30(2) CivC). Intellectual and volitional capacity is acquired gradually as minors develop, and they are therefore presumed to be capable of making juridical acts which are, as to their nature, appropriate to the intellectual and volitional maturity of the minors of their age (section 31 CivC).

148. As regards conflict of laws rules, under the general rule in section 29(1) PIL Act, legal personality and legal capacity of natural persons are governed by the law of the state in which a person is habitually resident. There has been a shift from the traditional connecting factor of nationality applied in the corresponding conflict of laws rule in the former PIL Act[89] towards the modern connecting factor of habitual residence. *In favorem validitatis* should a natural person lack legal capacity to undertake a legal act according to the law of the country of its habitual residence, it suffices when the person has legal capacity under the law of the country where the legal act is undertaken (section 29(2) PIL Act). Pursuant to this general conflict of laws rules, the law applicable to legal capacity is either the law of the state of the habitual residence or the *lex loci actus*.

149. Legal capacity is excluded from the material scope of Rome I Regulation with prejudice to Article 13 stipulating that in a contract between persons who are in the same country, a natural person who would have capacity under the law of that country may invoke his incapacity resulting from another law only if the other party to the contract was aware of this incapacity at the time of the conclusion of the contract or was not aware thereof as a result of negligence.

150. The general conflict of laws rules in section 29(1) and (2) PIL Act apply unless stipulated otherwise in the PIL Act. There are special conflict of laws rules on legal capacity of a person to conclude marriage, to conclude registered partnership, to draw or withdraw a disposition of property upon death, to assume obligations arising from bills of exchange and on legal capacity of a foreigner to act as an arbitrator. Under section 48(1) PIL Act the legal capacity of a person to conclude marriage as well as the conditions for the validity of marriage is governed by *lex patriae* of the person in question. Legal capacity to conclude and terminate registered partnership (or similar relationship) as well as the effects thereof is governed by the law of the state in which the registered partnership or similar relationship is being or has been celebrated (section 67(2) PIL Act). A special conflict of laws rule on legal capacity to draw and withdraw a disposition of property upon death is stipulated in section 77(1) PIL Act: the law applicable is the law of the state of which the deceased person is a citizen at the time of the disposition or where the deceased is habitually resident at that time. The application of this national conflict of laws rule is affected by the Succession Regulation[90] that contains special conflict of laws rules for substantive validity of dispositions of property upon death made in writing in Articles 24 and 25 (for the purposes of these rules the capacity of the person making a disposition of property upon death to make such a disposition pertains to substantive validity pursuant to Article 26(1)(a) Succession Regulation) and by a number of bilateral treaties on legal assistance in civil matters concluded with non-EU countries that contain special conflict of laws rules for legal capacity to draw or withdraw a will (e.g., Article 36 of the Treaty between the Czechoslovak Socialist Republic and the Socialist Republic of Vietnam on Legal Assistance in Civil and Criminal Matters according to which the law applicable to capacity of the deceased to make or revoke a will is his *lex patriae* at the time of its making or

89. PIL Act No. 97/1963 Coll., concerning PIL and the Rules of Procedure relating thereto, as amended.
90. Regulation (EU) No. 650/2012 of the European Parliament and of the Council on jurisdiction, applicable law, recognition and enforcement of decisions and acceptance and enforcement of authentic instruments in matters of succession and on the creation of a European Certificate of Succession (Succession Regulation).

revoking). Legal capacity of a person to obligations (to be legally bound) under bills of exchange or cheques is governed by the law of the state of which the person is a national (section 31(1) PIL Act), renvoi is admitted. Provided a foreigner habitually resident outside of the territory of the Czech Republic lacks legal capacity to obligations under bills of exchange or cheques under his *lex patriae*, it is sufficient if he has legal capacity pursuant to the law of the country where he signed the bill of exchange or cheque.

151. The capacity to incur liability in tort is not governed by the law determined pursuant to the conflict of laws rule on legal capacity to undertake legal acts in section 29 PIL Act; it is governed by the law applicable to non-contractual obligations determined pursuant to Rome II Regulation (*see* Recital 12 of the Preamble). Rome II Regulation that is applicable to events giving rise to damage which occurred after 11 January 2009 is based on the *lex loci damni infecti* principle. Unless provided otherwise the law applicable to non-contractual obligations arising out of a tort/delict is the law of the country in which the damage occurs irrespective of the country in which the event giving rise to the damage occurred and irrespective of the country in which the indirect consequences of that event occur (*see* for details Article 4(1) Rome II Regulation). The Czech PIL Act has no special rule on delictual capacity.

152. Under Czech law legal capacity of natural persons may only be restricted by court under conditions set out in section 55(1) CivC; declaration of incapacity is not admitted. The court may restrict the legal capacity of a person to the extent to which the person is unable to make juridical acts due to a mental disorder which is not only temporary and shall always define the extent to which the capacity of the person to undertake independent juridical acts has been restricted (section 57(1) CivC). Juridical acts undertaken by a person that lacks full legal capacity and is not eligible to undertake these acts are considered invalid as well as juridical acts undertaken by a person acting under a mental disorder that makes the person unable to make juridical acts (section 581 CivC).

153. As to the restriction of legal capacity of natural persons, the PIL Act provides for a conflict of laws rule in section 34. This provision that applies to guardianship also stipulates that the conditions for restriction of legal capacity as well as for incapacitation are governed by the law of the state where the person concerned (the ward) is habitually resident. The legal relations between the guardian and the ward are governed by *lex fori* (section 36 PIL Act). The obligation to accept and exercise guardianship is governed by the law of the state in which the guardian is habitually resident (section 35 PIL Act). The application of the relevant national conflict of laws rules is affected by the Hague Convention on International Protection of Adults that is binding for the Czech Republic.[91] Pursuant to Article 3 letter a) of the Convention measures within the material scope may deal with the determination of incapacity and the institution of a protective regime.

91. https://www.hcch.net/en/instruments/conventions/status-table/?cid=71 (accessed 14 Apr. 2018).

I. Name

154. Pursuant to section 77(1) CivC the name of natural person means his given name and surname (and where applicable his other names or maiden names that pertain to him on the basis of a statute). In general, every natural person has the right to use his name in legal transactions and the right to protection of and respect for his name (section 10(1) of the Charter of Fundamental Rights and Freedoms[92] and section 77(1) CivC). There are special provisions on the surname of married persons in sections 660–662 CivC, on the name of a child in sections 860–864 CivC and on the surname of an adopted person in section 835 CivC. Act on Registers, Name and Surname[93] regulates the recognition of decisions on changes of name and surname issued by bodies of foreign states (in particular, sections 77–79 of the Act). The Czech PIL Act contains a special conflict of laws rule on name of natural persons in section 29(3). The regulation of name is governed by the *lex patriae* of the person concerned unless the application of the law of the state in the territory of which the person is habitually resident is invoked. This is an important provision for international families whose members are of different nationalities but habitually resident in the same state. If *lex patriae* applies and the person concerned holds multiple nationalities, the rule in section 28 PIL Act applies to determine which nationality shall be considered relevant. The CJEU has delivered important decisions with respect to name (e.g., C-148/02 Garcia Avello that deals with issues of change of surname of children with multiple nationality).[94]

II. Nationality/Habitual Residence/Domicile

155. Nationality has traditionally been the most important connecting factor in Czech conflict of laws rules.[95] In the current PIL Act it has mostly given way to the connecting factor of habitual residence; however, there are still national conflict of laws rules based on this criterion to be found in the current PIL Act. There is therefore a special rule in section 28 PIL Act on multiple nationalities. A person with multiple nationalities that holds Czech nationality is considered a Czech national (section 28(1) PIL Act). Pursuant to section 28(2) PIL Act, if a person holds nationality of two or more foreign states, the nationality acquired last prevails unless there is a closer connection to another state whose national the person is. If the nationality of a person cannot be determined pursuant to paragraph 2 (e.g., a person has acquired multiple nationalities at birth), such person is regarded a national of the state in the territory of which he is habitually resident or provided the habitual residence cannot be determined, in the territory of which he resides. If his habitual residence or residence cannot be determined, for the purposes of PIL Act he is considered a Czech national (section 28(3) PIL Act). The rule in section 28 PIL Act

92. Constitutional Act No. 2/1993 Coll., Charter of Fundamental Rights and Freedoms, as amended.
93. Act No. 301/2000 Coll., on Registers, Name and Surname.
94. C-148/02 Carlos Garcia Avello, C-353/06 Stefan Grunkin, C-208/09 Ilonka Sayn-Wittgenstein, C-391/09 Mlagožata Runevič-Vardyn.
95. PIL Act No. 97/1963 Coll.

may be affected by provisions in bilateral treaties on legal assistance binding on the Czech Republic. Czech citizenship is regulated by Act on Czech Citizenship[96] that came into effect on 1 January 2014 and replaced the previous Act on Acquisition and Loss of Citizenship of the Czech Republic.[97] Habitual residence has no definition in the Czech legal system; it is a factual concept that is to be interpreted in line with the relevant decisions of the CJEU. Domicile is defined in section 80 CivC as a place where a person stays with the intention to live there permanently, subject to changes in circumstances; such intention may be evident from his declarations or from the circumstances of the case. A person with no domicile is considered to be domiciled at the place where he lives. If such a place cannot be determined or if it can be determined only with disproportionate difficulties, the place where a person has property or the place of his last domicile is considered to be his domicile.

III. Stateless Persons and Refugees

156. Pursuant to Czech law, if a person is stateless, he is regarded a national of the state in the territory of which he is habitually resident or provided the habitual residence cannot be determined, in the state in the territory of which he resides. If his habitual residence or residence cannot be determined pursuant to section 28(2) PIL Act, for the purposes of PIL Act he is considered a Czech national (section 28(3) PIL Act). If a person is an applicant for international protection, an asylum seeker or beneficiary of subsidiary protection or is stateless under another law or international agreement, the personal status of such a person is governed by provisions of international conventions determining the legal status of refugees and the legal status of stateless persons (section 28(4) PIL Act). Czech Republic is a party to the 1951 Convention Relating to Legal Status of Refugees, the 1954 Convention Relating to Legal Status of Stateless Persons and the 1961 Convention on the Reduction of Statelessness. Criteria for granting asylum in the Czech Republic are set in Act on Asylum.[98] Pursuant to its section 12 an asylum is granted to a foreign national if it is established during the course of international protection proceedings that the foreign national is either persecuted for exercising political rights and freedoms, or has legitimate fear of being persecuted on the grounds of race, gender, religion, nationality, belonging to a particular social group or for holding certain political opinions in the state of which he is a national, or, if the foreign national is a stateless person, in the state of his last permanent residence. Act on Temporary Protection of Aliens[99] sets out conditions for the admission and residence of aliens in the territory of the Czech Republic for the purposes of provision of temporary protection on account of armed conflict, civil war or ongoing violence, natural disaster, constant or massive violation of fundamental human rights and freedoms or constant or massive persecution on national or religious grounds (Article 1(1)(a) and Article 1(2) of the Act on Temporary Protection of Aliens).

96. Act No. 186/2013 Coll., on Czech Citizenship and on Amendment to Some Other Acts.
97. Act No. 40/1993 Coll. on Acquisition and Loss of Citizenship of the Czech Republic.
98. Act No. 325/1999 Coll., on Asylum.
99. Act No. 221/2003 Coll., on Temporary Protection of Aliens.

IV. Transsexuals

157. Change of sex is regulated by law since the recodification of Czech private law in 2012 (effective as of 2014).[100] The Czech substantive law stipulates surgery resulting in sterility as preconditions for a sex change. Under section 29(1) CivC the sex change of a person takes place by surgery in the course of which the genitalia is transformed and the reproductive function disabled. Sex change does not affect the personal status of a person or his property situation. However, by operation of law sex change triggers termination of both marriage and registered partnership (section 29(2) CivC). The rights and duties of a man and woman whose marriage terminated as a result of sex change to their common children as well as their property rights and duties are governed, by analogy, by provisions on the rights and duties of divorced spouses. There is no special conflict of laws rule in the PIL Act. The question of transsexuality is prima facie a question of personal status; therefore, the law of the state of the habitual residence of the person concerned shall apply (section 29(1) PIL Act).

§2. Legal Persons

158. Legal person is defined in section 20(1) CivC as an organized body whose legal personality is provided or recognized by statute. Legal persons under Czech law have legal personality (section 118 CivC) and capacity to acquire rights and duties consistent with their legal nature (section 20(1) CivC). There are three types of legal persons pursuant to the Czech CivC: corporations, endowed institutions and registered institutes.

I. Incorporated Organizations

159. Under Czech law all three types of legal persons: corporations, endowed institutions and registered institutes are incorporated upon registration in a public registry. Corporations include associations (section 214 CivC), associations of unit owners (section 1194 CivC) and business corporations. Business corporations that are regulated by special Act on Commercial Companies and Cooperatives (BCA)[101] include commercial companies and cooperatives. Commercial companies admitted by Czech law are an unlimited partnership, a limited partnership, a limited-liability company, a joint stock company, a European Company and a European Economic Interest Grouping (section 1(2) BCA). European Company and European Economic Interest Grouping are governed by the provisions of BCA only to the extent stipulated in the directly applicable legislation of the EU. Commercial companies are

100. In detail: B. Havelková, *The Legal Status of Transsexual and Transgender Persons in the Czech Republic*, in *The Legal Status of Transsexual and Transgender Persons* (J. Scherpe ed. Intersentia 2015).
101. Act No. 90/2012 Coll., on Commercial Companies and Cooperatives (BCA).

established for doing business or for managing their own assets unless provided otherwise. A cooperative is a community of an indefinite number of persons established for mutual support of its members or third parties or, where appropriate, for doing business (section 551(1) BCA).

160. The general conflict of laws rule to determine *lex societatis* is laid down in section 30 PIL Act. Legal personality and legal capacity of an entity, other than a natural person, are governed by the law of the state under which it was incorporated. The actual seat of the entity is of no relevance for the determination of *lex societatis* as this conflict of laws rule follows the incorporation principle. The law of incorporation applies regardless of whether or not such an entity has its actual seat in the state of its incorporation. The wording 'other than a natural person' widens the scope of applicability of the conflict of laws rule on foreign entities that are endowed with limited legal personality and capacity but are not considered as legal persons. However, for an entity to be bound by its usual acts it is sufficient if it has such capacity under the law applicable at the place where the legal act was undertaken (section 30(2) PIL Act). It is sufficient when the legal requirements of *lex loci actus* are met.

161. Czech law admits in principle only two types of associations which do not have legal personality and both of them can be formed only on a contractual basis: partnership (section 2716 CivC) and silent partnership (section 2747 CivC). As both partnerships are created on contractual basis only, conflict of laws rules on contracts apply.

II. Liability

162. Under Czech law *lex societatis*, the law of the state under which the entity was incorporated, is the law governing legal personality and legal capacity of the entity. Section 30(1) PIL Act contains a non-exhaustive list of issues included in the scope of *lex societatis*: trading name or name of an entity, internal relations of an entity, the relations between an entity and its partners or members, mutual relations of its partners or members, liability of its partners or members for obligations of an entity, determination of persons acting on behalf of an entity, winding up of an entity.

III. Cross-Border Transformation

163. Pursuant to section 26(1) PIL Act a foreign legal entity is a legal entity with its registered seat outside the territory of the Czech Republic, while a Czech legal entity is deemed to be an entity with a registered seat in the territory of the Czech Republic. A legal entity having its registered seat in Czech Republic may be established only under Czech law (section 30(3) PIL Act). Therefore, should a legal person be incorporated in the Czech Republic, it has to be in one of the legal forms laid down in Czech law. This rule does not affect the possibility to transfer the registered seat of a legal entity domiciled abroad and incorporated under the law of a foreign state to the Czech Republic, if so provided for in an international treaty, a directly applicable EU law or other legislation. General provisions on transfer of a registered seat to the Czech Republic are contained in sections 138–143 CivC. Pursuant to section 138(1) CivC the transfer of the registered seat of a legal person is possible unless prohibited under the legal order of the state in which the legal person has its registered seat or unless a legal person prohibited under section 145 CivC is involved. A legal person who intends to transfer its registered seat to the Czech Republic has to opt for one of the legal forms of legal persons provided for in Czech law and submit a relevant forming juridical act required by Czech law (section 138(2) CivC). After transferring its registered seat to the Czech Republic, internal legal relations within a legal person, as well as the liability of its members and the members of its bodies for debts of the person incurred after the effective date of the transfer, are governed by Czech law (section 138(3) CivC). Special provision on transfers of a registered seat from the territory of a EU Member State or any other state of the European Economic Area (EEA) to the Czech Republic are contained in sections 384a–384e Act on Transformations of Commercial Companies and Cooperatives.[102]

102. Act No. 125/2008, Coll., on Transformations of Commercial Companies and Cooperatives, as amended.

Chapter 2. Obligations

§1. Contractual Obligations

164. Conflict of laws rules for contracts are anchored in the Regulation (EC) No. 593/2008 of the European Parliament and of the Council of 17 June 2008 on the law applicable to contractual obligations (Rome I Regulation) that is currently the most relevant legal instrument in the Czech Republic for the determination of the law applicable for contracts. Rome I Regulation is applicable to contracts concluded on 17 December 2009 and later. Law applicable to contracts concluded before that date is determined according to conflict of laws rules of the Rome Convention on the Law Applicable to Contractual Obligations. Within the meaning of Article 17 of the Rome Convention, under which the Convention shall apply in a State party to contracts made after the date on which this Convention entered into force with respect to that state, in the Czech Republic the Rome Convention is applicable to contracts concluded after 1 July 2006. Contracts concluded before that date are subject to then relevant provisions of the Czech autonomous PIL. There are a number of bilateral treaties on legal assistance in civil matters concluded between the Czech Republic and non-EU countries that take precedence over the Rome I Regulation (Article 25(1)) and over the PIL Act rules (section 2 PIL Act). Some of them contain also rules on the law applicable to contractual obligations (e.g. the Treaty with Mongolia, No. 106/1978 Coll.). The PIL Act contains the rule for law applicable to contracts in its section 87. It applies: (a) provided the European unified conflict of laws rules do not apply, or (b) in amendment to the European unified conflict of laws rules or (c) to matters expressly excluded from the material scope of the Rome I Regulation or the Rome Convention or (d) provided there is no binding treaty unifying the relevant substantive law.[103]

I. Party Autonomy

165. Under Czech law and Czech legal theory, a contract is a bilateral or multilateral legal act based on consensus, on full and unconditional acceptance of an offer to conclude a contract. It is a bilateral or multilateral legal act from which an obligation arises.[104] Under section 1724 CivC, by a contract, parties express their will to enter into a mutual obligation and to adhere to the contents of the contract. Under an obligation a creditor has the right to a particular performance as a claim against the debtor, and the debtor has the duty to satisfy that right by discharging the debt (section 1721 CivC). Obligations arise of contracts, unlawful acts or other legal facts stipulated by the statute (section 1723(1) CivC). One of the most important principles of the law of contractual obligations, apart from the principle of

103. Rozehnalová in M. Pauknerová et al., *Zákon o mezinárodním právu soukromém. Komentář* [*Private International Law Act. Commentary*] 597 (Wolters Kluwer ČR 2013).

104. M. Hulmák, et al. *Občanský zákoník V. Závazkové právo. Obecná část (§ 1721 – 2054). Komentář* [*Civil Code V. Law of Obligations. General Part (ss 1721–2054). Commentary*] 18 (C.H. Beck 1st ed. 2014).

equality of the contractual parties, is the freedom to contract and the autonomy of will of the parties (section 1(2) CivC). The principle of autonomy of will applies accordingly in conflict of laws: contracting parties are, in principle, free to choose the applicable law.

166. Under Rome I Regulation parties may choose the law applicable to their contract irrespective of the fact whether or not it is the law of an EU Member State (Article 3 Rome I Regulation). The choice of law may be explicit or tacit, but it must be clearly demonstrated by the terms of the contract or circumstances of the case. The contractual parties are free to change the law to be applied after the conclusion of the contract. Partial choice of law is admitted; the parties can select the law applicable to part of the contract only. Unlike Czech autonomous law, Rome I Regulation expressly allows the choice of applicable law also in case of the so-called single-country contracts. Under Article 3(3) Rome I Regulation, where all other elements relevant to the situation at the time of the choice are located in a country other than the country whose law has been chosen, the choice of the parties shall not prejudice the application of provisions of the law of that other country which cannot be derogated from by an agreement.[105] Under Article 3(4) Rome I Regulation, where all other elements relevant to the situation at the time of the choice are located in one or more Member States of the EU, the parties' choice of applicable law other than that of a Member State shall not prejudice the application of provisions of European law, where appropriate as implemented in the EU Member State of the forum, which cannot be derogated from by an agreement.

167. Under Czech PIL Act the contracting parties may also choose which law will govern their contract. The choice of law can be made either expressly or tacitly (section 87(1) PIL Act). The choice of the law applicable to contracts under the Czech PIL Act is, except for certain special provisions implementing EU directives, unlimited.[106] Parties may choose any law to govern a contract, irrespective of whether there is a relevant link between the chosen law and contract, or not. The only condition is that the *lex electa* must be a law in force (e.g. the parties cannot choose the law of the former German Democratic Republic as the law applicable to contract). Under section 87(1) PIL Act, the choice of applicable law by the contracting parties may be concluded either in writing or orally.

II. Form

168. The law applicable to formal validity is determined pursuant to detailed rules in Article 11 Rome I Regulation. Provided the contractual parties or their

105. This is also possible under the Czech autonomous law by means of a so-called material choice of law, *see* Z. Kučera, *Mezinárodní právo soukromé* 132–133 (Brno-Plzeň 7th ed. 2009).

106. Section 87 para. 2 PILA (consumer contracts), s. 87 para. 3 PILA (insurance contracts), s. 87 para. 4 PILA (timeshares), ss 82–83 PILA (securities and investment instruments, ss 112–114 PILA (insolvency of financial institution), ss 115–116 PILA (insolvency of insurance undertakings).

agents are in the same country at the time of the conclusion of the contract, the contract is formally valid if it satisfies the formal requirements of the *lex causae* or of the *lex loci actus*. Provided the contractual parties or their agents are not in the same country at the time of the conclusion of the contract, the contract is formally valid if it satisfies the formal requirements of the *lex causae*, or of the law of either of the countries where either of the parties or their agent is present at the time of conclusion, or of the law of the country where either of the parties had his habitual residence at that time. The formal validity of consumer contracts is governed by the law of the country where the consumer is habitually resident. Any change in the law to be applied that is made after the conclusion of the contract by the parties shall not prejudice its formal validity under Article 11.

169. In Czech private substantive law the general principle of the informality of legal acts applies. Pursuant to section 559 CivC the form of a juridical act can be freely chosen unless restricted by an agreement or by a statute. The principle of the informality of legal acts is also reflected in conflict of laws rules. The general conflict of laws rule on law applicable to formal validity of juridical acts in section 42 PIL Act that also applies to contracts is designed *in favorem validitatis*. A contract is valid if its form is pursuant to (a) the law governing the contract and the legal relation established thereby, or (b) the law of the state in which one of the parties expressed (manifested) its will (intent), or (c) the law of the state in which one of the parties has habitual residence or seat or (d) the law of the state in which an immovable property concerned by the legal act is located. Furthermore, should the law which governs or should govern the contract, or the law of the state in which an immovable property concerned by the legal act is located, stipulate maintaining of a certain form as a prerequisite of validity, such a form has to be kept (section 42(2) PIL Act). Under this rather complicated provision the *lex causae* or the *lex rei sitae* in case of contracts with respect to immovables take precedence over the otherwise applicable law to formal validity that might be less strict.

III. Validity and Formation

170. The existence and validity of a contract, or of any term of a contract, is determined pursuant to the *lex causae*, the law which would govern the contract or term if valid (Article 10 Rome I Regulation). Nevertheless, a party, in order to establish that he did not consent, may invoke the law of the country in which he is habitually resident if it appears from the circumstances that it would not be reasonable to determine the effect of his conduct in accordance with *lex causae*. The Czech PIL Act has a general conflict of laws rule on existence and material validity of juridical acts in section 41 PIL Act that applies also to contracts. Under Czech law the law applicable to the question of whether a contract has been validly made, the existence of a contract (including consequences of its invalidity) is also governed by the law which would govern the contract if valid.

IV. Performance

171. Performance of obligations is governed by *lex causae*. Under Article 12(1)(b) Rome I Regulation performance of obligations falls into the scope of applicable law. According to the Giuliano-Lagarde Report on Rome Convention the following falls within this provision: the diligence with which the obligation must be performed; conditions relating to the place and time of performance; the extent to which the obligation can be performed by a person other than the party liable; the conditions as to performance of the obligation both in general and in relation to certain categories of obligation (joint and several obligations, alternative obligations, divisible and indivisible obligations, pecuniary obligations); where performance consists of the payment of a sum of money, the conditions relating to the discharge of the debtor who has made the payment, the appropriation of the payment, the receipt.[107]

172. There is no special provision on scope of law applicable to contracts in the Czech PIL Act.

V. Breach of Contractual Obligations (Including Damages)

173. The *lex causae* governs the consequences of breach of contractual obligations. Pursuant to Article 12(1)(c) Rome I Regulation the consequences of a total or partial breach of obligations, including the assessment of damages, fall into the scope of applicable law. The assessment of damages is included to the extent that this is governed by rules of law and lies within the limits of the powers conferred upon the court by its procedural law. The expression 'consequences of breach' refers to the consequences which the law or the contract attaches to the breach of a contractual obligation, whether it is a matter of the liability of the party to whom the breach is attributable or of a claim to terminate the contract for breach. Any requirement of service of notice on the party to assume his liability also comes within this context.[108]

174. Under Czech autonomous law the consequences of breaches of contracts are governed by the law applicable to contract (section 91(2) PIL Act).

VI. Rescission

175. Rescission of contract is one of the ways of extinction of obligations. Ways of extinguishing obligations fall into the scope of the law applicable to contract under Article 12(1)(d) Rome I Regulation.

107. Report on the Convention on the law applicable to contractual obligations. OJ 31.10.80, No. C 282/32.
108. Report on the Convention on the law applicable to contractual obligations. OJ 31.10.80, No. C 282/33.

VII. Representation

176. Under Czech civil substantive law, a representative or an agent is a person that is authorized to act in the name of another; the rights and duties arising from such an agency are acquired directly by the represented person (section 436(1) CivC). Agency (representation) is created by virtue of law on the basis of a decision by a state authority (the so-called statutory agency) or on contractual basis (sections 441 et seq. CivC). By virtue of law, for example, parents have the right and duty to make juridical acts in the name of their children provided the children lack legal capacity to make such acts (sections 892 et seq. CivC) or a spouse has the right to act in the name of the other spouse in usual matters (section 696(1) CivC).

177. Agency created by virtue of a decision of a court or other state authority is, for example, the guardianship. The court appoints a guardian for an individual if it is necessary to protect his interest, or if required by a public interest. A court appoints a guardian in particular for a person whose legal capacity has been limited by the court, for a person of unknown whereabouts, an unknown person participating in certain juridical acts or a person whose health condition is causing him difficulties in administering his assets and liabilities or defending his rights (section 465(1) CivC). Another example is an insolvency administrator appointed by court for the purposes of the insolvency proceedings (sections 21 et seq. of the Insolvency Act (InsA)). Agency by virtue of contract is anchored in sections 441 et seq. CivC. The principal states the scope of the authority to represent in a power of attorney. Unless the agency is related to a particular juridical act only, the power of attorney is granted in writing. Where the law requires special form for a certain juridical act, the power of attorney has to be granted in the same form. But where the law requires the form of an authentic instrument, it is sufficient if the power of attorney related to this juridical act is granted in writing with an officially certified signature.

178. The Czech PIL Act contains conflict of laws rules for agency in its section 44. For agency by virtue of law or by a decision of a court (or other authority) as well as for the effects thereof, either the law which contains the provision on agency by operation of law applies or the law of the state the court or authority of which has given the judgment upon which the agency is based. For the effects of agency in usual acts, a compliance with the law applicable in place where the act was undertaken (performed) is sufficient (section 44(1) PIL Act). This conflict of laws rule does not apply to guardianship or curatorship, as there are special conflict of laws rules in sections 34 and 65 PIL Act.

179. In case of agency by contract, a legal act undertaken by an agent has effects for the principal if it complies with at least one of the following laws: the law applicable in place where the agent undertook the act, or where the principal has his seat or his habitual residence, or where the agent has his seat or his habitual residence, or where an immovable property is located if the legal act concerns such an immovable property or the law which governs the legal relationship established by a juridical act of the agent (section 44(2)–(3) PIL Act). The power of attorney is formally valid if it satisfies the formal requirements of the laws referred to above or of the law applicable in place where the power of attorney was granted (section 44(4) PIL Act). In case the agent acts exceeding the scope of the authority granted or acts without authority, the relation between the agent and a third party established as a result of such acting is governed by the law applicable in place where the agent has his seat or habitual residence. A third party may invoke the application of the law applicable in place where the agent was acting (section 44(5) PIL Act). There is a special conflict of laws rule in section 45 PIL Act that determines the law applicable to effects of acts based on authority granted by an entrepreneur to make juridical acts associated with the operation of a business enterprise or to carry out certain activities within the operation of a business enterprise. The applicable law is the law of the state in which the principal has the respective business plant, a branch or an establishment within whose operation the activities are carried out. However, it is sufficient if these effects are in conformity with the law applicable in place where the authorized person undertook a legal act towards a third person and, when the legal act concerns an immovable property, also with the law applicable in place where the immovable property is located.

180. The unified rules on law applicable to contracts in Rome I Regulation apply to the relation principal–agent and agent–third person in contractual agency. The question whether an agent is able to bind a principal, or an organ to bind a company or other body corporate or unincorporated, in relation to a third party is excluded from the material scope of the Rome I Regulation (Article 1(2)(g)). In case the agent acts without authority and a non-contractual obligation arises out of his acting, the conflict of laws rule on *negotiorum gestio* in Article 11 Rome II Regulation determines the law applicable.

181. Relevant international treaties with respect to statutory agency binding for the Czech Republic are the 1996 Convention on Jurisdiction, Applicable Law, Recognition, Enforcement and Cooperation in Respect of Parental Responsibility and Measures for the Protection of Children and the 2000 Convention on the International Protection of Adults (*see* §8).

VIII. Interpretation

182. A contract should be interpreted in conformity with the law applicable to contract, that is, either with the law selected by the parties or with the otherwise applicable law pursuant to default conflict of laws rules. Pursuant to Article 12(1)(a) Rome I Regulation interpretation of the contract falls into the scope of the applicable law. However, the contracting parties are free to choose another law to govern the interpretation of their contract. Pursuant to Czech PIL Act that contains the principles of application of foreign law for Czech courts, a foreign governing law shall be interpreted by courts in the same manner as in the country of its origin (section 23(1) PIL Act). Account shall be taken not only to the wording but also to the broader legal framework, including case law (for details *see* Part I Chapter 1 §4 *supra*).

IX. Third Parties and Multiparty Agreements

183. Czech civil law is based on the principle of autonomy of will and the principle of *neminem laedere* (section 3(1) CivC). The Civil Code includes provisions on contracts concluded for the benefit of a third person in sections 1767 et seq. Parties may enter into a contract in favour of a third person. If a debtor is to perform in favour of a third person, the creditor may require that the debtor discharges his debt to that person. The debtor has contractual defence not only against the creditor but also against the third person. If the third person rejects a right acquired under such a contract, he is considered to have never acquired such right to performance. A contract for the benefit of a third person does not represent a special type of contract under Czech law; it is considered a modification of other contractual types, for example a sales contract, loan contract, etc. Contracts for the benefit of a third person are frequent in business-to-business service relations, e.g. contracts concluded between the buyer and the issuing bank to open letter of credit in favour of the beneficiary. Generally, juridical act of one person cannot create an obligation of another person unless the latter agrees.[109] Section 1769 CivC stipulates how to interpret contracts on performance by a third party. Provided a person undertakes to ensure that a third person discharges a debt in favour of a third party, such person is obliged to induce the third party to provide the agreed performance. Provided a person undertakes that a third person discharges the debt, such person shall compensate the creditor for the damage in case of non-fulfilment. Vicarious liability is anchored in section 2914 CivC. A person that in his activities uses an agent, employee or another helper shall compensate for damages caused by such person as if he caused it himself.

184. With respect to conflict of laws rules, the Czech PIL Act does not contain any special provision related to third parties. The only exception is the rule in section 91 PIL Act on the law applicable to security of obligations. Pursuant to section 91(1) PIL Act parties or a party providing the security interest unilaterally may choose the law applicable to the security of obligation. This choice of law or its modification shall not prejudice the rights of third parties.

X. Assignment and Subrogation

185. The relevant conflict of laws rules are anchored in the Rome I Regulation. Czech autonomous PIL has no special rule. Article 14 Rome I Regulation applies to voluntary assignment and contractual subrogation of a claim against another person (the debtor), and it contains different conflict of laws rules for the relationship assignor–assignee (Article 14(1) Rome I Regulation) and assignee–debtor (Article 14(2) Rome I Regulation). The relationship between assignor and assignee is governed by the law that applies to the contract between the assignor and assignee. The

109. M. Hulmák, et al. *Občanský zákoník V. Závazkové právo. Obecná část (§ 1721 – 2054). Komentář* [*Civil Code V. Law of Obligations. General Part (ss 1721–2054). Commentary*] 246 (C.H. Beck 1st ed. 2014).

relationship between the assignee and the debtor and other aspects affecting the debtor (assignability, conditions under which the assignment or subrogation can be invoked against the debtor, whether the debtor's obligations have been discharged) are governed by the law governing the assigned or subrogated claim. The concept of assignment includes outright transfers of claims, transfers of claims by way of security and pledges or other security rights over claims (Article 14(3) Rome I Regulation).

186. Law applicable to legal subrogation is determined pursuant to the conflict of laws rule in Article 15 Rome I Regulation. Where a person (the creditor) has a contractual claim against another (the debtor) and a third person has a duty to satisfy the creditor, or has in fact satisfied the creditor in discharge of that duty, the law which governs the third person's duty to satisfy the creditor shall determine whether and to what extent the third person is entitled to exercise against the debtor the rights which the creditor had against the debtor under the law governing their relationship.

§2. Particular Contracts

I. Sales Contract

187. Czech Republic is bound by the 1980 United Nations Convention on Contracts for the International Sales of Goods (CISG) that unifies substantive law of international sales contracts and by the 1974 United Nations Convention on the Limitation Period in the International Sale of Goods that unifies limitations periods in international sales contracts.

188. The CISG governs formation of the sales contract and the rights and obligations of the seller and the buyer arising from such a contract. Unless the contracting parties exclude the application of CISG pursuant to Article 6, it applies to sales contracts concluded between parties whose places of business are in different states provided both states are CISG contracting states (Article 1(1)(a) CISG) or provided that rules of PIL lead to the application of the law of a contracting state regardless the location of place of business of the contracting parties (Article 1(1)(b) CISG). Czech Republic declared pursuant to Article 95 CISG that it was not bound by the Article 1(1)(b) CISG, thus applying the CISG only to sales contracts provided the place of business of the contracting parties was in contracting states; however this declaration has been recently withdrawn.

189. Where the CISG does not apply, the law applicable to sales contract is determined based on the rules in the Rome I Regulation. Parties are free to choose the law applicable to sales contract pursuant to Article 3 Rome I Regulation. In the absence of choice of law there is a special rule that applies to contracts for sales of goods in Article 4(1)(a) Rome I Regulation. The law applicable to contracts for sale of goods is the law of the country where the seller is habitually resident unless it is clear from the circumstances that the contract is manifestly more closely connected with another country; the law of this country applies based on the escape clause in Article 4(3) Rome I Regulation.

190. There is no special conflict of laws rules on the law applicable to sales contracts in the Czech PIL Act.

II. Service Contract

191. Pure service contracts are excluded from the material scope of the CISG. In case of mixed contracts, the CISG applies to those contracts that include services provided the supply of labour or other services does not constitute the preponderant part of the obligations of the seller (Article 3(2) CISG).

192. The law applicable to service contracts is determined according to Rome I Regulation. The Czech autonomous PIL has no special provision. Pursuant to Article 3 Rome I Regulation a service contract is governed by the law chosen by the parties or, when the parties do not choose the applicable law, by the law of the state where the service provider has his habitual residence (Article 4(1)(b) Rome I Regulation).

III. Consumer Contracts

193. Under the Czech Civil Code, consumer contracts are contracts concluded between a consumer and an entrepreneur (section 1810 CivC). A consumer is any individual who, outside his trade, business or profession, enters into a contract or has other dealings with an entrepreneur (section 419 CivC), and an entrepreneur is a person who, on his own account and responsibility, carries out independently a trade or similar activity with the intention to do so consistently for profit with regard to this activity (section 420(1) CivC). The contractual clauses in consumer contracts derogating from the statutory provisions on consumer protection are disregarded. This also applies where a consumer waives a special right conferred upon him by a statute (section 1812(2) CivC). If the contents of a consumer contract allow differing interpretations, the interpretation most favourable to the consumer is used (section 1812(1) CivC)). Moreover, in consumer contracts, stipulations which establish, contrary to the requirement of proportionality, a significant imbalance in the rights or duties of the parties to the detriment of the consumer are prohibited (section 1813 CivC). In addition, the provisions of the Consumer Protection Act[110] as well as protective provisions of the Civil Code may come into consideration as overriding mandatory rules.

110. Act No. 634/1992 Coll., on Consumer Protection, as amended.

194. The law applicable to consumer contracts is determined according to Rome I Regulation that contains special conflict of laws rules applicable to certain consumer contracts (Article 6(1) Rome I Regulation). Consumers are always protected by such rules of the country of their habitual residence that cannot be derogated from by an agreement, provided the contract was concluded by a natural person for a purpose which can be regarded as being outside his trade or profession (the consumer) with another person acting in the exercise of his trade or profession (the professional) who pursues his commercial or professional activities in the country where the consumer has his habitual residence; or by any means, directs such activities to that country or to several countries including that country, and the contract falls within the scope of such activities. Pursuant to Article 6(2) Rome I Regulation parties can choose any law as the law applicable to their consumer contract, but such a choice shall not have the result of depriving the consumer of the protection afforded to him by the mandatory rules of the law of the country in which the consumer has his habitual residence. In the absence of choice of law the law of the state where the consumer is habitually resident applies (Article 6(1) Rome I Regulation). In other cases, the law applicable to a contract between a consumer and a professional is determined pursuant to general rules (Articles 3 and 4 Rome I Regulation). The special rules do not apply to contracts explicitly listed in Article 6(4) Rome I Regulation as, for example, a contract for the supply of services where the services are to be supplied to the consumer exclusively in a country other than that in which he has his habitual residence; a contract of carriage other than a contract relating to package travel; a contract relating to a right in rem in immovable property or a tenancy of immovable property other than a contract relating to the right to use immovable properties on a timeshare basis.

195. The Czech PIL Act contains a special rule on consumer contracts in section 87(2) that is not a conflict of laws rule. It stipulates that, provided a consumer contract is closely connected with the territory of a EU Member State and court proceedings have been initiated in the Czech Republic, a consumer shall not be deprived of the protection granted under the Czech law regardless of the fact that a law of a third state has been chosen or otherwise determined to apply to the contract. Given the broad material scope of application of rules on law applicable to consumer contracts in the Rome I Regulation, the practical relevance of this provision is rather questionable.[111]

IV. Employment Contracts

196. The law applicable to employment contracts is determined pursuant to the rules of the Rome I Regulation. It contains special conflict of laws rules for individual employment contracts that fall within its scope of application. Individual employment contracts under the Rome I Regulation belong to contracts concluded with parties regarded as being weaker, and those parties are protected by conflict of

111. Břicháček, Bříza in P. Bříza, et al. *Zákon o mezinárodním právu soukromém. Komentář* [*Act on Private International Law. Commentary*] 537 (C.H. Beck 1st ed. 2014).

laws rules that are more favourable to their interests than the general rules (Recital 23 of the Preamble to the Rome I Regulation). Parties may choose law applicable to an employment contract but by this choice employees cannot be deprived of the protection afforded to them by provisions which cannot be derogated from by an agreement or which can only be derogated from to their benefit under the law applicable in the absence of choice of law (Article 8 Rome I Regulation). Provided the parties do not choose applicable law, the employment contract is governed by the law of the country in which or, failing that, from which the employee habitually carries out his work in performance of the contract. The country where the work is habitually carried out is not deemed to have changed if he is temporarily employed in another country. Where the law applicable cannot be determined, the contract shall be governed by the law of the country where the place of business through which the employee was engaged is situated. Where it appears from the circumstances as a whole that the contract is more closely connected with a country other than that indicated, the law of that other country applies (Article 8(2–4) Rome I Regulation).

197. As regards individual employment contracts, work carried out in another country should be regarded as temporary if the employee is expected to resume working in the country of origin after carrying out his tasks abroad. The conclusion of a new contract of employment with the original employer or an employer belonging to the same group of companies as the original employer should not preclude the employee from being regarded as carrying out his work in another country temporarily (Recitals 34–36 of the Preamble to the Rome I Regulation).

198. Under Czech law, an employment contract is a contract between an employer and an employee in which they agree on what kind of work the employee will perform, the place where the work will be performed and the date on which the employee will begin to work (section 34 Labour Code).[112] An employment relationship can be established by contract, election or appointment (section 33 Labour Code).

199. Czech autonomous PIL does not have a special conflict of laws rule on employment contracts, but section 89 PIL Act contains a special conflict of laws rule on law applicable to employment relations except of those established by an employment contract. Such employment relations are governed by the law of the state under which the employment was established.

200. With regard to employment contracts, Czech public law contains a number of provisions that may be considered as overriding mandatory rules. Under the Employment Act[113] a foreign national may only be recruited and employed provided he has a valid work permit and a valid permit to reside on the territory of the Czech Republic, or provided he is a holder of a green card unless otherwise stipulated by this Act. A work permit is also required if a foreign national works for a

---

112. Act No. 262/2006 Coll., Labour Code, as amended.
113. Act No. 435/2004 Coll., on Employment, as amended.

foreign employer, when posted to work on the territory of the Czech Republic by his employer on the basis of a contract with a Czech legal entity or natural person. For the purposes of employment pursuant to this Act, a citizen of the EU or his family member and a family member of a citizen of the Czech Republic are not deemed a foreigner (sections 85(1), 89 and 95 Employment Act). An employment contract concluded without the required permits is considered invalid.

201. A number of mandatory rules on security and health protection of workers, which form part of Czech public labour law, may also be considered as overriding mandatory rules that might be applied by Czech courts irrespective of the applicable law. In addition to this, where an employee of an employer from another EU Member State is posted to perform work within the framework of transnational provision of services in the Czech Republic,[114] the regulation of the Czech Republic applies to his work performance as regards, for example, the maximum length of working hours and the minimum length of rest periods; the minimum length of annual leave; the minimum wage rates and overtime premiums; occupational safety and health; the working conditions for pregnant employees; equal treatment for male and female employees and prohibition of discrimination, etc. (section 319 Labour Code).

V. Contracts of Carriage

A. Carriage of Persons and Carriage of Goods

202. Czech civil law differentiates between contracts for the carriage of persons and of goods. Pursuant to section 2550 CivC by a contract for the carriage of a person, a carrier undertakes to carry a passenger to his destination, and a passenger undertakes to pay the fare. Pursuant to section 2555(1) CivC by a contract for the carriage of goods, a carrier undertakes to carry a consignor's goods as a consignment from the point of dispatch to the destination, and a consignor undertakes to pay freight to the carrier. Special conflict of laws rules on contracts of carriage are anchored in Rome I Regulation. There are no conflict of laws rules on contracts of carriage in the Czech PIL Act.

203. There is a number of relevant unifying international conventions in the field of transport law binding for the Czech Republic; the EU conflict of laws rules only apply where no uniform law applies, mainly in carriage contracts concerning inland waterway and multimodal transports, forwarding contracts, charter-parties and lease contracts. Under Article 5 Rome I Regulation the choice of the law applicable to a contract for the carriage of goods is unlimited, while the law applicable to a contract for the carriage of passengers is subject to limitations protecting the passenger as a weaker party. The contractual parties may choose as the law applicable to a contract for the carriage of passengers the law of the country where: (a) the passenger

114. Directive 96/71/EC of the European Parliament and of the Council of 1996 concerning the posting of workers in the framework of the provision of services.

has his habitual residence; or (b) the carrier has his habitual residence; or (c) the carrier has his place of central administration; or (d) the place of departure is situated; or (e) the place of destination is situated (Articles 3 and 5 Rome I Regulation). Under the Rome I Regulation, to the extent that the law applicable to a contract for the carriage of goods has not been chosen, the law applicable is the law of the country of habitual residence of the carrier, provided that the place of receipt or the place of delivery or the habitual residence of the consignor is also situated in that country. If those requirements are not met, the law of the country where the place of delivery as agreed by the parties is situated applies. To the extent that the law applicable to a contract for the carriage of passengers has not been chosen by the parties, the law applicable is the law of the country where the passenger has his habitual residence, provided that either the place of departure or the place of destination is situated in that country. If these requirements are not met, the law of the country where the carrier has his habitual residence applies. The escape clause in Article 5(3) Rome I Regulation enables to apply the law of another country if it is clear from all the circumstances of the case that the contract, in the absence of a choice of law, is manifestly more closely connected with this country.

204. Czech Republic is a contracting party to the following international transport law conventions, the regulation of which takes precedence over Rome I Regulation (Article 25 Rome I Regulation):

- Convention concerning International Carriage by Rail (COTIF) (Berne, 1980) as amended by the Vilnius Protocol (1999).
- Convention on the Contract for the International Carriage of Goods by Road (CMR) (Geneva, 1956).
- Convention on the Contract for the International Carriage of Passengers and Luggage by Road (CVR) (Geneva, 1973).
- Convention for the Unification of Certain Rules Relating to International Carriage by Air (Warsaw, 1929), as amended by the Hague Protocol of 1955.
- Convention Supplementary to the Warsaw Convention for the Unification of Certain Rules Relating to International Carriage by Air Performed by a Person Other than the Contracting Carrier (Guadalajara, 1961).
- Convention for the Unification of Certain Rules for International Carriage by Air (Montreal, 1999).
- Convention on the Carriage of Goods by Sea (Hamburg, 1978).
- Convention on the Contract for the Carriage of Goods by Inland Waterway (CMNI) (Budapest, 2001).

Within the EU provisions of the Regulation (EC) No. 261/2004 establishing common rules on compensation and assistance to passengers in the event of denied boarding and of cancellation or long delay of flights, and of the Regulation (EC) No. 2027/97 on air carrier liability in the event of accidents are of substantial practical relevance. Provisions on carriage of passengers by sea are included in the Regulation (EC) No. 392/2009 on the liability of carriers of passengers by sea in the event of accidents, which incorporates provisions of the Athens Convention relating to the Carriage of Passengers and their Luggage by Sea, 1974 and the Protocol thereto of 2002.

VI. Insurance Contract

205. An insurance contract is defined in section 2758 CivC as a contract whereby the insurer undertakes to provide the policyholder or a third person with insurance indemnity in the case of a random event covered by insurance and the policyholder undertakes to pay a premium to the insurer. Except where contracts are concluded for less than a year, the insurance contract must be concluded in writing. Where reference is made in the contract to insurance terms and conditions, the insurer is obliged to familiarize the policyholder before the contract is concluded except when concluded distantly (section 2774 CivC). Insurance terms and conditions shall generally include the details of the duration period of insurance, define the insured event, exclusions from insurance and the manner of determining the scope of insurance indemnity and its due date. Insurance companies which undertake insurance as their business activity must comply with the Insurance Act[115] that harmonizes the Czech law with EU directives.

206. The Czech PIL Act contains a special rule on law applicable to insurance contracts in section 87(3) that has a limited scope of application. It applies only to insurance contracts that are excluded from the material scope of Rome I Regulation (Article 1(2)(j) Rome I Regulation) which are insurance contracts arising out of operations carried out by organizations other than undertakings referred to in Article 2 of Directive 2002/83/EC of the European Parliament and of the Council of 5 November 2002 concerning life assurance, the object of which is to provide benefits for employed or self-employed persons belonging to an undertaking or group of undertakings, or to a trade or group of trades, in the event of death or survival or of discontinuance or curtailment of activity, or of sickness related to work or accidents at work. It may also be applicable in connection with Article 7(3) Rome I Regulation that in cases under letters (a), (b) and (e) gives parties to insurance contract the freedom to choose the law applicable to insurance contract based on a national conflict of laws rules. Pursuant to section 87(3) PIL Act contractual parties are free to make an unlimited choice of law with the exception of cases when the insurance contract falls within the material scope of a directly applicable regulation of EU. In such a case the parties may only make a choice of law admitted by such a regulation. In the absence of choice of law by the parties, insurance contracts are governed by the law of the state where the policyholder is habitually resident.

207. The Rome I Regulation contains special conflict of laws rules for insurance contracts in Article 7 applicable to insurance contracts covering risks situated inside the territory of EU Member States and to insurance contracts covering a large risk

115. Act No. 277/2009 Coll., on the Insurance Industry, as amended.

as defined in Article 5(d) of the First Council Directive 73/239/EEC on the coordination of laws, regulations and administrative provisions relating to the taking-up and pursuit of the business of direct insurance other than life assurance regardless of whether or not the risk covered is situated in a EU Member State.

208. The law applicable to other insurance contracts covering risk outside of the territory of the EU Member States and reinsurance contracts is determined pursuant to general rules in Articles 3, 4 and 6 Rome I Regulation. The country in which the risk is situated is determined in accordance with Article 2(d) of the Second Council Directive 88/357/EC on the coordination of laws, regulations and administrative provisions relating to direct insurance other than life assurance and laying down provisions to facilitate the effective exercise of freedom to provide services and, in the case of life assurance, the country in which the risk is situated shall be the country of the commitment within the meaning of Article 1(1) (g) of Directive 2002/83/EC. An insurance contract covering a large risk shall be governed by the law chosen by the parties in accordance with Article 3 Rome I Regulation. To the extent that the applicable law has not been chosen by the parties, such an insurance contract is governed by the law of the country where the insurer has his habitual residence. Where it is clear from all the circumstances of the case that the contract is manifestly more closely connected with another country, the law of that other country shall apply. In the case of an insurance contract other than a contract covering a large risk, the choice of law is limited by a list of laws in Article 7(3) Rome I Regulation (the law of any Member State where the risk is situated at the time of conclusion of the contract; the law of the country where the policy holder has his habitual residence; in the case of life assurance, the law of the Member State of which the policy holder is a national, etc.) To the extent that the law applicable has not been chosen by the parties, such a contract is governed by the law of the EU Member State in which the risk is situated at the time of conclusion of the contract (Article 7 Rome I Regulation).

VII. IP Contracts

A. License Agreement

209. Under Czech civil law by a license agreement a licensor grants to a licensee an authorization to exercise intellectual property rights within the stipulated limited or unlimited extent, and a licensee undertakes to pay remuneration to the licensor (section 2358 CivC). As to formal requirements the license agreement has to be in writing if an exclusive license is granted or if the license is to be registered in a public register.

210. The law applicable to license agreements is determined based on the rules in Rome I Regulation. The parties may choose the law applicable to a license agreement pursuant to Article 3 Rome I Regulation. In the absence of choice of law, unless it is clear from the circumstances that the license agreement is manifestly more closely connected with another country and the law of this country applies based on the escape clause in Article 4(3) Rome I Regulation, the law applicable to a license agreement is the law of the state where the party required to effect the characteristic performance of the contract has his habitual residence (Article 4(2) Rome I Regulation). The determination of the party that effects the characteristic performance is in this case rather controversial, pursuant to the prevailing opinion the characteristic performance is effected by the licensor.[116] Pursuant to the interpretation of the CJEU contracts under which the owner of an intellectual property right grants its contractual partner the right to use that right in return for remuneration are not a service,[117] and Article 4(1)(b) Rome I Regulation should not therefore be applied to determine the applicable law to license agreements.

B. Trademark Agreement

211. Transfer trademark agreement is not an agreement specifically provided for by the Czech Civil Code; it is to be classified as innominate contract under section 1746(2) CivC. The law applicable to transfer trademark agreements is either the law chosen by parties (Article 3 Rome I Regulation), or, in the absence of choice of law, the law of the state where the party required to effect the characteristic performance of the contract, the transferor, has his habitual residence (Article 4(2) Rome I Regulation), unless it is clear from the circumstances that the agreement is manifestly more closely connected with another country whose law applies based on the escape clause in Article 4(3) Rome I Regulation.

212. The protection of trademarks, as intellectual property rights, is based on the principle of territoriality and subject to *lex loci protectionis*, the law of the country where the right is protected. Pursuant to section 80 PIL Act intellectual property rights are governed by the law of the state which recognizes such rights and provides for their protection.

VIII. Hybrid Contracts

A. Leasing

213. Financial leasing can be defined as a transaction in which one party (the lessor), on the specifications of another party (the lessee), enters into an agreement with a third party (the supplier) under which the lessor acquires a plant, capital goods or other equipment on terms approved by the lessee so far as they concern its interests, and enters into an agreement (the leasing agreement) with the lessee, granting to the lessee the right to use the equipment in return for the payment of

---

116. P.A. De Miguel Asensio, *The Law Governing International Intellectual Property Licensing Agreements (A Conflict of Laws Analysis*. In *Research Handbook on Intellectual Property Licensing* 327 (J. de Werra ed., Edward Elgar Publishing 2013).

117. Judgment of the European Court of Justice of 23 Apr. 2009. Falco Privatstiftung and Thomas Rabitsch v Gisela Weller-Lindhorst (C-533/07).

rentals.[118] Czech civil law does not contain special provisions on leasing; leasing contracts can be concluded as innominate contracts pursuant to section 1746(2) CivC. As regards conflict of laws rules, neither the autonomous Czech PIL nor the unified European law provides for special regulation. General conflict of laws rules on contracts in the Rome I Regulation apply. In the absence of choice of law, the governing law pursuant to the default rules will in most cases be the law of the state where the lessor has his habitual residence at the time of the conclusion of the contract (Article 4(2) Rome I Regulation).

B. Factoring

214. A factoring contract can be defined as a contract concluded between one party (the supplier) and another party (the factor), pursuant to which the supplier may or will assign to the factor receivables arising from contracts on sales of goods made between the supplier and its customers (debtors), other than those who bought the goods primarily for their personal use, and the factor is to perform at least two of the following functions: finance for the supplier, maintenance of accounts relating to the receivables, collection of receivables, protection against default in payment by debtors.[119] Czech civil law does not contain special provisions on factoring contracts; they can be concluded as innominate contracts pursuant to section 1746(2) CivC. With regard to conflict of laws rules, special rules are contained neither in the unified European law nor in the Czech PIL Act. General rules on the determination of the law applicable to contracts in Rome I Regulation apply. In the absence of choice of law, the law applicable to a factoring contract in most cases will be the law of the state where the factor has his habitual residence at the time of the conclusion of the contract (Article 4(2) Rome I Regulation).

C. Franchise

215. By a franchise contract the franchisee carries on the licensed business under the franchisor's name, trademarks, etc. in accordance with a system developed by the franchisor. Despite the fact that franchising contracts are relatively frequent in Czech Republic, Czech civil law does not contain special provisions with respect to this type of contract; they are concluded in the framework of section 1746(2) CivC as innominate contracts, with elements of a license and mandate contract. Under the European law franchising agreement was defined in Regulation No. 4087/88 on competition protection which is however no longer in force.[120] Law

118. *See* Art. 1 of the UNIDROIT Convention on International Financial Leasing (Ottawa 1988). The Czech Republic is not a Contracting State to this Convention.
119. *See* Art. 1 of the UNIDROIT Convention on International Factoring (Ottawa 1988). The Czech Republic is not a Contracting State to this Convention.
120. Commission Regulation (EEC) No. 4087/88 on the application of Art. 85(3) of the Treaty to categories of franchise agreements. In this respect, *see also* the Commission Regulation (EC) No. 2790/1999 on the application of Art. 81(3) of the Treaty to categories of vertical agreements and concerted practices.

applicable to franchising agreements is determined pursuant to the rules on law applicable to contracts in Rome I Regulation. Parties are free to choose the law applicable to the franchising agreement under Article 3 Rome I Regulation. In the absence of a choice of law, the law applicable to a franchising agreement is determined pursuant to a special conflict of laws rule in Article 4(1)(e) Rome I Regulation. To the extent that the law applicable to the contract has not been chosen, a franchise contract is governed by the law of the country where the franchisee has his habitual residence, unless it is clear from the circumstances that the franchising agreement is manifestly more closely connected with another country; the law of this country applies based on the escape clause in Article 4(3) Rome I Regulation.

D. Publishing Contract

216. Publishing contracts are concluded between a publisher and an author (owner of the intellectual property) to publish the author's work. Czech law contains provisions on publishing contract as a special type of contract in sections 2384–2389 CivC. Law applicable to publishing contracts is determined pursuant to the rules on law applicable to contracts in Rome I Regulation. Parties are free to choose the law applicable to the publishing contract under Article 3 Rome I Regulation. In the absence of a choice of law, unless it is clear from the circumstances that the publishing contract is manifestly more closely connected with another country and the law of this country applies based on the escape clause in Article 4(3) Rome I Regulation, the law applicable to a publishing contract is determined pursuant to Article 4(2) Rome I Regulation; it is the law of the state where the party required to effect the characteristic performance of the contract has his habitual residence. The performance of the publisher is the economic purpose of the contract and therefore the publisher is to be considered the party effecting the characteristic performance.[121]

IX. Negotiable Instruments

A. Bill of Exchange and heques

217. Czech Republic is not bound by Geneva Conventions relating to bills of exchange and cheques concluded in the early 1930s: Convention Providing a Uniform Law for Bills of Exchange and Promissory Notes, Convention Providing a Uniform Law for Cheques, Convention for the Settlement of Certain Conflict of Laws in Connection with Bills of Exchange and Promissory Notes, Convention for the Settlement of Certain Conflict of Laws in Connection with Cheques, Convention on the Stamp Laws in Connection with Bills of Exchange and Promissory

121. P.A. De Miguel Asensio, *The Law Governing International Intellectual Property Licensing Agreements (A Conflict of Laws Analysis*, in *Research Handbook on Intellectual Property Licensing)* 329 (J. de Werra ed., Edward Elgar Publishing 2013).

Notes and Convention on the Stamp Laws in Connection with Cheques. The above-listed conventions concerning bills of exchange and promissory notes and conventions relating to cheques were signed by the then Czechoslovakia but were never ratified. Nevertheless, the contents, except for certain provisions, were incorporated into the Czech autonomous law, by Act on Bills of Exchange, Promissory Notes and Cheques,[122] including conflict of laws rules that are now part of the Czech PIL Act.

218. Section 31 PIL Act contains a special rule on the law applicable to the capacity of a person to obligations (to be legally bound) under bills of exchange or cheques. The law applicable is the *lex patriae* of such a person (section 31(1) PIL Act). *Renvoi* is admitted. Should the conflict of laws rules of the applicable law claim that the law of another state is applicable, the law of the other state applies. Pursuant to section 31(2) PIL Act a person without a capacity to obligations under bills of exchange or cheques under the law referred to in paragraph 1 is nevertheless validly bound should he sign the bill of exchange or cheque in the state under the law of which he would have the capacity to obligations under bills of exchange or cheques. This is not applicable provided a citizen of the Czech Republic or a person habitually resident in the Czech Republic is concerned. Who is to be considered a drawee is governed by the law of the state in which the cheque is payable (section 32 PIL Act). Should the cheque be, under such a law, invalid due to the drawee, obligations under signatures written on the cheque in the state the law of which does not stipulate invalidity for such a reason shall nevertheless be valid.

219. Further special conflict of laws rules on bills of exchange are stipulated in sections 93–97 PIL Act. Pursuant to section 93(1) PIL Act the effects of binding declarations of a bill of exchange recipient are governed by *lex loci actus* (section 93(2) PIL Act). The limits for exercising recourse rights by all persons bound by a bill of exchange are governed by the law of the place where the bill of exchange was issued (section 94 PIL Act). This law governs also whether a bill of exchange owner acquires a claim which forms the basis for the issuance of the bill of exchange (section 95 PIL Act). The law of the state of the payment place governs whether it is possible to limit the acceptance of bills of exchange to a part of the bill of exchange sum and whether the owner is obliged to accept a partial payment (section 96 PIL Act). It also governs measures which have to be undertaken should the bill of exchange get lost or stolen (section 97 PIL Act).

220. Conflict of laws rules relevant for cheques are contained in addition to the above-mentioned section 31 PIL Act in its sections 98–100. The effects of cheque declarations are governed by the law of the state in which they were made (section 98 PIL Act). Time limits for exercising recourse rights by all persons bound by a cheque are governed by the law of the state on the territory of which the cheque was issued (section 100 PIL Act). Pursuant to section 101 PIL Act the law of the state in which a cheque is payable governs (a) whether the cheque must be payable at sight or whether it can be exposed to a certain time after sight and what effects occur when the cheque lists a later day than an actual date of issuance, (b) the period

122. Act No. 191/1950 Coll. on Bills of Exchange, Promissory Notes and Cheques.

for submission, (c) whether it is possible to accept a cheque, verify, confirm or authorize it, and what effects such clauses shall have, (d) whether the owner may request a partial payment and be obliged to accept it, (e) whether a cheque may be crossed or provided with an 'only to settlement' certificate or a certificate of the same meaning and what effects crossing or a settlement certificate or a certificate of the same meaning shall have, (f) whether the owner is vested with special rights for coverage and what is the content of such rights, (g) whether the issuer can revoke a cheque or state opposition against the payment of a cheque, (h) the measures which have to be undertaken should the cheque get lost or stolen, (i) whether a protest or a finding of the same meaning is necessary to preserve recourse rights against the endorser, the issuer and other persons bound by the cheque.

B. Letters of Credit

221. Under Czech civil law (section 2682 ff. CivC) by a letter of credit contract, the issuer of the letter of credit undertakes to issue to the mandator, at his request, on his account, and in favour of a third person (beneficiary) a letter of credit, and a mandator undertakes to remunerate the issuer of the letter of credit contract. Unless otherwise expressly provided by a letter of credit, it may by changed or cancelled by the issuer of the letter of credit only with the consent of the beneficiary and the mandator. In case of a documentary letter of credit, the issuer of the letter of credit provides a performance to the beneficiary when it is presented with documents determined by the letter of credit in accordance with the terms of the letter of credit. This also applies if the documents are presented to the issuer authorized by a letter of credit. There are no special conflict of laws rules in Czech autonomous law with respect to letters of credit.

222. The operation of letters of credit in the Czech Republic is very often governed by the Uniform Customs and Practice for Documentary Credits. It is a set of detailed rules published by the ICC in Paris (the latest revision is from 2007). As soft law, it applies when incorporated into the contract by the parties in accordance with the applicable law.

X. Agency Contracts

223. Commercial agency contract under the Czech civil law (section 2483 CivC) is a contract by which a commercial agent, as an independent entrepreneur, undertakes to pursue long-term activities for the principal aimed at facilitating the conclusion of a certain type of business transactions by the principal or negotiating business transactions in the name of the principal and on his account, and a principal undertakes to pay the commercial agent a commission. It must be concluded in a written form. Pursuant to section 2485 CivC when the relevant geographical area is not set in the contract and the commercial agent is a foreign person, the country of the commercial agent's registered seat at the time of the conclusion of the contract is considered the agreed geographical area.

224. National rules on commercial agency contracts within the EU are partially harmonized based on the EC Directive 86/653 on self-employed agents[123] and contain a number of mandatory provisions protecting the commercial agent as a weaker party. According to the ruling of the CJEU Articles 17 and 18 of this Directive, which guarantee certain rights to commercial agents after termination of agency contract, must be applied by courts in EU Member States as overriding mandatory rules where the commercial agent carried on his activity in an EU Member State although the principal is established in a non-member country, and the parties chose the law of the non-member country to govern the contract.[124] The Directive lays down the minimum protection requirements only, and some Member States grant protection to commercial agents that goes even beyond the requirements set in the Directive. If parties choose the law of a EU Member State which meets the minimum protection requirements laid down by Directive as law applicable to their commercial agency contract it may be rejected by the court of the forum state in favour of the *lex fori* rules governing the situation of self-employed commercial agents, owing to the mandatory nature, but only if the court finds, on the basis of a detailed assessment, that, in the course of the transposition, the legislature of the state of the forum held it to be crucial to grant the commercial agent protection going beyond that provided for by the directive, taking account in that regard of the nature and of the objective of such mandatory provisions.[125]

225. The law applicable to commercial agency contracts is to be determined according to Rome I Regulation. Parties may choose the law applicable (Article 3 Rome I Regulation). If they do not choose the applicable law, unless it is clear from the circumstances that the agency contract is manifestly more closely connected with another country and the law of this country applies based on the escape clause in Article 4(3) Rome I Regulation, the law of the state where the commercial agent has his habitual residence applies.). According to CJEU in a commercial agency contract, which is to be considered a contract for provision of services, it is the commercial agent who performs the obligation which characterises that contract and who provides the services.[126]

§3. Non-Contractual Obligations

226. In situations involving conflict of laws, the law applicable to non-contractual obligations in civil and commercial matters is determined based on the rules laid down in the Regulation (EC) No. 864/2007 on the law applicable to non-contractual obligations (Rome II Regulation), provided the events giving rise to

123. Council Directive 86/653/EEC of 18 Dec. 1986 on the coordination of the laws of the Member States relating to self-employed commercial agents.
124. Judgment of the European Court of Justice of 9 Nov. 2000. *Ingmar GB Ltd v. Eaton Leonard Technologies Inc.* (C-381/98).
125. Judgment of the European Court of Justice of 17 Oct. 2013. *United Antwerp Maritime Agencies (Unamar) NV v. Navigation Maritime Bulgare.* (C-184/12).
126. Judgment of the European Court of Justice of 11 March 2010. *Wood Floor Solutions Andreas Domberger.* (C-19/09).

damage occurred after 11 January 2009 (Article 31 Rome II Regulation). The provisions of the Rome II Regulation are based on the principle of universal application. The law determined by the Rome II Regulation is applied whether or not it is the law of an EU Member State (Article 3 Rome II Regulation).

227. The non-contractual liability arising from traffic accidents is governed by the law determined based on the conflict of laws rules in the 1971 Hague Convention on the Law Applicable to Traffic Accidents, which takes precedence over the provisions of the Rome II Regulation (Article 28 Rome II Regulation) and by which the Czech Republic is bound. With respect to liability for nuclear damage, Czech Republic is bound by the 1963 Vienna Convention on Civil Liability for Nuclear Damage. Relevant conflict of laws rules can also be found in bilateral treaties on legal assistance in civil matters concluded by the Czech Republic with non-EU countries.

228. The Czech PIL Act contains only one residual rule to determine the law applicable to non-contractual obligations arising out of violations of privacy and rights relating to personality, including defamation in section 101 as this matter is explicitly excluded from the material scope of the Rome II Regulation (Article 1(2)(g)).

I. Party Autonomy

229. Under the Rome II Regulation choice of law is admitted. The parties may agree to submit non-contractual obligations to the law of their choice: by an agreement entered into after the event, giving rise to the damage occurred; or where all the parties are pursuing a commercial activity, also by an agreement freely negotiated before the event giving rise to the damage occurred (Article 14 Rome II Regulation). Limited choice of law is admitted in case of liability for environmental damage. Choice of law is excluded in case of non-contractual obligations arising from an infringement of an intellectual property right (Article 8(3) Rome II Regulation) and of non-contractual obligations arising out of an act of unfair competition (Article 6(4) Rome II Regulation).

230. The Czech PIL Act allows in its section 101 unilateral limited choice of law in case of non-contractual obligations arising out of violations of privacy and rights relating to personality, including defamation. The affected (injured) person may choose the law of the state in which (a) the affected person has habitual residence or seat, (b) the violation initiator (perpetrator) has habitual residence or seat, or (c) the result of a violating conduct appeared (manifested itself) provided the violation initiator was able to predict it.

II. Objective Connection

231. The general objective connecting factor in Rome II Regulation is the place where the damage occurred, irrespective of the country in which the event giving rise to the damage occurred and irrespective of the country or countries in which the indirect consequences of that event occur (Article 4(1) Rome II Regulation). The law applicable to non-contractual obligations pursuant to this general default rule of Rome II Regulation is the *lex loci damni.*

232. Where the person claimed to be liable and the person sustaining damage both have their habitual residence in the same country at the time when the damage occurs, the relevant connecting factor is their common habitual residence and the law of that country applies (Article 4(2) Rome II Regulation). The connecting factor of the closest connection is applied in the escape clause in Article 4(3) Rome II Regulation. Where it is clear from all the circumstances of the case that the tort/delict is manifestly more closely connected with another country, the law of that other country applies. A manifestly closer connection with another country might be based in particular on a pre-existing relationship between the parties, such as a contract, that is closely connected with the tort/delict in question.

233. The Rome II Regulation lays down specific conflict of laws rules for special torts/delicts, namely for product liability, unfair competition and acts restricting free competition, environmental damage, infringement of intellectual property rights, and industrial action (for details *see* Articles 5–9 Rome II Regulation).

234. Non-contractual obligations arising out of nuclear damage and non-contractual obligations arising out of violations of privacy and rights relating to personality, including defamation, are explicitly excluded from the material scope of the Rome II Regulation. Czech Republic is a contracting state to the 1963 Vienna Convention on Civil Liability for Nuclear Damage.

III. Law of Torts

A. Lex loci delicti

235. Lex loci delicti, the law of the state in which the event giving rise to the damage occurred, is applicable to non-contractual obligations arising out of environmental damage or damage sustained by persons or property as a result of such damage provided the person seeking compensation for damage chooses this law to apply (Article 7 Rome II Regulation).

B. Scope of Application

236. The Rome II Regulation does not apply, in particular, to revenue, customs or administrative matters or to the liability of the state for acts and omissions in the exercise of state authority (*acta iure imperii*). Other issues excluded from its scope of application are listed in Article 1(2) Rome II Regulation. It does not apply to non-contractual obligations arising:

237. - out of family relationships and relationships deemed by the law applicable to such relationships to have comparable effects, including maintenance obligations;

238. - out of matrimonial property regimes, property regimes of relationships deemed by the law applicable to such relationships to have comparable effects to marriage, and wills and succession;

239. - under bills of exchange, cheques and promissory notes and other negotiable instruments to the extent that the obligations under such other negotiable instruments arise out of their negotiable character;

240. - out of the law of companies and other bodies corporate or unincorporated regarding matters such as the creation, by registration or otherwise, legal capacity, internal organization or winding up of companies and other bodies corporate or unincorporated, the personal liability of officers and members as such for the obligations of the company or body and the personal liability of auditors to a company or to its members in the statutory audits of accounting documents;

241. - out of the relations between the settlors, trustees and beneficiaries of a trust created voluntarily;

242. - out of nuclear damage;

243. - out of violations of privacy and rights relating to personality, including defamation.

C. Damages (Compensation)

244. The existence, nature and assessment of the damage, including remedies that can be claimed, are governed by the law applicable to non-contractual obligations determined under the rules of the Rome II Regulation (Article 15(c) Rome II Regulation).

IV. Unfair Competition

245. There is a special conflict of laws rule to determine the law applicable to a non-contractual obligation arising out of an act of unfair competition in Article 6 Rome II Regulation. The governing law is the law of the country where competitive relations or the collective interests of consumers are, or are likely to be, affected (Article 3(3)(a) Rome II Regulation). Where an act of unfair competition affects exclusively the interests of a specific competitor, *lex loci damni* applies (Article 3(2) Rome II Regulation).

246. The law applicable to a non-contractual obligation arising out of a restriction of competition is the law of the country where the market is, or is likely to be, affected. When the market is, or is likely to be, affected in more than one country, the person seeking compensation for damage who sues in the court of the domicile of the defendant, may instead choose to base his claim on the law of the court seized, provided that the market in that EU Member State is among those directly and substantially affected by the restriction of competition out of which the non-contractual obligation on which the claim is based arises; where the claimant sues, in accordance with the applicable rules on jurisdiction, more than one defendant in that court, he can only choose to base his claim on the law of that court if the restriction of competition on which the claim against each of these defendants relies directly and substantially affects also the market in the Member State of that court (Article 3(3)(b) Rome II Regulation).

247. There is no special conflict of laws rule on unfair competition in the Czech PIL Act.

V. *Negotiorum gestio*

248. *Negotiorum gestio* (agency without mandate) relates to obligations arising out of the so-called quasi-contracts.[127] Under Czech law a person who interferes in the affairs of another person without due authority bears the consequences (section 3006 CivC). If a person, without being called upon to do so, arranges a matter of another person to prevent imminent damage, the person whose matter was arranged shall reimburse the reasonably incurred costs, even where no result was achieved for reasons not attributable to the agent without mandate (section 3007 CivC).

249. In accordance with Rome II Regulation, if a non-contractual obligation arising out of an act performed without due authority in connection with the affairs of another person concerns a relationship existing between the parties, such as the one arising out of a contract or a tort/delict, that is closely connected with that non-contractual obligation, it is governed by the law that governs that relationship. Where the law applicable cannot be determined, and the parties have their habitual residence in the same country when the event giving rise to the damage occurs, the

127. Czech Civil Code does not use the term 'quasi-contract'.

law of that country applies. Where the law applicable cannot be determined on the basis of the preceding provisions, it is the law of the country in which the act was performed. And where it is clear from all the circumstances of the case that the non-contractual obligation arising out of an act performed without due authority in connection with the affairs of another person is manifestly more closely connected with another country, the law of that other country applies (Article 11 Rome II). A choice of the applicable law is admitted under Article 14 Rome II.

250. There is no special conflict of laws rule on agency without mandate in the Czech PIL Act.

VI. Unjust Enrichment

251. Under Czech Civil Code a person who is enriched at the expense of another without a just cause must, to the extent of his enrichment, make restitution to the impoverished person (2991–3005 CivC).

252. Rome II Regulation lays down special conflict of laws rules on unjust enrichment in Article 10. If a non-contractual obligation arising out of unjust enrichment, including payment of amounts wrongly received, concerns a relationship existing between the parties, such as the one arising out of a contract or a tort/delict, that is closely connected with that unjust enrichment, it shall be governed by the law that governs that relationship. Where the law applicable cannot be determined and the parties have their habitual residence in the same country when the event giving rise to unjust enrichment occurs, the law of that country shall apply. Where the law applicable cannot be determined on the basis of preceding rules, it shall be the law of the country in which the unjust enrichment took place. And where it is clear from all the circumstances of the case that the non-contractual obligation arising out of unjust enrichment is manifestly more closely connected with another country, the law of that other country shall apply. A choice of the applicable law is admitted under Article 14 Rome II Regulation.

253. There is no special conflict of laws rule on unjust enrichment in the Czech PIL Act.

VII. *Culpa in contrahendo*

254. The characterization of pre-contractual liability may differ in national laws ; it can be characterized either as contractual or as non-contractual. For the purposes of Rome II Regulation *culpa in contrahendo* is an autonomous concept that is to be characterized as non-contractual, as a quasi-tort, and should not necessarily be interpreted within the meaning of national law. It should include the violation of the duty of disclosure and the breakdown of contractual negotiations (Recital 30 of the Preamble of the Rome II Regulation). There is a special conflict of laws rule to determine the law applicable to a non-contractual obligation arising out of dealings prior to the conclusion of a contract, regardless of whether the contract was actually concluded or not, in Article 12 Rome II Regulation. Pursuant to this rule the law that applies to the contract or that would have been applicable to it had it been entered into applies. Where the *lex causae* cannot be determined the law (a) of the country in which the damage occurs, irrespective of the country in which the event giving rise to the damage occurred and irrespective of the country or countries in which the indirect consequences of that event occurred; or (b) where the parties have their habitual residence in the same country at the time when the event giving rise to the damage occurs, the law of that country; or (c) where it is clear from all the circumstances of the case that the non-contractual obligation arising out of dealings prior to the conclusion of a contract is manifestly more closely connected with a country other than that indicated in points (a) and (b), the law of that other country, applies.

255. There is no special conflict of laws rule on *culpa in contrahendo* in the Czech PIL Act.

VIII. Violations of Privacy and Rights Relating to Personality, Including Defamation

256. Non-contractual obligations arising out of violations of privacy and rights relating to personality, including defamation are governed by the law determined pursuant to section 101 PIL Act. Pursuant to this conflict of laws rule non-contractual obligations arising out of violations of privacy and rights relating to personality, including defamation, are governed unless the affected (injured) person chooses the applicable law, by the law of the state in which the violation occurred. The affected (injured) person may choose among the law of the state in which the affected person has habitual residence or seat; the law of the state in which the violation initiator (perpetrator) has habitual residence or seat; and the law of the state in which the result of a violating conduct appeared (manifested itself) provided the violation agent could have predicted it.

Chapter 3. Property

257. Law of property is usually understood as a category paired with the law of obligations. Under Czech law there are three fundamental attributes distinguishing rights in rem from obligations: (1) these rights are absolute, effective *erga omnes*; (2) an obligation corresponding to a right in rem is always an obligation to refrain from doing something; and (3) the secondary object of the right *in rem* is a tangible asset.[128] The rights *in rem* are divided into two basic groups: rights of ownership (*iura in re sua*) (sections 1011–1114 CivC) and rights over other property, encumbrances (*iura in re aliena*) (sections 1240–1399 CivC) that include e.g., a lien or a right of retention.

§1. *Lex rei sitae*

258. Under the general conflict of laws rule in section 69(1) PIL Act rights *in rem* in immovable property as well as in tangible movable property are governed unless otherwise stipulated by other statutory provisions, by the law of a state on the territory of which the property is located. *Lex rei sitae* also determines whether a property is immovable or movable and governs all questions relating to rights in rem, in particular, types of rights in rem, their contents and effects, how they are established and how they extinguish.

259. An exception to the *lex rei sitae* rule applies to succession and to property relations between spouses. The law applicable to succession pursuant to Articles 21–22 of the Succession Regulation applies to both immovable and movable assets of the estate and governs among others the transfer of the assets forming part of the estate to the heirs and, as the case may be, to the legatees of the assets (Article 23(2)(e) Succession Regulation). The law applicable to matrimonial property is from 29 January 2019 determined based on the rules of the Regulation on Matrimonial Property Regimes which takes precedence over the autonomous PIL rules in section 49(3–4) PIL Act (*see* Chapter 5 §3). To avoid fragmentation, the law applicable to the matrimonial property regime governs that regime as a whole, irrespective of the nature of the assets and regardless of whether the assets are located in another EU Member State or in a third state. In the above-mentioned relations, the *lex rei sitae* is substituted by another applicable law that is mostly connected with personal elements of the respective legal relationship.

§2. Movable Property

260. The *lex rei sitae* applies to both immovable and tangible movable property, unless stipulated otherwise (section 69(1) PIL Act). In case of movable tangible

128. Kindl T. Commentary on s. 979. In J. Švestka, et al. *Občanský zákoník – Komentář* (Civil Code – Commentary) (Wolters Kluwer 2014).

property, mobile conflicts may arise when the place where it is located changes. Therefore, there are special rules for avoiding such a conflict of laws.

261. The creation and extinguishment of rights in rem to tangible movable property is governed by the law of the place where the property was located at the time of occurrence of an event giving rise to the creation or extinguishment of the right unless the creation and extinguishment of an ownership right in tangible movable property is transferred by contract. In such a case the governing law is *lex causae* (section 70(1–2) PIL Act). For *res in transitu see* Chapter 3, §2, II).

262. A mobile conflict does not arise if all the prerequisites for the creation of the respective property right had been completed under the *lex rei sitae* before the asset was moved to another state; the right to such asset was created in the legal framework of the state of the original location of the asset. The law of its new location applies with respect to the contents and effects of the newly established right in rem. If, for example, a lien (pledge) had been established in a foreign state under its law and the respective movable asset was moved to the territory of the Czech Republic thereafter, in the Czech Republic a lienor (pledgee) may only assert those rights of pledge to such a movable asset which are assigned to lienors under Czech law.[129]

263. There is a special conflict of laws rule in section 69(2) PIL Act with respect to property rights to vessels and aircrafts registered in a public register. The creation and extinguishment of such property rights is governed by the law of the state that administers the respective register. Provisions on records in public registers applicable in place where the movable property is located apply, no matter what is the law applicable to its creation, extinguishment, limitation or transfer (section 71 PIL Act).

264. Pursuant to a special conflict of laws rule in section 72 PIL Act an acquisitive prescription is governed by the law of the state on the territory of which the asset was at the beginning of the course of the prescription period unless the person entitled from acquisitive prescription invokes the law of the state in the territory of which the acquisitive prescription took place. This law may only be invoked provided all prerequisites for acquisitive prescription stipulated by the law of this state have been met after the asset was moved to the territory of this state.

265. As regards possible rights in rem which are known by the Czech civil law and which could lead to a classification problem, the term 'rights in rem' used in the Czech conflict of laws rule is to be interpreted broadly enough to include such rights.

---

129. Z. Kučera, *Mezinárodní právo soukromé*, 2009, pp. 277–278.

I. Collateral

266. For the purposes of the determination of the law applicable to security interest, it has to be differentiated under the Czech law between security interest that has an obligation nature and security interest that has a right in rem nature.[130] The Czech PIL Act contains a special conflict of laws rule on law applicable to security interest for an obligation in its section 91. Pursuant to this provision the party that unilaterally provided the security interest may choose the governing law; the choice of law is not limited. In the absence of choice of law, the law applicable to the security interest for an obligation is generally the law governing the secured obligation due to the accessorial relationship of most types of security interest to the secured obligation.

267. However, there are exceptions to this rule. The *lex causae* of the secured obligation does not apply if a right in rem is concerned or if it follows otherwise from law or nature of the matter. In case of a pledge, a sub-pledge and a retention right, the conflict of laws rules for property law apply to determine the law applicable to these types of security interest. Pursuant to the general rule in section 69 PIL Act the *lex rei sitae* of the security interest applies. Pursuant to Czech law security interest using real estate as collateral has to be registered in public registry and arises upon its registration (section 1316 CivC). *Lex rei sitae* is not applicable to title retention; *lex causae* applies in accordance with section 70(2) PIL Act.

268. Pledging of claims (or other rights) is governed either by *lex electa* or, in the absence of choice of law, by *lex causae* of the claim (or other right) over which the pledge was established. A choice or change of the applicable law shall not prejudice the rights of third parties and only rights following from the law governing the secured obligation may be exercised against the debtor (section 91(1) PIL Act).

269. Another exception is the law applicable to pledging of securities, cases when securities are used as collateral. Pursuant to section 83(2) PIL Act a pledge of securities is governed by the law applicable in place of habitual residence or a seat of the pledge creditor in the relevant time period unless the parties choose another law; *renvoi* is excluded. In case of securities that must be submitted in order to obtain and handle the asset in question, the law of the place where the securities are located in the relevant time period applies.

270. The scope of application of the relevant Czech autonomous conflict of laws rules is limited by Rome I Regulation that applies to agreements on security interests (Article 3–4 Rome I Regulation).

130. Rozehnalová in M. Pauknerová et al., *Zákon o mezinárodním právu soukromém. Komentář*, *supra*, p. 623.

II. Goods in Transit

271. Goods during transit are goods transported from one state to another, i.e. if the transportation has already started but it has not been completed yet. The Czech PIL Act contains a special conflict of laws rule to determine the law governing rights in rem to goods during transit. For *res in transitu*, the creation and extinguishment of a right in rem to tangible movable property are governed by the law of the place from which the goods were dispatched, provided the relevant legal act of creating or extinguishing these rights was undertaken after the commencement of the transport and within its duration. The governing law is *lex loci expeditionis*. Provided the creation and extinguishment of rights in rem to this property occur by means of disposition of a security which has to be submitted in order to release the property and dispose of it (a bill of lading), the law of the place where the security is located at the time of the disposal applies (section 70(3) PIL Act). In this case the transfer of rights in rem is governed by the law of the situs of the respective security (*lex situs chartae*), not by the law of the situs of the goods in question.

III. Cultural Property

272. Czech PIL does not have any special provision on law applicable to cultural property; general rules apply. With respect to the export of cultural property the Czech Act on the Sale and Export of Objects of Cultural Value[131] contains mandatory provisions pursuant to which objects of cultural value can only be exported when certified for export (either for a limited period of time or permanently) by the relevant authority (e.g., a museum, gallery, Ministry of Culture). Objects of cultural value under this Act are natural objects or human artefacts or sets of these, which are significant for history, literature, art, science or technology and meet criteria specified in Annex I to this Act.

§3. Immovable Property

273. Under the general conflict of laws rule in section 69(1) PIL Act rights in rem in immovable property as well as in tangible movable property are governed, unless otherwise stipulated by other statutory provisions, by the law of a state on the territory of which the property is located.

274. Pursuant to a special conflict of laws rule in section 72 PIL Act the acquisitive prescription is governed by the law of the state on the territory of which the asset was at the beginning of the course of the prescription period unless the person entitled from acquisitive prescription invokes the law of the state in the territory of which the acquisitive prescription took place. This law may only be invoked provided all prerequisites for acquisitive prescription stipulated by the law of this state have been met after the asset had been moved to the territory of this state.

131. Act No. 71/1994 Coll., on the Sale and Export of Objects of Cultural Value.

I. Mortgage

275. Pursuant to Czech law, a mortgage is a special type of security interest using real estate as collateral. Mortgage is therefore governed by *lex rei sitae* (section 91 PIL Act).

II. Emissions

276. Under Czech law anything that would cause waste, water, smoke, dust, gas, odour, light, shadow, noise, vibration and other similar effects is an immission (section 1013(1) CivC). A plot owner shall refrain from immissions to infiltrate the plot of land of another owner (neighbour) to the extent disproportionate to the local circumstances and substantially restricting normal use of his land; this also applies to animals entering the plot of land of another person.

277. The Czech PIL Act contains no special conflict of laws rule to determine the law applicable to cross-border immissions. Claims based on cross-border immissions can be classified based either on property law or on tort law. If classified as part of tort law, liability would be determined pursuant to conflict of laws rules of Rome II Regulation (*see* Chapter 2, §3). If classified as part of property law, the PIL Act conflict of laws rule on property rights would apply and the governing law would be *lex rei sitae*.

III. Easements

278. Easements are rights in rem. Under Czech law the general conflict of laws rules for property rights in section 69 PIL Act apply.

§4. Securities

279. Conflict of laws rules concerning securities are contained in sections 82–83 of the Czech PIL Act. Pursuant to section 82 PIL Act whether a security is validly issued, whether there are rights associated with it in such a manner that they cannot be exercised after the issuance of a security throughout the term of its validity without the security concerned, and what rights and what legal effects are connected thereto are governed according to the nature of the security by the law governing the legal capacity and internal relations of a legal entity which issued the security (*lex societatis*), or by the law governing the legal relation for which an issuance of a security is stipulated (*lex causae*), or by the law applicable in place where the security was issued (*lex loci actus*), or by the law of the state in which an entity issuing the security has a seat or habitual residence unless the nature of the security corresponds to an application of another law, or by the law determined in a security provided the nature of the security admits it (*lex electa*). The choice among the alternative connecting factors within this conflict rule is based on the nature of the instrument.[132]

280. Pursuant to section 83(1) PIL Act, unless stipulated otherwise by law, a right to a security is governed by *lex rei sitae*, while a transfer of a right to a security is governed by the law applicable in place where the security is located at the time of its disposition. The law applicable to a statutory lien over a security is determined pursuant to section 83(2) PIL Act; the governing law is the law applicable in place of habitual residence or a seat of a lien creditor in a decisive time period unless the parties choose another law; *renvoi* is excluded. Should a security which must be submitted in order to give out and handle properties be concerned, the law applicable in place where the security is located in the decisive time period applies. Section 83(8) PIL Act contains a special conflict of laws rule to determine the law applicable to existence and transition of a statutory lien over shares and securities issued by any of the legal entities participating in a cross-border transformation (a merger or similar transaction). The rule refers to Act on Transformations of Commercial Companies and Cooperatives; its section 59g contains the relevant conflict of laws rule. Notwithstanding the provisions of section 83(1–2) PIL Act, handling book-entry or immobilized securities or other securities entered in a depository, or handling a depository-entered right which acts as a book-entry security is governed by the law of the state in which the entry is undertaken; *renvoi* is excluded. A choice of law is admissible only if it concerns a law of a state in which the entity administering the depository has its seat or branch at the time of the choice of law and administering a depository belongs among usual activities of such an entity.

281. Section 83 paragraphs 4–7 PIL Act implement the EU Directive 98/26/EC of the European Parliament and of the Council on settlement finality in payment and securities settlement systems, the Directive 2002/47/EC of the European Parliament and of the Council on financial collateral arrangements and the Directive 2004/25/EC of the European Parliament and of the Council on takeover bids. Pursuant to section 83(4) PIL Act if investment instruments, including the rights associated thereto, are determined to secure the rights of (a) a participant in or an operator of a payment system with settlement finality, of a foreign payment system with settlement finality, of a settlement system with settlement finality or of a foreign settlement system with settlement finality provided such rights arose from his or her participation in or operating of the system, or (b) a central bank of a Member State of the EU or the countries of the EEA or the European Central Bank, the rights of such entities or entities acting on their behalf from a collateral security shall be governed by the law of the state where a depository of investment instruments is administered in which entries establishing legal effects of these acts are undertaken. Pursuant to section 83(5) PIL Act if investment securities, collective investment securities or money market instruments to which a proprietary right or another right in rem is evidenced by an entry in a depository are provided as a subject of a financial collateral security, or if rights arising from an entry of investment securities, collective

132. Horák in P. Bříza et al., *Zákon o mezinárodním právu soukromém. Komentář*, *supra*, p. 475.

investment securities or money market instruments in a depository are provided as a subject of a financial collateral security and enabling an authorized entity to dispose of such a security or instrument directly or indirectly in at least a similar manner as a legitimate holder, (a) a legal nature of the subject of a financial collateral security as well as the property-law effects of such a financial collateral security; (b) conditions required for a financial collateral security creation, for providing of such a subject of a financial collateral security, as well as other conditions for the financial collateral security to become effective with respect to the third persons; (c) proprietary or other rights over the subject of a financial collateral security arising from their entry in a depository, as well as the condition of acquisition from a person other than the owner; (d) conditions and a manner of satisfaction from the subject of a financial collateral security provided a decisive event comes, shall be governed by the law of the state in which the depository is administered. Pursuant to section 83(6) PIL Act a takeover bid intended for owners of securities of a participating nature issued by a public limited-liability company with a seat in the Czech Republic the securities of which are admitted to be traded on a regulated market in the Czech Republic, as well as legal issues related to a takeover bid with an international element, is governed by the Czech law. A choice of a different law in the cases referred to in paragraph 4, as well as a choice of a different law and *renvoi* in the cases referred to in paragraph 5 are excluded.

§5. Trust

282. Trusts are a relatively new concept to Czech law that was introduced in the 2012 recodification of private law. Pursuant to Czech civil law (section 1448 CivC) a trust fund is created by setting aside part of the property owned by the founder in such a way that the owner entrusts the administrator with the property for a particular purpose through a contract or disposition *mortis causa*, and the trustee undertakes to keep and administer the property. The creation of a trust establishes separate and independent ownership of the part of the property set aside and the trustee is obliged to administer it. The rights arising from the right of ownership in the property in a trust are exercised by the trustee in his own name and on the account of the trust; however, the property in a trust is not owned by the administrator or the founder, or the person entitled to receive benefits from the trust fund.

283. Czech PIL Act reflects the introduction of this concept to Czech civil law and contains a special conflict of laws rules with respect to trust funds in its section 73. The scope of the provision is formulated widely so that not only trust funds in the sense of section 1448 CivC but also similar institutions fall under the scope of this rule. The founder of the trust fund may choose the law governing a trust fund provided the chosen law regulates trust funds, or may be applied thereto. In the absence of choice of law, the traditional connecting factor of the closest connection is applied to determine the governing law. The PIL Act lists a number of facts that shall be considered when determining the state to which the trust fund is most closely connected: a place from which the trust fund is administered; a place in which the property the trust fund consists of is predominantly located; a place of seat or habitual residence of the trustee; the purpose of the trust fund as well as the place where it is to be fulfilled. The PIL Act explicitly allows *dépecage* with respect to trust funds in its section 73(3).

284. Trust funds established abroad will be recognized according to Czech law provided they fulfil the essential requirements stipulated for trust funds in the national substantive law (section 1448 CivC). Pursuant to section 1452(3) CivC trust fund by-laws require the form of an authentic instrument, but if such a formal requirement of the Czech regulation is not fulfilled and the trust fund fulfils other requirements of section 1448(1–2) CivC, it should not be considered a non-recognition ground.[133]

§6. EXPROPRIATION

285. The question whether property rights have been acquired and who is entitled to exercise these rights is determined pursuant to the autonomous conflict of laws rules in the Czech PIL Act regarding property rights (*see* Chapter 3).

---

133. Svoboda in P. Bříza et al., *Zákon o mezinárodním právu soukromém. Komentář*, *supra*, p. 382.

Chapter 4. Intangible Property Rights

286. Intangible property rights are traditionally very closely connected with the territory that grants them protection. The principle of territoriality also impacts the national conflict of laws solutions, including the Czech. Pursuant to section 80 PIL Act intellectual property rights are governed by the law of the state which recognizes such rights and grants them protection. *Lex loci protectionis* governs the intellectual property rights as subjective rights that may be invoked *erga omnes*, not the relative subjective rights concerning individual intangible property rights. *Lex loci protectionis* governs *inter alia* creation of such a right, conditions under which such a right is granted, time limit for which it is granted, its extinction. [134]

287. Czech Republic is bound by a number of international treaties concerning intellectual property.[135] Among the most relevant ones are the following multilateral international treaties:

- Paris Convention for the Protection of Industrial Property (1883).
- Madrid Agreement Concerning the International Registration of Marks (1891) and Protocol (1989).
- Lisbon Agreement for the Protection of Appellations of Origin and their International Registration (1958).
- Washington Patent Cooperation Treaty (1970).
- Geneva Universal Copyright Convention (1952).
- Berne Convention for the Protection of Literary and Artistic Works (1886).
- Rome Convention for the Protection of Performers, Producers of Phonograms and Broadcasting Organizations (1961).
- Berne Convention for the Protection of Literary and Artistic Works (1886).

The EU law does not unify the conflict of laws rules for intellectual property; however a number of regulations has been adopted introducing, e.g. the Community trademark,[136] the Community design[137] or the European Patent with unitary affect.[138] The application date of the Regulation implementing enhanced cooperation in the area of the creation of unitary patent protection, that was adopted in 2012 and in which the Czech Republic is taking part, is tied to the date of entry into force of the Agreement on a Unified Patent Court.

134. Břicháček in P. Bříza et al., *Zákon o mezinárodním právu soukromém. Komentář*, *supra*, p. 466.
135. For details, *see* the website of the Czech Intellectual Property Office: https://www.upv.cz/en/legislation.html.
136. In particular, Regulation (EC) No. 207/2009 on the Community trademark.
137. In particular, Council Regulation (EC) No. 6/2002 of 12 Dec. 2001 on Community designs.
138. Regulation (EU) No. 1257/2012 of the European Parliament and of the Council of 17 Dec. 2012 implementing enhanced cooperation in the area of the creation of unitary patent protection.

288. With respect to infringements of intellectual property rights, the conflict of laws rules are anchored in Rome II Regulation. Pursuant to Article 8 Rome II Regulation the law applicable to a non-contractual obligation arising from an infringement of an intellectual property right is *lex loci protectionis*. In the case of a non-contractual obligation arising from an infringement of a unitary Community intellectual property right, the law applicable is, for any question that is not governed by the relevant Community instrument, the law of the country in which the act of infringement was committed. No choice of law is admitted.

§1. Rights of Personality

289. Pursuant to the Czech civil law, personality of an individual including all his natural rights, is protected, particularly life and dignity of an individual, his health and the right to live in a favourable environment, his respect, honour, privacy and expressions of personal nature (section 81 CivC). An individual whose personality rights have been affected has the right to claim that the unlawful interference be refrained from or its consequence remedied. The post-mortal protection of personality rights can be claimed by any of the persons close to the deceased (section 82 CivC).

I. Applicable Law and Remedies

290. Non-contractual obligations arising out of violations of privacy and rights relating to personality, including defamation, are excluded from the material scope of Rome II Regulation; the governing law is determined pursuant to section 101 PIL Act. The affected (injured) person can choose the law of the state in which (a) the affected person has habitual residence or seat, (b) the violation initiator (perpetrator) has habitual residence or seat, or (c) the result of a violating conduct appeared (manifested itself) provided the violation agent could predict it. In the absence of choice of law, the governing law is the law of the state in which the violation occurred.

§2. Industrial Designs

291. *See* above Chapter 4.

Chapter 5. Family Law

292. The Czech PIL Act contains conflict of laws rules for the following family law matters: (1) marital regimes (sections 47–66 PIL Act); (2) parent–child regimes including determination of paternity, rights of unmarried mother and adoption (sections 53–58 PIL Act); and (3) guardianship and curatorship of minors (sections 64–66 PIL Act). Conflict of laws rules on registered partnership are contained in section 67 PIL Act. *Renvoi* is not excluded in family matters with the exception of choice of law provided the parties did not expressly agreed on *renvoi* (section 21 PIL Act).

293. European law and a number of international treaties and conventions binding on the Czech Republic, which have precedence over the national conflict rules in the PIL Act (section 2 PIL Act and Article 10 of the Constitution of the Czech Republic), play a predominant role in the regulation of international family law.

294. Law applicable to maintenance is determined pursuant to the Regulation on Jurisdiction, Applicable Law, Recognition and Enforcement of Decisions and Cooperation in Matters relating to Maintenance Obligations (Maintenance Regulation)[139] in connection with the Hague Protocol from 2007 on the law applicable to maintenance obligations (2007 Hague Protocol). Some other relevant EU regulations unifying conflict of laws rules in family matters are binding only for those Member States that take part in the so-called enhanced cooperation. Czech Republic does not take part in the enhanced cooperation in the area of the law applicable to divorce and legal separation and therefore the Regulation implementing enhanced cooperation in the area of the law applicable to divorce and legal separation (Rome III Regulation)[140] is not applicable in the Czech Republic. The situation is different in the area of the law applicable to matrimonial property regimes and property consequences of registered partnership where the Czech Republic takes part in the enhanced cooperation. Both the Regulation implementing enhanced cooperation in the area of jurisdiction, applicable law and the recognition and enforcement of decisions in matters of matrimonial property regimes (Regulation on Matrimonial Property Regime) and the Regulation implementing enhanced cooperation in the area of jurisdiction, applicable law and the recognition and enforcement of decisions in matters of the property consequences of registered partnerships (Regulation on Property Consequences of Registered Partnership)[141] are applicable in the Czech Republic as of 29 January 2019.

139. Regulation No. 4/2009 on Jurisdiction, Applicable Law, Recognition and Enforcement of Decisions and Cooperation in Matters relating to Maintenance Obligations (Maintenance Regulation).

140. Council Regulation (EU) No. 1259/2010 of 20 Dec. 2010 implementing enhanced cooperation in the area of the law applicable to divorce and legal separation (Rome III Regulation).

141. Council Regulation (EU) No. 2016/1103 of 24 Jun. 2016 implementing enhanced cooperation in the area of jurisdiction, applicable law and the recognition and enforcement of decisions in matters

295. Czech Republic is a contracting state to many international conventions unifying substantive and conflict of laws rules in family law matters, such as, *inter alia*, the 1967 Strasbourg European Convention on the Adoption of Children, the 1975 Strasbourg European Convention on the Legal Status of Children Born Out of Wedlock, the 1989 New York Convention on Rights of a Child, the 1993 Hague Convention on the Protection of Children and Cooperation in Respect of Intercountry Adoption, and the 1996 Strasbourg European Convention on the Exercise of Children's Rights, the 1996 Hague Convention on Jurisdiction, Applicable Law, Recognition, Enforcement and Cooperation in respect of Parental Responsibility and Measures for Protection of Children, the 1980 Hague Convention on Civil Aspects of International Child Abduction or the 2003 Strasbourg Convention on Contact with Children.

296. Special conflict of laws rules in the field of family law are also included in numerous bilateral treaties on mutual legal assistance binding for the Czech Republic.[142] With respect to the citizens of the other contracting party such rules have precedence not only over the PIL Act provisions but also over international conventions, except for rules on some very special subject matters in multilateral conventions to which both contracting states are parties. Regarding the EU Regulations, only the bilateral treaties concluded with non-EU countries take precedence over the Regulations provided they concern matters governed by the respective Regulation.

§1. State Law: Religious Law

297. Czech civil law allows both civil and church wedding ceremony. Pursuant to section 657 CivC where the marriage is entered into before a public body performing the wedding ceremony in the presence of a registrar, it is a civil wedding; where the marriage is entered into before a body of a church or religious society authorized to do so pursuant to section 7(1) of the Act on Churches and Religious Societies,[143] it is a church wedding.

---

of matrimonial property regimes (Regulation on Matrimonial Property Regime) and Council Regulation (EU) No. 2016/1104 of 24 Jun. 2016 implementing enhanced cooperation in the area of jurisdiction, applicable law and the recognition and enforcement of decisions in matters of the property consequences of registered partnerships (Regulation on Property Consequences of Registered Partnership).

142. Bilateral treaties with Albania, Bulgaria, North Korea, Cuba, Hungary, Mongolia, Poland, Romania, the former Yugoslavia (still in force with respect to some former Member States of the Yugoslav Federation), the former Union of Soviet Socialist Republics (still in force with respect to some former Member States of the Union), Ukraine, Uzbekistan and Vietnam.

143. Act No. 3/2002 Coll., on Churches and Religious Societies. The list of churches and religious societies authorized to perform a wedding ceremony in the Czech Republic is available at the website of the Czech Ministry of Culture (https://www.mkcr.cz/zvlastni-prava-33.html).

§2. MARRIAGE

I. Engagement

298. Engagement to marry is not explicitly regulated by Czech law; it is a factual concept. Nevertheless, it might be possible to consider the liability for breach of good morals, in case the marriage does not take place based on fault (section 2909 CivC). Moreover, the Czech Civil Code provides for contracts of a man and a woman wishing to marry on administration of future marital property (section 722 CivC).

299. The Czech PIL Act does not have any special conflict of laws rule with regard to the engagement to marry. In general, there are two possibilities: such a relationship can either be classified under the conflict of laws rules relating to marriage (sections 48–49 PIL Act), or under conflict of laws rules relating to validity of legal acts in general (sections 41–42 PIL Act).

II. Heterosexual Marriage

300. Czech law is based on the principle of monogamy. Under section 674 CivC marriage cannot be entered into by a person who has previously entered into marriage or by a person who has previously entered into a registered partnership or into another similar union abroad while this marriage, registered partnership or other similar union entered into abroad still lasts.

301. In certain cases, the effects of the application of a foreign law permitting polygamy can invoke the reservation of public order under section 4 PIL Act. Provisions of a foreign law, which is to be applied pursuant to the provisions of PIL Act, are applied only if the effects of such application are not manifestly incompatible with the public policy of the forum. For example, monogamy is considered as a principle of Czech law whose observance is required without exception, therefore if a Czech woman intends to marry a citizen of Iran who has already married another woman in Iran and under Iranian law has the capacity to conclude another marriage, the *lex fori* (Czech law) provisions under which a marriage impediment exists are applied instead of the non-applicable provisions of Iranian law.

A. Substance and Form

302. The capacity of a person to celebrate marriage as well as the conditions for its validity are governed by *lex patriae* (section 48(1) PIL Act).

303. The capacity to marry should be assessed separately with respect to both persons. If their nationality is different, the capacity of each fiancée should be assessed in conformity with the respective legal system.

304. The Act on Register of Births, Marriages and Deaths[144] requires a fiancée, who is a foreigner, to submit a certificate (not older than six months) of his or her capacity to marry issued by the respective body of the state of his or her nationality.

305. A decision of a foreign court declaring as invalid a marriage of a foreign citizen with a Czech citizen cannot be considered inconsistent with public policy of the Czech Republic only for the reason that Czech law does not consider the legal ground of invalidity on the basis of which the invalidity of a marriage was determined by the foreign court as marriage impediment under Czech law. Such a decision can therefore be recognized in the territory of the Czech Republic (R 27/1991).[145]

306. The form of the wedding ceremony is governed by the law of the place where the marriage is being concluded (section 48(2) PIL Act). Some legal systems allow the so-called consular marriages that are entered into at the premises of embassies. Czech law allows Czech citizens to enter into marriage abroad at a diplomatic mission or consular office of the Czech Republic (section 668 CivC). Pursuant to section 48(3) PIL Act the conclusion of such a marriage is governed by Czech law. Czech citizens are not allowed to enter into marriage at an embassy of a foreign state in the Czech Republic (section 48(4) PIL Act). Such a marriage would not be considered validly concluded in the territory of the Czech Republic.[146]

III. Same-Sex Marriage

307. The Czech law does not permit same-sex marriages. Pursuant to section 655 CivC marriage is a permanent union of a man and a woman formed in a manner provided for by the CivC. Same-sex marriages concluded abroad in countries that allow their celebration are not recognized in the Czech Republic and cannot be registered as marriages in the Czech Register of Marriages.[147]

IV. Personal Effects of Marriage

308. The law applicable to personal relations of spouses is determined pursuant to a special conflict of laws rule in section 49(1) PIL Act. The governing law is the

144. Act No. 301/2000 Coll., on Register of Births, Marriages and Deaths.
145. Decision of the Supreme Court of Czechoslovakia which recognized the decision of the Civil Court in B. (Italy), Collection of Decisions of the Supreme Court No. 6/1991, 253. The reason of invalidity was the fact that the conclusion of marriage was only pretended without the intention of living together (*see* Art. 128 of Italian Civil Code in connection with Italian Act of 19 May 1975).
146. *See* for details: M. Pauknerová, *Private International Law in the Czech Republic: Tradition, New Experience and Prohibition of Discrimination on Grounds of Nationality*, 4 J. Private Int. Law, 83 (2008).
147. Decision of the Czech Supreme Administrative Court from 30 May 2018 (As 230/2017).

lex patriae, provided both of them are nationals of the same state, or failing that the law of the state of their common habitual residence, or failing that Czech law.

V. Dissolution

309. As the Czech Republic is not bound by Rome III Regulation that unifies conflict of laws rules for divorce, the autonomous national conflict rules in PIL Act apply. Conflict of laws rules regarding the dissolution of marriage are anchored also in a number of bilateral treaties on legal assistance that take precedence over the PIL Act rules (section 2 PIL Act).

A. Annulment

310. Pursuant to Czech Civil Code if a marriage has been entered into despite the existence of a legal impediment, the court declares the marriage invalid on the application of anyone having a legal interest therein, unless the marriage was impeded by limited legal capacity (section 680 CivC). The national conflict of laws rules on legal capacity to enter into marriage and its validity and on the form of the wedding ceremony are to be applied with respect to the law applicable to annulment of a marriage.[148] Pursuant to section 50(3) PIL Act when annulling marriage the capacity to celebrate marriage and the form of its celebration shall be governed by laws applicable to them at the time of marriage celebration.

B. Divorce

311. The relevant conflict of laws rules are anchored in a number of bilateral treaties on legal assistance that apply to divorces with respect to nationals of contracting parties and that take precedence over the rules in the Czech autonomous PIL. If no bilateral treaty is applicable, the law governing divorce is determined pursuant to section 50(1) PIL Act in connection with section 49(1) PIL Act. Dissolution of marriage through divorce is governed by the law of the state of the common nationality of the spouses at the time the divorce proceedings are initiated. If the spouses are nationals of two different states, the law of the state of their common habitual residence applies, or failing Czech law (*lex fori*) applies. Czech law also applies if the foreign law applicable based on these conflict of laws rules does not allow divorce at all or under extremely onerous circumstances only and at least one of the spouses is a Czech national or habitually resident in the Czech Republic (section 49(2) PIL Act). The application of this rule should be restrictive and exceptional as the non-application of foreign law bears the risk that a decision on divorce based on Czech substantive law will be denied recognition abroad.[149]

---

148. Zavadilová in M. Pauknerová, et al. *Zákon o mezinárodním právu soukromém. Komentář*, *supra*, p. 343.
149. Fišerová in P. Bříza, et al. *Zákon o mezinárodním právu soukromém. Komentář*, *supra*, p. 265.

312. Unified EU rules on law applicable to divorce in Rome III Regulation do not apply in Czech Republic.

C. Legal Separation of Marriage

313. Czech legal system does not know legal separation of marriage. Czech courts that would acquire jurisdiction (based on the rules of the Brussels II*bis* Regulation) to decide on an application for legal separation of a marriage would most probably determine the governing law *per analogiam* pursuant to the national conflict of laws rule on divorce in section 50(1) PIL Act.

§3. MATRIMONIAL PROPERTY

314. Under Czech autonomous PIL the law governing property relations between spouses is the law of the state of their common habitual residence; or failing that, the law of the state of the common nationality of the spouses; or failing that Czech law. This hierarchical conflict of laws rule is anchored in section 49(3) PIL Act. Unlike the conflict of laws rule on divorce (section 50(1) in connection with section 49(1) PIL Act), the conflict rule on property relations between spouses does not fix the moment to which the habitual residence or nationality of the spouses should be assessed. Due to this wording, mobile conflicts cannot be excluded, as both habitual residence and nationality of the spouses may change in course of a marriage. In general, the moment when a respective right is established or extinguished is decisive.

315. Spouses and future spouses may also contractually agree on their matrimonial property regime different from the statutory one. Under Czech law such an agreement must be concluded in the form of an authentic instrument (section 716 CivC). The law governing the contractual matrimonial property regimes of spouses is determined pursuant to a special conflict of laws rule in section 49(4) PIL Act. In the absence of choice of law, the governing law to agreements on matrimonial property regime is the law applicable to the property regimes of spouses at the time of the conclusion of the agreement.

316. Relevant conflict of laws rules on matrimonial property regime are also included in a number of bilateral treaties on legal assistance that take precedence over the national rules.

317. From 29 January 2019 the Regulation on Matrimonial Property Regimes applies in the Czech Republic. The Regulation introduces, among others, harmonized conflict of laws rules to determine the law applicable to matrimonial property regime (as defined in Article 3(1)(b) Regulation on Matrimonial Property Regimes), that take precedence over the relevant national rules in PIL Act and in bilateral treaties concluded with another EU Member State that is bound by this Regulation.

However, the autonomous conflict of laws rules still remain relevant after 29 January 2019 as the Chapter III of the Regulation on Applicable Law applies only to spouses who marry or who specify the law applicable to the matrimonial property regime on or after 29 January 2019 (Article 69(3) Regulation on Matrimonial Property Regimes). Marriage is not defined by the Regulation; legal definitions of marriage in national laws of the EU Member States apply.

318. In the absence of a choice of law agreement pursuant to Article 22, the conflict of laws rules in Article 26 of the Regulation on Matrimonial Property Regimes apply. The law governing the matrimonial property regime is (a) the law of the state of the spouses' first common habitual residence after the conclusion of the marriage; or failing that (b) the law of the spouses' common nationality at the time of the conclusion of the marriage; or failing that (c) the law with which the spouses jointly have the closest connection at the time of the conclusion of the marriage, taking into account all the circumstances. If the spouses have more than one common nationality at the time of the conclusion of the marriage, the conflict of laws rule using nationality as a connecting factor does not apply.

319. There is an escape clause in Article 26(3) of the Regulation on Matrimonial Property Regimes according to which the courts having jurisdiction may exceptionally deviate from the law of the state of the spouses' first common habitual residence after the conclusion of the marriage determined as applicable law pursuant to Article 26(1)(a) if the applicant demonstrates that the spouses had their last common habitual residence in another state for a significantly longer period of time than in the state designated pursuant to point (a); and both spouses had relied on the law of that other state in arranging or planning their property relations. Then the law of this other state applies as from the conclusion of the marriage, unless one spouse disagrees. In the latter case, the law of that other state shall have effect as from the establishment of the last common habitual residence in that other state. The application of the law of the other state shall not adversely affect the rights of third parties deriving from the law applicable pursuant to point (a). The escape clause does not apply when the spouses have concluded a matrimonial property agreement before the establishment of their last common habitual residence in that other state.

320. For reasons of legal certainty and in order to avoid the fragmentation of the matrimonial property regime, the law applicable to a matrimonial property regime governs that regime as a whole, irrespective of the nature of the assets and regardless of whether the assets are located in another EU Member State or in a third state (Recital 43 Preamble of the Regulation on Matrimonial Property Regimes).

321. The law determined by the Regulation on Matrimonial Property Regimes applies even if it is not the law of an EU Member State (Article 20 of the Regulation on Matrimonial Property Regimes). *Renvoi* is excluded (Article 33 Regulation on Matrimonial Property Regimes).

I. Choice of Law Agreement

322. Under the Czech PIL Act a limited choice of law is admitted when the spouses contractually agree on their matrimonial property regime (section 49(4) PIL Act). They can choose that their property regime will be governed either by the law of the state of which one of the spouses is a national or in which one of the spouses is habitually resident, or by the law of the state in which an immovable property is located (if applicable), or by Czech law. The form of an authentic instrument is required for such an agreement on choice of law if concluded abroad.

323. The Regulation on Matrimonial Property Regimes allows a limited choice of law in its Article 22. The spouses or future spouses may choose, regardless of the nature or location of the property, among the laws with which they have close links because of their habitual residence or their nationality. They can choose either the law of the state where the spouses or future spouses, or one of them, is habitually resident or the law of a state of nationality of either spouse or future spouse. The decisive moment for the assessment of the habitual residence or nationality is the time of the conclusion of the agreement. The choice of law may be made at any moment, before the marriage, at the time of conclusion of the marriage or during the course of the marriage. Unless the spouses agree otherwise, a change of the law applicable to the matrimonial property regime made during the marriage shall have prospective effect only. If they agree on a retroactive effect of such a change of the applicable law, it should not adversely affect the rights of third parties deriving from that law.

324. The Regulation also contains conflict of laws rules on existence and validity (both material and formal) of the choice of law agreement (Articles 23–24).

II. Relationship to Succession Law

325. Under Czech law (section 764(1) CivC) if a marriage were to terminate by a spouse's death, the property rights and duties of the former spouses would be assessed under succession proceedings according to the property regime which existed between the spouses, or, where applicable, according to the instructions which the deceased spouse had given during his life regarding his property upon death; otherwise, the community property is settled according to the statutory rules, unless the surviving spouse agrees with the heirs on a settlement otherwise. The settlement of the community property upon death of a spouse is dealt with as a preliminary question within the succession proceedings. The court (in the Czech Republic the notary as court commissioner) applies different conflict of laws rules to determine the law applicable to matrimonial property regime and to succession which may result in different substantive laws being applied to the settlement of the regime of community property terminated upon the death of one of the spouses (the deceased) and subsequently to succession of the estate of the deceased. The succession of the estate of the deceased spouse is expressly excluded from the material scope of the Regulation on Matrimonial Property Regimes. And vice versa questions relating to matrimonial property regimes are expressly excluded from the material scope of the Succession Regulation.

§4. Registered Partnership: Partnership/Civil Unions

326. Registered partnership has been part of the Czech legal system since July 2006. It is regulated by an Act on registered partnership.[150] It is defined as a permanent partnership of two individuals of the same sex established in the manner set out by law. Pursuant to section 4(2) of this Act at least one of the persons entering into a registered partnership has to be a Czech national, thus two foreign nationals cannot validly enter into a registered partnership in the Czech Republic.[151] The Czech PIL Act contains special conflict of laws rules with respect to registered partnership in section 67(2). The law applicable to registered partnership and similar relationships (regimes) is the law of the state in which the registered partnership or a similar regime is being or has been celebrated. With respect to the scope of applicable law, the governing law applies to the effects of the registered partnership or of a similar regime, the capacity to celebrate and terminate them, their annulment and non-existence as well as to the personal and property relations of the partners.

I. Personal Effects

327. Czech PIL Act contains special conflict of laws rules with respect to registered partnership in section 67(2). The law applicable to registered partnership and similar relationships (regimes) is the law of the state in which the registered partnership or a similar regime is being or has been celebrated. The governing law applies among others to the personal effects of the registered partnership.

II. Dissolution

328. The Czech PIL Act contains special conflict of laws rules with respect to registered partnership in section 67(2). The law applicable to registered partnership and similar relationships (regimes) is the law of the state in which the registered partnership or a similar regime is being or has been celebrated. The governing law applies among others to its dissolution.

---

150. Act No. 115/2006 Coll., on registered partnership and on amendments to some related acts.
151. Zavadilová, Grygar in M. Pauknerová et al., *Zákon o mezinárodním právu soukromém. Komentář*, *supra*, p. 441.

III. Property

329. Pursuant to section 67(2) PIL Act the law applicable to property relations of registered partners is the law of the state in which the registered partnership or a similar regime is being or has been celebrated.

330. From 29 January 2019, the Regulation on Property Consequences of Registered Partnership applies in the Czech Republic. The Regulation introduces, among others, harmonized conflict of laws rules to determine the law applicable to matters arising from the property consequences of registered partnerships (as defined in its Article 3(1)(a)) that are directly applicable and take precedence over the national rule in PIL Act. However, the autonomous conflict of laws rule still remains relevant after 29 January 2019 as the Chapter III of the Regulation on Applicable Law applies only to partners who register their partnership or who specify the law applicable to the property consequences of their registered partnership on or after 29 January 2019 (Article 69(3) Regulation on Property Consequences of Registered Partnership).

331. Pursuant to the Regulation partners or future partners may choose the law applicable to the property consequences of their registered partnership among the laws with which they have close links because of their habitual residence or nationality: the law of the state where the partners or future partners, or one of them, is habitually resident at the time the agreement is concluded, or the law of a state of nationality of either partner or future partner at the time the agreement is concluded, or the law of the state under whose law the registered partnership was created. However, in order to avoid depriving the choice of law of any effect and thereby leaving the partners in a legal vacuum, such choice of law should be limited to a law that attaches property consequences to registered partnerships (Article 22(1) of the Regulation on Property Consequences of Registered Partnership). This choice can be made at any moment, before the registration of the partnership, at the time of the registration of the partnership or during the course of the registered partnership (Recital 44 of the Preamble). The law applicable governs the property consequences of the registered partnership as a whole, that is to say, all the property consequences covered by the registered partnership, irrespective of the nature of the assets and regardless of whether the assets are located in another Member State or in a third state (Recital 42 of the Preamble). The Regulation also contains conflict of laws rules on existence and validity (both material and formal) of the choice of law agreements (Articles 23–24).

332. In the absence of choice of law by the partners, the law applicable to property consequences of the registered partnership is determined pursuant to Article 26 of the Regulation on Property Consequences of Registered Partnership. The governing law is the law of the state under whose law the registered partnership was created (Article 26(1)). By way of exception and upon application by either partner, the judicial authority having jurisdiction to rule on matters of the property consequences of a registered partnership may decide that the law of a state other than the state whose law is applicable pursuant to paragraph 1 shall govern the property consequences of the registered partnership if the law of that other state attaches property consequences to the institution of the registered partnership and if the applicant demonstrates that: (a) the partners had their last common habitual residence in that other state for a significantly long period of time; and (b) both partners had relied on the law of that other state in arranging or planning their property relations. The law of that other state applies as from the creation of the registered partnership unless one partner disagrees. In the latter case, the law of that other state has effect as from the establishment of the last common habitual residence in that other state. *Renvoi* is excluded (Article 31 of the Regulation on Property Consequences of Registered Partnership).

§5. Extra-Marital Cohabitation

I. Property

333. Extra-marital cohabitation is not explicitly regulated in Czech law. The Civil Code contains only general provisions on, e.g., co-ownership, common lease or association agreement. Maintenance obligations with respect to children arise regardless of whether or not the parents are married. The Civil Code uses the term 'common household' relating to persons living together permanently. In the law of succession, persons who lived with the decedent in the common household for at least one year before his death and, as a result, cared for the common household or were dependent in maintenance on the decedent are included in the second class of heirs (section 1636(1) CivC).

334. Pursuant to Czech legal literature and practice the Civil Code provisions on community property regime of spouses cannot be applied to cohabitants.[152]

335. Czech PIL does not contain any special conflict of laws rule with respect to cohabitants. Before Czech courts extra-marital cohabitation could probably be classified as falling into the scope of the conflict of laws rules on personal and property relations between spouses, applying these *per analogiam* (section 49(1, 3–4) PIL Act).

§6. Maintenance Law

I. Spousal Maintenance

336. Regarding spousal maintenance the Czech PIL Act contains a reference provision only. Pursuant to section 49(3) PIL Act maintenance obligations between

152. O. Jehlička et al., *Občanský zákoník, Komentář* [*Civil Code, Commentary*, in Czech] 485 (6th ed. C.H. Beck 2001); and S. Radvanová & M. Zuklínová, *Kurs občanského práva, Instituty rodinného práva* [*Civil Law Course, Institutions of Family Law*] 203 (C.H. Beck 1999).

spouses are governed by the law determined under an international treaty, the application of which is stipulated by a directly applicable instrument of the EU law. Spousal maintenance falls under the scope of Maintenance Regulation that applies to maintenance obligations arising from a family relationship, parentage, marriage or affinity. The law governing maintenance obligations is determined based on its Article 15 in accordance with the 2007 Hague Protocol in the EU Member States bound by that instrument, including Czech Republic.[153]

337. Based on its universal character, the 2007 Hague Protocol applies even if the applicable law is that of a non-contracting state. In accordance with the general conflict of laws rule in Article 3 of the 2007 Hague Protocol, maintenance obligations are governed by the law of the state of the habitual residence of the creditor. The applicable law changes with the change of the habitual residence of the creditor; the law of the state of the new habitual residence applies as from the moment when the change occurs. Articles 5 and 6 of the 2007 Hague Protocol lay down a special rule with respect to spouses and ex-spouses: in the case of a maintenance obligation between spouses, ex-spouses or parties to a marriage which has been annulled, Article 3 does not apply if one of the parties objects and the law of another state, in particular the state of their last common habitual residence, has a closer connection with the marriage. In such a case, the law of that other state applies. In case of spousal maintenance obligations, the debtor may contest a claim from the creditor on the ground that there is no such obligation under both the law of the state of the habitual residence of the debtor and the law of the state of the common nationality of the parties if there is one.

338. The 2007 Hague Protocol allows a limited choice of the law applicable to spousal maintenance obligations with the exception of cases provided for in Article 8(3) of the 2007 Hague Protocol. The maintenance creditor and debtor may at any time choose the law of any state of which either party is a national at the time of the designation; or the law of the state of the habitual residence of either party at the time of designation; or the law designated by the parties as applicable, or the law in fact applied, to their property regime, divorce or legal separation. Such an agreement shall be in writing or recorded in any medium, the information contained in which is accessible to be usable for subsequent reference, and shall be signed by both parties. Notwithstanding the law designated by the parties, the question of whether the creditor can renounce his or her right to maintenance is determined by the law of the state of the habitual residence of the creditor at the time of the designation. Unless at the time of the designation the parties were fully informed and aware of the consequences of their designation, the law designated by the parties does not apply where the application of that law would lead to manifestly unfair or

153. The 2007 Hague Protocol was approved on behalf of the European Community (now European Union) by the Council Decision No. 2009/941/EC of 2009 on the conclusion by the European Community of the Hague Protocol of 2007 on the Law Applicable to Maintenance Obligations.

unreasonable consequences for any of the parties (Article 8 of the 2007 Hague Protocol). Pursuant to Article 7(1) of the 2007 Hague Protocol the maintenance creditor and debtor for the purpose only of a particular proceeding in a given state may expressly designate *lex fori* as applicable to a maintenance obligation.

II. Partnership Maintenance

339. According to Czech law, registered partners have mutual maintenance obligations. The maintenance obligations between partners and ex-partners are stipulated in sections 10–12 of the Act on registered partnership. With respect to applicable law, it is a controversial issue. Maintenance obligations are explicitly excluded from the material scope of the Regulation on Property Consequences of Registered Partnership (Article 1(2)(c)). The autonomous conflict of laws rule on registered partnership in section 67(2) PIL Act does not expressly include maintenance obligations between partners in its scope. Maintenance obligations could thus be classified in accordance with the Czech traditional doctrine as part of personal relations between partners, which would result in the application of the autonomous general conflict of rule in section 67(2) PIL Act to determine the law applicable to maintenance obligations between partners; or the scope of the 2007 Hague Protocol could be interpreted widely so that partnership maintenance would be included into its material scope and the law applicable to maintenance obligations between partners would be determined pursuant to the conflict of laws rules in the 2007 Hague Protocol.

III. Maintenance of Cohabitees

340. As extra-marital cohabitation is not explicitly regulated in Czech law; there is no regulation regarding maintenance obligations of cohabitees. The 2007 Hague Protocol is silent on whether maintenance obligations arising out of such relationships are included within its scope. Pursuant to the Bonomi Report on the 2007 Hague Protocol the states that are willing to recognize institutions similar to marriage may make them subject to the rule under Article 5. It would be up to the Czech court concerned whether it would on a case-by-case basis admit the application of foreign law determined based on the 2007 Hague Protocol that recognizes a maintenance obligation arising from an extra-marital cohabitation.

§7. Child Law

I. Determination of Parenthood

341. The Czech substantive law deals only with establishment and denial of fatherhood (sections 776 et seq. CivC); the mother is the woman that gave birth to the child (section 775 CivC). The Czech PIL Act, however, reflects the developments in the field of family law and contains conflict of laws rules on establishment and denial of parenthood (not only fatherhood).

342. The law applicable to establishment and denial of parenthood is in most cases determined pursuant to Czech autonomous conflict of laws rules. There is neither an EU Regulation unifying conflict of laws rules in this area nor any multilateral international treaty binding for Czech Republic. Some of the bilateral treaties on legal assistance may contain relevant conflict rules that take precedence over the Czech PIL Act rules. In accordance with section 54(1) PIL Act the law applicable to the establishment and denial of parenthood is the law of the state of which the child was a national at birth (*lex patriae*). If the child acquired more than one nationality by birth, Czech law (*lex fori*) applies irrespective of the fact whether Czech nationality is one of the multiple nationalities or not. As the court always has to consider the best interest of the child, if it is in the interest of the child, either the law of the state in which the mother was habitually resident at the time of the conception of the child (section 54(1) PIL Act) or, provided the child is habitually resident in the Czech Republic, the Czech law applies (section 54(2) PIL Act). It is not laid down in the PIL Act what is to be understood under the interest of the child; the application of these special conflict of laws rules is up to the court's consideration with respect to the factual circumstances of each case.[154] In *favorem validitatis*, the parenthood is also validly established if the declaration of parenthood satisfies legal requirements of the *lex loci actus* or if the parenthood was denied by one person and established by another person in court proceedings or out of court in a foreign state in compliance with its law (section 54(4) PIL Act).

II. Custody and Access Rights

343. Custody of minors and access rights are essential parts of parental responsibility. The Czech PIL Act contains a reference provision in section 57(2) according to which the law applicable to parental rights and obligations (with the exclusion of maintenance) and of measures for protection of person or property of the child is determined under the 1996 Hague Convention on Jurisdiction, Applicable law, Recognition, Enforcement and Cooperation in Respect of Parental Responsibility and Measures for the Protection of Children (Hague Convention on Protection of Children). The Convention applies to children from the moment of their birth until they reach the age of 18 years and relates to, *inter alia*, the attribution, exercise, termination or restriction of parental responsibility, as well as its delegation; rights of custody, including rights relating to the care of the person of the child and, in particular, the right to determine the child's place of residence, as well as rights of access, including the right to take a child for a limited period of time to a place other than the child's habitual residence; guardianship, curatorship and analogous institutions (Articles 1–3 of the Hague Convention on Protection of Children). Pursuant to its

154. J. Grygar, in M. Pauknerová et al., *Zákon o mezinárodním právu soukromém. Komentář, supra*, p. 365.

Article 20 the conflict of laws rules laid down by the Convention apply even if the law designated by them is the law of a non-contracting state. Under Article 15 of the Hague Convention on Protection of Children in exercising their jurisdiction under the Convention, the authorities of the contracting states apply their own law (*lex fori*). The jurisdiction of Czech courts in matters of parental responsibility is not determined under the Convention but under the jurisdiction rules in the Brussels II*bis* Regulation. According to the prevailing opinion among experts, Article 15 of the Convention on Protection of Children is to be interpreted widely and applied provided the grounds for the court's jurisdiction correspond with those of the Hague Convention on Protection of Children.[155] Pursuant to its Article 15(2) the law of another state with which the situation has a substantial connection may exceptionally be applied or taken into consideration insofar as the protection of the person or the property of the child requires. If the child's habitual residence changes to another contracting state, the law of that other state governs, from the time of the change, the conditions of application of the measures taken in the state of the former habitual residence. The exercise of parental responsibility (who has parental responsibility and the conditions of its exercise) is governed by the law of the state of the child's habitual residence (Article 17 of the Convention on Protection of Children). Under Article 21 of the Convention on Protection of Children the *renvoi* is excluded unless the applicable law is determined pursuant to Article 16.

344. The respective provisions in bilateral treaties concluded by the Czech Republic that have priority over the Convention on Protection of Children may also be relevant.

III. Guardianship

345. Pursuant to Czech substantive law when there is a conflict of interests between the child and another person, the court appoints a guardian (in Czech '*opatrovník*') to a child if the legal representative (in most cases the parent) of the child fails to defend sufficiently the interests of the child, if it is in the interests of the child for another reason, or where provided by a statute (section 943 CivC). When the parents of a minor child die or they live but do not exercise full parental responsibility, the court appoints a curator (in Czech '*poručník*') to a child. In principle, a curator has all the rights and duties towards the child as a parent except of maintenance obligations (section 928 CivC).

346. The law applicable to both the guardianship and curatorship is determined under the conflict of laws rules of the Hague Convention on Protection of Children that is binding for the Czech Republic. For the purposes of the Convention the term 'parental responsibility' includes, *inter alia*, guardians or other legal representatives in relation to the person or the property of the child (Article 1(2)). Under Article 15 of the Hague Convention on Protection of Children in exercising their jurisdiction

155. Zavadilová, M. Nováková in M. Pauknerová et al., *Zákon o mezinárodním právu soukromém. Komentář*, *supra*, p. 392.

under the Convention, the authorities of the contracting states apply their own law (*lex fori*). Pursuant to its Article 15(2) the law of another state with which the situation has a substantial connection may exceptionally be applied or taken into consideration insofar as the protection of the person or the property of the child requires. If the child's habitual residence changes to another contracting state, the law of that other state governs, from the time of the change, the conditions of application of the measures taken in the state of the former habitual residence. The exercise of guardianship or curatorship is governed by the law of the state of the child's habitual residence (Article 17).

347. The Czech PIL Act contains special conflict of laws rules in section 65 in connection with sections 35–36. The Convention rules take precedence over the PIL Act rules and given the universal applicability of the Convention, the PIL Act rules on the law applicable to guardianship or curatorship are practically out of application. However, the respective provisions in bilateral treaties concluded by the Czech Republic that have priority over the Convention on Protection of Children may be relevant.

IV. Adoption

348. Under Czech civil law, both children and adults can be adopted. Upon adoption of a minor child, the adoptive parents are registered as parents and have parental responsibility (section 832(2) CivC). The family relations between the adopted child and the original family are extinguished (section 833(1) CivC). The adoption of a minor is decided by a court on application of the person who wishes to adopt the child. Where an application to adopt a child from a foreign country is filed, the applicant has to attach a decision of a competent public body of that state consenting to the adoption (section 796(1) CivC). Under Czech substantive law, the adoption of a child to a foreign country always requires the consent of the Office for International Legal Protection of Children (section 35(2)(i) Act on Social and Legal Protection of Children[156]). The Office for International Legal Protection of Children (ÚMPOD) is the Czech Central Authority pursuant to the 1993 Hague Convention on Protection of Children and Cooperation in Respect of Intercountry Adoption binding for the Czech Republic. Czech Republic is also bound by the 1967 European Convention on the Adoption of Children.

349. The law applicable to adoption is determined pursuant to the Czech autonomous PIL rules; they are applicable to adoption of both children and adults. Under section 61(1–2) PIL Act an adoption is subject to conditions laid down in the law of the state of nationality of both the adoptee and the adopter. Should the adopting spouses have different nationalities, the conditions laid down in the law of the state of nationality of both spouses have to be satisfied. The cumulative application of up to three applicable laws is justified by the intent to ensure that the adoption will be

156. Act No. 359/1999 Coll., as amended, on Social and Legal Protection of Children.

recognized in all systems to which the adopters and the adoptee have a relevant relationship.[157] Provided the adoptee or the adopter (or at least one of the adopting spouses) is habitually resident in the Czech Republic and foreign law applicable under the section 61(1–2) PIL Act does not allow adoption or admits it only under extremely onerous circumstances, Czech law applies (section 61(3) PIL Act).

350. The effects of adoption are governed by the law determined pursuant to the conflict of laws rule in section 62(1) PIL Act that lays down a hierarchy of connecting factors. The effects of an adoption are governed by the law of the state of which all the parties are nationals at the time of adoption or, failing that, by the law of the state in which all parties are habitually resident at the time of adoption or, failing that, by the law of the state of the nationality of the adoptee. Pursuant to section 62(2) PIL Act the relations between the adopter (the adopting spouses) and the adoptee in matters of parental responsibility are governed by the law applicable to parental responsibility of parents towards children, and in matters of maintenance obligations by the law applicable to maintenance obligations of parents towards children.

V. Artificial Insemination, Surrogacy

351. Questions concerning artificial insemination are regulated by Act on Specific Health Services;[158] its sections 3–11 stipulate legal requirements for artificial insemination. With respect to presumptions of paternity, under section 778 CivC if a child conceived through artificial insemination is born to an unmarried woman, the man who gave consent to the artificial insemination is presumed to be the child's father. Paternity may not be denied with respect to a child born at a period between the one hundred and sixtieth day and three hundredth day after artificial insemination carried out with the consent of the mother's husband, or with the consent of another man if the mother is not married, regardless of the genetic substance used. This does not apply if the child's mother got pregnant in a different way (section 787 CivC). The Czech PIL Act does not provide for any special conflict of laws rule with respect to artificial insemination. As regards questions of paternity, conflict of laws rules concerning the establishment and denial of parenthood apply.

352. Pursuant to section 775 CivC a mother is a woman who has given birth to a child. As for surrogacy (a surrogate mother), Czech Civil Code does not deal with surrogacy at all with the exception of one single provision with respect to adoption. Under section 804 CivC the exclusion of adoption among persons related in direct line and between siblings does not apply in cases of surrogate motherhood. Regarding conflict of laws rules, there are no special provisions in the Czech PIL Act. With

157. M. Nováková, in M. Pauknerová, et al. *Zákon o mezinárodním právu soukromém. Komentář*, *supra*, p. 423.
158. Act No. 373/2011 Coll., on Specific Health Services.

respect to systematic classification, the conflict of laws rules on the establishment and denial of parenthood and on adoption could be applied accordingly.[159]

VI. Child Support

353. The Czech PIL Act contains a reference provision in its section 57(1) PIL Act. Maintenance obligations between parents and children are governed by the law determined under an international treaty, the application of which is stipulated by a directly applicable instrument of the EU law. Maintenance obligations of parents towards children fall under the scope of the Maintenance Regulation that applies to maintenance obligations arising from a family relationship, parentage, marriage or affinity. The law governing maintenance obligations is determined based on its Article 15 in accordance with the 2007 Hague Protocol in the EU Member States bound by that instrument, including Czech Republic.[160]

354. Based on its universal character, it applies even if the applicable law is that of a non-contracting state. Limited choice of the law applicable admitted by Article 6(1) of the 2007 Hague Protocol is excluded in cases of maintenance obligations in respect of a person under the age of 18 (Article 6(3) 2007 Hague Protocol). The only choice of law that is admitted in these cases is the choice of law pursuant to Article 7(1), under which the maintenance creditor and debtor for the purpose only of a particular proceeding in a given state may expressly designate *lex fori* as applicable to a maintenance obligation.

355. In accordance with the general conflict of laws rule in Article 3 of the 2007 Hague Protocol, maintenance obligations are governed by the law of the state of the habitual residence of the creditor. The applicable law changes with the change of the habitual residence of the creditor, and the law of the state of the new habitual residence applies as from the moment when the change occurs. Special conflict of laws rules that apply in case of maintenance obligations of parents towards children (and children towards parents) are laid down in Article 4. If the creditor is unable, by virtue of the law referred to in Article 3, to obtain maintenance from the debtor, the law of the forum applies. Notwithstanding Article 3, if the creditor has seized the competent authority of the State where the debtor has his habitual residence, the law of the forum shall apply. However, if the creditor is unable, by virtue of this law, to obtain maintenance from the debtor, the law of the State of the habitual residence of the creditor applies. If the creditor is unable, by virtue of the laws referred to in Article 3 and paragraphs 2 and 3 of this Article, to obtain maintenance from the debtor, the law of the State of their common nationality, if there is one, applies.

---

159. For details *see also* M. Pauknerová & M. Pfeiffer, *National Report on Surrogacy: Czech* in *International Surrogacy Arrangements: Legal Regulation at the International Level* 105–117 (Paul Beaumont & Katarina Trimmings eds. Hart Publishing 2013).

160. The 2007 Hague Protocol was approved on behalf of the European Community (now European Union) by the Council Decision No. 2009/941/EC of 2009 on the conclusion by the European Community of the Hague Protocol of 2007 on the Law Applicable to Maintenance Obligations.

356. The Maintenance Regulation does not affect the application of bilateral or multilateral conventions and treaties to which one or more Member States are party at the time of adoption of this Regulation and which concern matters governed by the Regulation (Article 69 of the Maintenance Regulation).

357. Under the section 155(2) of the Czech (CCP[161] the court may give judgment for a sum of money expressed in a foreign currency, provided that it does not contradict the circumstances of the case and one of the parties is resident abroad. The determining criterion for whether or not to fix the amount of maintenance in a foreign currency is especially the fact whether such a decision shall lead to the quick and effective protection of rights of the minor child. In those cases, in which the court arrives at the conclusion that such a procedure would not lead to the expected objective, the court will fix the amount of maintenance in Czech crowns (R 26/87, p. 171).

VII. Child Abduction

358. Czech Republic is bound by the 1980 Hague Convention on the Civil Aspects of International Abduction (Abduction Convention). The objects of the Abduction Convention are to secure the prompt return of children wrongfully removed to or retained in any contracting state and to ensure that rights of custody and of access under the law of one contracting state are effectively respected in the other contracting states (Article 1 Abduction Convention); it applies to any child under 16 years of age who was habitually resident in a contracting state immediately before any breach of custody or access rights. It does not contain any conflict of laws rules. The rules of the Abduction Convention are complemented by additional stricter provisions in the Brussels II*bis* Regulation on jurisdiction in international abduction cases (Article 10) and on return of the child (Article 11). The Regulation introduced the so-called overriding return mechanism. Pursuant to Article 11(8) Brussels II*bis* Regulation notwithstanding a judgment of non-return pursuant to Article 13 Abduction Convention, any subsequent judgment which requires the return of the child issued by a court having jurisdiction under the Regulation is enforceable in other Member States without an exequatur requirement in order to secure the return of the child.[162] The rules in the Brussels II*bis* Regulation take priority over the rules in the Abduction Convention, in relations between the EU Member States in cases when an abduction of a child takes place between EU Member States (with the exception of Denmark). Similarly, Article 7 of the Convention on Protection of Children also contains jurisdiction rules aiming at complementing and increasing the effectiveness of the Abduction Convention. It applies where an abduction of a child takes place between the contracting states. When, e.g. a child habitually resident in the Czech Republic (who is a contracting party to the Convention on Protection of Children) is abducted to another contracting state,

161. Act No. 99/1963 Coll., Civil Procedure Code, as amended.
162. Changes of the current wording of Art. 11 are expected to be adopted in the forthcoming recast of the Brussels II*bis* Regulation.

Czech courts preserve their jurisdiction to decide on custody rights pursuant to its Article 7. The respective provisions in both the Brussels II*bis* Regulation and the Convention on Protection of Children provide that the jurisdiction in matters of parental responsibility in cases of international abduction of a child stay in principle with courts of the state of the child's habitual residence prior to the wrongful removal or retention.

§8. Protection of Adults

359. Under Czech civil law, legal capacity of a person can only be restricted, not removed (sections 55 et seq. CivC). Czech Republic is a contracting party to the 2000 Hague Convention on the International Protection of Adults (Convention on Protection of Adults) that applies to the protection in international situations of adults (persons who have reached the age of 18 years) who, by reason of an impairment or insufficiency of their personal faculties, are not in a position to protect their interests. It contains rules to determine the law applicable to representation of an adult; determination of incapacity and the institution of a protective regime; the placing of an adult under the protection of a judicial or administrative authority; to guardianship, curatorship and analogous institutions; to the designation and functions of any person or body having charge of the adult's person or property, representing or assisting the adult; to the placement of the adult in an establishment or other place where protection can be provided; to the administration, conservation or disposal of the adult's property; to the authorization of a specific intervention for the protection of the person or property of the adult (Articles 1 and 3 Convention on Protection of Adults). The rules of this Convention apply even if the law designated by them is the law of a non-contracting state. Any restriction on the capacity of an adult or even on the free disposal of his rights can only be the result of a measure of protection; the Convention on Protection of Adults does not apply to *ex lege* representation of the adult.[163] *Renvoi* is excluded by Article 19 of the Convention on Protection of Adults.

360. Pursuant to its Article 13 the courts or other authorities in exercising their jurisdiction under the provisions of this Convention apply *lex fori*. However, in so far as the protection of the person or the property of the adult requires, they may exceptionally apply or take into consideration the law of another state with which the situation has a substantial connection.

361. The Czech PIL Act has special conflict of laws rules on guardianship and determination of incapacity in its sections 34–37. Pursuant to section 37 PIL Act, Czech courts apply Czech law unless provided otherwise in sections 34–36 PIL Act. Pursuant to section 34 PIL Act the conditions for an establishment and termination of guardianship and conditions for limitation of legal capacity as well as for incapacitation are governed by the law of the state in which the ward has his habitual

163. Explanatory Report on the 2000 Hague Protection of Adults Convention by prof. Paul Lagarde, p. 69. (https://www.hcch.net/en/publications-and-studies/details4/?pid=2951&dtid=3).

residence. The guardianship concerns the ward and his property, irrespective of its location, provided the state where the property is located recognizes the effects of such a guardianship. This conflict of laws rule applies to cases where Czech courts lack jurisdiction.[164] Pursuant to section 35 PIL Act an obligation to accept and exercise guardianship is governed by the law of the state in which the guardian is habitually resident. The law of the state in which the guardianship court or authority has its seat governs legal relations between the guardian and the ward (section 36 PIL Act).

362. Article 15 of the Convention on Protection of Adults contains special conflict of laws rules to determine the law applicable to representation of an adult. The existence, extent, modification and extinction of powers of representation granted by an adult, either under an agreement or by a unilateral act, to be exercised when such adult is not in a position to protect his or her interests, are governed by the law of the State of the adult's habitual residence at the time of the agreement or act unless one of the following laws has been designated expressly in writing: the law of the state of which the adult is a national; the law of the state of a former habitual residence of the adult or the law of the state in which property of the adult is located, with respect to that property. The manner of exercise of such powers of representation is governed by the law of the state in which they are exercised.

363. Relevant conflict of laws rules are also contained in a number of bilateral treaties on legal assistance binding for the Czech Republic.

---

164. Ptáček in P. Bříza, et al. *Zákon o mezinárodním právu soukromém. Komentář*, *supra*, p. 207.

Chapter 6. Succession Law

364. Under the Czech Civil Code, a right to inheritance is acquired upon the decedent's death. A person may inherit by means of statute, by testament or by an agreement as to succession (sections 1475–1720 CivC). The application of Czech autonomous conflict of laws rules on succession in sections 76–78 PIL Act, that follow unitary principle arising from the concept of universal succession, is significantly affected by the Succession Regulation that applies to the succession of persons who died on or after 17 August 2015. Conflict of laws rules as well as rules on jurisdiction regarding succession matters are also contained in a number of bilateral treaties on mutual legal assistance. Czech Republic is a contracting party of the 1973 Hague Convention Concerning the International Administration of the Estates of Deceased Persons.

§1. *Lex Successionis*

365. According to the general conflict of laws rule in Article 21(1) Succession Regulation the law applicable to succession as a whole is the law of the state in which the deceased had his habitual residence at the time of death. The Succession Regulation also follows the unitary principle; there is in principle no scission with respect to the law applicable to succession of movable and immovable assets of the estate. Article 21(2) of the Succession Regulation contains an escape clause pursuant to which the court, where it is clear from all the circumstances of the case that, at the time of death, the deceased was manifestly more closely connected with a state other than the state of the decedent's last habitual residence, applies the law of that other state. The law determined based on these rules is applied whether or not it is a law of an EU Member State.

§2. Scope of Application

366. Pursuant to Article 23 of the Succession Regulation the *lex successionis* governs among others: the causes, time and place of the opening of the succession; the determination of the beneficiaries, of their respective shares and of the obligations which may be imposed on them by the deceased, and the determination of other succession rights, including the succession rights of the surviving spouse or partner; the capacity to inherit; disinheritance and disqualification by conduct; the transfer to the heirs and, as the case may be, to the legatees of the assets, rights and obligations forming part of the estate, including the conditions and effects of the acceptance or waiver of the succession or of a legacy; the powers of the heirs, the executors of the wills and other administrators of the estate, in particular as regards the sale of property and the payment of creditors, without prejudice to the powers referred to in Article 29(2–3) of the Succession Regulation; liability for the debts under the succession; the disposable part of the estate, the reserved shares and other restrictions on the disposal of property upon death as well as claims which persons close to the deceased may have against the estate or the heirs; any obligation to restore or account for gifts, advancements or legacies when determining the shares of the different beneficiaries; and the sharing-out of the estate.

§3. Testamentary Disposition

367. Pursuant to Czech substantive succession law a disposition of property upon death is a testament, an agreement as to succession or a testamentary clause on legacy (section 1491 CivC). For the purposes of the Succession Regulation, dispositions of property upon death include wills, joint wills or agreements as to succession. Joint will is to be understood as a will that is drawn up in one instrument by two or more persons. An agreement as to succession under the Succession Regulation is an agreement, including an agreement resulting from mutual wills, which, with or without consideration, creates, modifies or terminates rights to the future estate or estates of one or more persons party to the agreement. There is no autonomous definition of a will in the Succession Regulation.

I. Legal Capacity

368. Legal capacity to inherit falls within the scope of the law applicable to succession. Pursuant to Article 23(1)(c) of the Succession Regulation the capacity to inherit is governed by the *lex successionis*, whereas pursuant to Article 26(1)(a) of the Succession Regulation the capacity of the person making the disposition of property upon death to make such a disposition is governed by the law applicable to substantive validity of such a disposition determined in accordance with Articles 24–25 of the Succession Regulation. Where a person has the capacity to make a disposition of property upon death under the law applicable pursuant to Article 24 or 25, a subsequent change of the law applicable does not affect his capacity to modify or revoke such a disposition.

II. Choice of Law

369. Pursuant to Article 22(1) of the Succession Regulation a person may choose the law of the state whose nationality he possesses at the time of making the choice or at the time of death to govern his succession as a whole. A person possessing multiple nationalities may choose the law of any of the states whose nationality he possesses at the time of making the choice or at the time of death. The choice can be made expressly in a declaration in the form of a disposition of property upon death or can be demonstrated by the terms of such a disposition.

370. The Czech PIL Act conflict of laws rule in section 77(4) PIL Act also admits a limited choice of law in succession matters. The deceased person can choose in a testament his *lex patriae* at the moment of the disposition or the law of the state of his habitual residence at the time of the disposition as the law applicable to succession. This autonomous conflict of laws rule providing for wider choice of law than the respective rule in the Succession Regulation retains its relevance with respect to choices of applicable law made prior to 17 August 2015. Pursuant to Article 83(2) of the Succession Regulation such a choice of law is valid if it meets the conditions laid down in Chapter III of the Succession Regulation or if it is valid in application of the rules of PIL which were in force, at the time the choice was made, in the state in which the deceased had his habitual residence or in any of the states whose nationality he possessed.

III. Compulsory Portion

371. Czech law provides for forced heirship rules in sections 1642–1645 CivC. Forced heirs that are entitled to a forced share of the decedent's estate include the decedent's children or, if they do not inherit, their descendants. If a forced heir is a minor, he must inherit at least three-quarters of his statutory inheritance share. If a forced heir is an adult, he must inherit at least a quarter of his statutory inheritance share.

372. There is no Czech case law (known to the authors) with respect to whether the application of foreign succession law that excludes forced heirship would be considered contrary to the Czech public policy.

IV. Interpretation

373. The interpretation of dispositions of property upon death is governed by the law governing the substantive validity of the dispositions determined pursuant to Articles 24–25 of the Succession Regulation (Article 26(1)(d) Succession Regulation).

V. Last Will

374. The admissibility of a will is governed either by *lex patriae* of the deceased at the time of disposition, when this law was chosen by the person disposing of the property upon death, or in the absence of choice of law by the law which, under the Succession Regulation, would have been applicable to the succession of the person who made the disposition if he had died on the day on which the disposition was made.

A. Formal Validity

375. The conflict of laws rules on formal validity of dispositions upon death made in writing are contained in Article 27 Succession Regulation. They do not apply to the formal validity of dispositions of property upon death made orally. In these rather rare cases, the national rule of conflict of laws in section 77(2) PIL Act would apply. Pursuant to Article 27(1) of the Succession Regulation a disposition of property upon death made in writing shall be valid as regards form if its form complies with the law: of the State in which the disposition was made or the agreement as to succession concluded; or of a State whose nationality the testator or at least one of the persons whose succession is concerned by an agreement as to succession possessed, either at the time when the disposition was made or the agreement concluded, or at the time of death; or of a State in which the testator or at least one of the persons whose succession is concerned by an agreement as to succession had his domicile, either at the time when the disposition was made or the agreement concluded, or at the time of death; or of the State in which the testator or at least one of the persons whose succession is concerned by an agreement as to succession had his habitual residence, either at the time when the disposition was made or the agreement concluded, or at the time of death; or in so far as immovable property is concerned, of the State in which that property is located. The same applies to their modification or revocation. Pursuant to section 77(2) PIL Act a will is valid as regards form provided the form complies to the law of the state of which the deceased person was a citizen at the time of making an expression of intent or at the time of death; or in the territory of which the will was disposed; or in which the deceased person was habitually resident at the time of making an expression of intent or at the time of death; or which shall be applied to legal relations of succession or it was supposed to be applied to them at the time of disposing a will; or in which an immovable property is located, should the immovable property be concerned.

376. Czech Republic is not bound by the 1961 Hague Convention on the Conflict of Laws Relating to the Form of Testamentary Dispositions.

B. Substantive Validity

377. The substantive validity of a will is governed by either *lex patriae* of the deceased at the time of disposition as the law chosen by the person disposing of the property upon death, or in the absence of choice of law by the law which under the Succession Regulation would have been applicable to the succession of the person who made the disposition if he had died on the day on which the disposition was made. This law governs, *inter alia*, the capacity of the person making the disposition of property upon death to make such a disposition; the particular causes which bar the person making the disposition from disposing in favour of certain persons or which bar a person from receiving succession property from the person making the disposition; the admissibility of representation for making a disposition of property upon death; the interpretation of the disposition; fraud, duress, mistake and any other questions relating to the consent or intention of the person making the disposition.

VI. Legacy

378. Under Czech substantive succession law, a decedent may allocate a legacy by ordering a person in a disposition *mortis causa* to surrender the bequeathed thing to a legatee. Only a person having the capacity to inherit may be a legatee. If a decedent designates an heir and determines that the heir is not to inherit a particular thing, it is considered an allocation of legacy to statutory heirs (sections 1594–1641 CivC). The Czech law provides only for legacies by damnation creating only an obligation of the heir to transfer the right of property to the legatee.

379. As legacy is included in a disposition of property upon death, the law governing the validity of the respective disposition of property *mortis causa* applies to legacy.

A. *Formal Validity*

380. See § 3, Chapter V, Paragraphs 377-378

B. *Substantive Validity*

381. See § 3, Chapter V, Paragraph 379

VII. Testamentary Contract (Agreements As to Succession)

382. The admissibility of an agreement to succession is governed by the law chosen by the parties pursuant to Article 25(3) Succession Regulation. Based on a limited choice the parties can choose *lex patriae* of the person or one of the persons whose estate is involved. In the absence of choice of law, the Succession Regulation stipulates in its Article 25(1–2) a different conflict of laws regime for agreements as to succession regarding succession of one person and of several persons. The admissibility of an agreement to succession regarding succession of one person is governed by the *lex successionis* that would have been applicable to the succession of that person if he had died on the day on which the agreement was concluded. The agreement to succession regarding succession of several persons is admissible only if it is admissible under all the laws which, under the Succession Regulation, would have governed the succession of all the persons involved if they had died on the day on which the agreement was concluded.

A. *Formal Validity*

383. See supra formal validity of wills.

B. Substantive Validity

384. Conflict of laws rules on substantive validity of agreements as to succession, its binding effects between the parties, including the conditions for its dissolution are contained in Article 25 of the Succession Regulation. The parties may choose as the governing the law which the person or one of the persons whose estate is involved could have chosen in accordance with Article 22 of the Succession Regulation on the conditions set out therein.

385. In the absence of choice of law, in case of agreements as to succession regarding the succession of one person the governing law is the law which, under the Succession Regulation, would have been applicable to the succession of that person if he had died on the day on which the agreement was concluded. In case of an agreement as to succession regarding the succession of several persons which is admissible pursuant to the governing law, its substantive validity and its binding effects between the parties, including the conditions for its dissolution are governed by the law, from among those applicable to its admissibility, with which it has the closest connection.

§4. Inheritance and Liability

386. Liability for debts under the succession falls within the scope of the law applicable to succession. Pursuant to Article 23(2)(g) of the Succession Regulation the liability for debts under the succession is governed by *lex successionis*.

Part III. Annex: International Civil Procedure

Chapter 1. Sources of International Civil Procedure

§1. National Law

387. The provisions governing international civil procedure are contained in the PIL Act. Part Two of the PIL Act, titled 'General Provisions of International Procedural Law' (sections 6–19), deals with 'Jurisdiction' (Title I), 'Provisions on Proceedings' (Title II) as, for example, status of foreigners and foreign entities in proceedings, foreign public documents and reciprocity, 'Recognition and Enforcement of Foreign Judgments' (Title III) and 'Special Provisions for Recognition and Enforcement of Certain Foreign Judgments' (Title IV). Special provisions on international civil procedure are contained in Part Four of the PIL Act, 'Provisions Concerning Individual Types of Private-Law Relations' (sections 29–101), including rules on jurisdiction and recognition and enforcement, if any, in particular fields. Part Five of the PIL Act, 'Judicial Cooperation in Relations with Foreign States' (sections 102–110), contains rules on judicial legal assistance, public documents and opinions of Ministry of Justice.

388. As a supplementary legislation, for example with respect to provisions concerning the competence of Czech courts (*see* section 6(2) PIL Act), the Czech CCP[165] and the Code of Civil Procedure in Special Cases (CCPSC) [166] shall be applied. Provisions of the Act on Notaries and their Activity (Code of Notarial Practice) may also be relevant.[167]

§2. European Union Law

389. On 1 May 2004 (the date of accession to the EU) EU law became part of the Czech law unifying many issues of international civil procedure. The EU (EC) Regulations in international civil procedure law are binding in its entirety and

165. Act No. 99/1963 Coll., as amended, CCP.
166. Act No. 292/2013 Coll., as amended, CCPSC.
167. Act No. 358/1992 Coll., as amended, Code of Notarial Practice.

directly applicable before Czech courts. The most significant regulations are: Regulation No. 1215/2012 on jurisdiction and the recognition and enforcement of judgments in civil and commercial matters (recast) (Brussels I Recast); Regulation No. 2201/2003 concerning Jurisdiction and the Recognition and Enforcement of Judgments in Matrimonial Matters and the Matters of Parental Responsibility, repealing Regulation (EC) No. 1347/2000 (Brussels II*bis* Regulation); Regulation No. 1206/2001 on Cooperation between the Courts of the Member States in the Taking of Evidence in Civil or Commercial Matters; Regulation No. 1393/2007 on the Service in the Member States of Judicial and Extrajudicial Documents in Civil and Commercial Matters (Service of Documents), and repealing Council Regulation No. 1348/2000; Regulation No. 805/2004 creating a European Enforcement Order for Uncontested Claims; Regulation No. 1896/2006 creating a European Order for Payment Procedure; Regulation No. 861/2007 establishing a European Small Claims Procedure; Regulation No. 4/2009 on Jurisdiction, Applicable Law, Recognition and Enforcement of Decisions and Cooperation in Matters relating to Maintenance Obligations (Maintenance Regulation); Regulation No. 650/2012 on jurisdiction, applicable law, recognition and enforcement of decisions and acceptance and enforcement of authentic instruments in matters of succession and on the creation of a European Certificate of Succession (Succession Regulation); Regulation No. 655/2014 establishing a European Account Preservation Order procedure to facilitate cross-border debt recovery in civil and commercial matters; Regulation No. 2015/848 on Insolvency Proceedings (Recast); Regulation No. 2015/2421 Amending Regulation (EC) No. 861/2007 establishing a European Small Claims Procedure and Regulation (EC) No. 1896/2006 creating a European order for payment procedure; Regulation No. 2016/1103 implementing enhanced cooperation in the area of jurisdiction, applicable law and the recognition and enforcement of decisions in matters of matrimonial property regimes; Regulation No. 2016/1104 implementing enhanced cooperation in the area of jurisdiction, applicable law and the recognition and enforcement of decisions in matters of the property consequences of registered partnerships; and Regulation No. 2016/1191 on Promoting the Free Movement of Citizens by Simplifying the Requirements for Presenting Certain Public Documents in the EU and Amending Regulation (EU) No. 1024/2012.

390. EU law takes preference over Czech national law in its application (*see* section 2 PIL Act). Unlike uniform European conflict rules, uniform European civil procedure rules are not universally applicable and, in principle, with some exceptions, only apply in relations to other EU Member States.

391. In relations between EU and certain states that are members of the European Free Trade Association (EFTA) (Iceland, Norway and Switzerland) Lugano Convention on jurisdiction and the recognition and enforcement of judgments in civil and commercial matters of 2009 applies. Lugano Convention extends the rules laid down in Brussels I Regulation to the territory of the three EFTA States.

§3. International Conventions

392. The provisions of PIL Act apply only if an international treaty binding on the Czech Republic does not provide otherwise (*see* section 2 PIL Act and Article 10 of the Constitution of the Czech Republic). Czech Republic is a contracting state to many international conventions concerning international procedure law, both bilateral (treaties on legal assistance) and multilateral, in particular the Hague conventions on the service abroad of judicial and extrajudicial documents, the taking of evidence abroad, the abolishment of requirements of legalization for foreign public documents, on recognition and enforcement of decisions in family matters, maintenance obligations, divorces, or the London convention on information on foreign law, etc. Particular attention deserves the Hague Convention on Choice of Court Agreements of 2005 (Choice of Court Convention).[168] In addition to this, procedural rules are also contained in other international conventions, for example numerous conventions on international transport law, the Vienna Convention on Consular Relations of 1963, bilateral consular conventions and others.

168. *See* Council decision 2014/887/EU.

Chapter 2. The Principle of *Lex Fori*

393. In proceedings pursuant to section 8(1) PIL Act, Czech courts act in accordance with Czech autonomous procedural rules, while the parties enjoy an equal status when exercising their rights. This rule anchors the *lex fori* principle; Czech courts apply Czech procedural law.

394. However, there are some exceptions to the principle of the *lex fori.* For example, foreign procedure law shall be applied with respect to the procedural capacity of a foreigner to act. Capacity of a foreigner to be a party to proceedings as well as the procedural capacity shall both be governed by the law of the state of the foreigner's habitual residence; it shall however be sufficient for the foreigner to possess such a capacity under the Czech law. Similarly, capacity of foreign entities other than natural persons to be a party to proceedings as well as their procedural capacity shall both be governed by the law under which the entity has been established; it shall however be sufficient for the entity to possess such a capacity under the Czech law (section 9 PIL Act).

395. Another example of the exceptional application of foreign procedural law relates to public documents being used as evidence. Pursuant to section 12 PIL Act a document executed by a court, a notary or an authority in a foreign state, which is in the place of its origin deemed to be a public document, or a public document executed by a diplomatic officer or consular agent in the Czech Republic, shall be considered a public document evidence in the Czech Republic, provided it is accompanied by the required legalization. Should the document executed abroad fail to include the required legalization in accordance with international practice and should the respective embassy of the Czech Republic have no doubts about its authenticity, the embassy issues a certificate declaring that the embassy has no doubts about the authenticity of the document.

396. The most frequent examples of the exceptional application of foreign procedure law are to be found in the sphere of legal assistance. Under section 104 PIL Act, requested legal assistance (i.e., in the Czech Republic) shall be provided under Czech regulations; however, if so requested, a foreign procedural rule may be applied if the requested procedure is not contrary to the Czech public policy. If requested by the foreign authority, witnesses, experts and parties may be heard under an oath (this procedure is not known in the Czech national procedural law). This also applies when a sworn declaration must be submitted abroad concerning facts relevant to the making or keeping of claims.[169]

---

169. Consequently, an oath or a cross-examination, which belongs to institutions not recognized by Czech domestic law (the *lex fori*), may be executed before the Czech court, for details *see* s. 104 PIL Act.

397. Finally, under section 107 PIL Act, service effected upon a request of a Czech court by a foreign authority as well as evidence taken before it shall be effective even when not in accordance with the provisions of the respective foreign law, provided they comply with Czech law.

Chapter 3. National Jurisdiction

398. The rules governing jurisdiction of Czech courts in relations with an international element are provided by the PIL Act and/or by the directly applicable EU legislation or by international treaties and conventions. The courts shall ensure, at any time in the course of proceedings, that the procedural conditions are fulfilled (section 103 CCP). The Czech court system[170] is composed of district courts, regional courts, two high courts (with jurisdiction in Bohemia and Moravia), the Supreme Court and the Supreme Administrative Court. The Constitutional Court, with its special role, is outside of this court system.[171]

399. The first instance courts are either district courts or, *ratione causae*, regional courts. Under section 9(1) CCP, competence in the first instance belongs to district courts unless provided otherwise by the law. Disputes arising from relations with a foreign element in civil and commercial law[172] shall be decided in the first instance by the district courts unless otherwise provided by the law. Regional courts act as first instance courts only if expressly stipulated by the law (*see* section 9(2) CCP), as for example in cases concerning intellectual property, cases involving a foreign state, or persons enjoying diplomatic immunity and privileges, if such disputes are within the jurisdiction of the Czech Republic's courts, etc. In commercial matters, regional courts decide, *inter alia*, disputes concerning commercial corporations, transformations of legal entities, disputes in matters of securities and investment instruments, etc. The Supreme Court acts as a Court of First Instance if special statutory provisions so provide (section 9(3) CCP). Appeals for cases first heard in district courts go to regional courts, and appeals for cases first heard in regional courts go to high courts. The Supreme Court has general jurisdiction over all matters for which any other court is competent.[173] It decides on, *inter alia*, extraordinary remedies as third instance, and delivers unifying opinions on the interpretation of laws and other legal regulations.

400. The Civil Procedure in Special Cases concerns e.g. personhood issues, declaration of missing and death, succession, matrimonial and partnership issues, parenthood, adoption, minor persons' care, and some cases on execution (section 2 CCPSC). Competence in the first instance belongs to the district courts unless otherwise provided by law. Regional courts decide, *inter alia*, on status issues of legal persons, custodianship of legal persons, capital market issues, etc. (section 3 CCPSC).

---

170. Act No. 6/2002 Coll., as amended, on Courts and Judges.
171. Constitutional Act No. 1/1993 Coll., as amended, Constitution of the Czech Republic, and Act No. 182/1993 Coll., as amended, on Constitutional Court.
172. Including disputes in which the jurisdiction of Czech courts was chosen by the agreement of the parties.
173. Except for the Supreme Administrative Court and the Constitutional Court.

Chapter 4. International Jurisdiction

§1. Statutory Forums

401. The jurisdiction of Czech courts within the Czech autonomous international procedure law is laid down by the PIL Act. The general provision on the 'Jurisdiction of Czech courts' (section 6 PIL Act) states that Czech courts shall have jurisdiction in proceedings when the (Czech) procedural provisions stipulate local jurisdiction (venue) of a court in the territory of the Czech Republic, without prejudice to the application of other provisions of this Act or other legislation. When the Czech courts have jurisdiction, their jurisdiction shall apply also on a counterclaim arising from the same legal relation or the same factual circumstances. There are special jurisdiction rules for proceedings on declaration of a person as dead or missing (section 39 PIL Act), divorce and marriage annulment (section 47 PIL Act), parentage (section 53 PIL Act), custody and care of minors (section 56 PIL Act),[174] adoption (section 60 PIL Act), termination or annulment of registered partnership and similar regimes (section 67 PIL Act), relating to rights in immovable properties (section 68 PIL Act), on document amortization matters (section 81 PIL Act), and relating to obligations and other property rights (section 85 PIL Act). Pursuant to section 2 PIL Act, these autonomous rules are superseded by the EU legislation and/or international treaties and conventions within the scope of their applicability.

402. Under the general rule in Brussels I Recast, which is in Czech courts the most frequently used instrument on international jurisdiction, persons domiciled in an EU Member State shall, whatever their nationality, be sued in the courts of that Member State. Persons who are not nationals of the Member State in which they are domiciled shall be governed by the rules of jurisdiction applicable to nationals of that State (*see* Article 4 Brussels I Recast). The Brussels I Recast stipulates in Article 7 special jurisdiction of courts of the Member States in matters relating to obligations (courts of the place of performance of such obligation); torts or delicts (courts for the place where the harmful event occurred or may occur); disputes arising out of the operations of branch, agency or other establishment (courts for the place in which such establishment is situated), etc. A person domiciled in a Member State may also be sued where he is one of a number of defendants, in the courts for the place where any one of them is domiciled, provided the claims are so closely connected that it is expedient to hear and determine them together to avoid the risk of irreconcilable judgments resulting from separate proceedings (for details *see* Article 8 Brussels I Recast). Special jurisdiction rules relate to weaker party contracts – insurance contracts, consumer contracts, and employment contracts. Basically, the proceedings against the weaker party may only be brought in the courts of the Member State in which such party is domiciled (for details *see* Articles 10–23 Brussels I Recast).

---

174. Jurisdiction in maintenance is fully covered by the Maintenance Regulation (with preferential application of some bilateral agreements).

403. When Czech courts shall have exclusive jurisdiction, then only a Czech court shall be competent to decide on certain types of matters, and proceedings on such matters conducted before a foreign court shall not have any effects with respect to the territory of the Czech Republic. In the autonomous Czech law, the exclusive jurisdiction of Czech courts relates in particular to the declaration of the death or absence of a missing Czech citizen (*see* section 39 PIL Act), to certain matters of adoption (if a minor concerned is a citizen of the Czech Republic and is habitually resident in the Czech Republic, section 60 PIL Act), and to rights in immovable properties located in the territory of the Czech Republic (section 68 PIL Act). A foreign decision is not recognized, nor executed, if, *inter alia*, Czech courts have exclusive jurisdiction to decide on the matter concerned (section 15(1) lit. (a) PIL Act).

404. Exclusive jurisdiction is also laid down in Article 24 Brussels I Recast, pursuant to which the following courts shall have exclusive jurisdiction, regardless of domicile of the defendant: in proceedings, which have as their object rights in rem in immovable property or tenancies of immovable property, the courts of the Member State in which the property is situated; in proceedings, which have as their object the validity of the constitution, the nullity or the dissolution of companies or other legal persons or associations of natural or legal persons, or of the validity of the decisions of their organs, the courts of the Member State in which the company, legal person or association has its seat; in proceedings, which have as their object the validity of entries in public registers, the courts of the Member State in which the register is kept; in proceedings concerned with the registration or validity of patents, trademarks, designs, or other similar rights required to be deposited or registered, the courts of the Member State in which the deposit or registration has been applied for, has taken place or is deemed to have taken place; and in proceedings concerned with the enforcement of judgments, the courts of the Member State in which the judgment has been or is to be enforced (for details *see* Article 24 Brussels I Recast).

405. In majority of cases the jurisdiction of Czech courts is not exclusive. Foreign decision delivered by courts of a foreign state in matters that do not fall under exclusive jurisdiction of Czech courts may be recognized and enforced by Czech courts under conditions set in sections 14–16 PIL Act.[175] Under Brussels I Recast, on the application of any interested party, the recognition of a judgment shall be refused, if the judgment conflicts with provisions on exclusive jurisdiction (*see* Article 45 Brussels I Recast).

175. The condition for such an observation of a foreign decision is to be deduced from s. 15 (1) lit. a) PIL Act. Under this provision, a final foreign decision may not be recognized or executed if its recognition is hindered by the exclusive jurisdiction of the Czech courts, or if the proceedings could not be implemented by any authority of a foreign state, should the provisions on jurisdiction of the Czech courts apply to assess the jurisdiction of a foreign authority unless the party to the proceedings against which the foreign judgment is focused voluntarily submits to the jurisdiction of a foreign authority.

406. In exceptional cases, the jurisdiction of Czech courts may be excluded. Provisions on jurisdictional immunity are contained in section 7 PIL Act. Other States shall have immunity with respect to the jurisdiction of the Czech courts as regards proceedings arising out of the state's acts and actions undertaken while exercising their state, governmental or other public powers and functions, including their property used or intended for such acts. Immunity with respect to the jurisdiction of Czech courts shall not apply to other acts, actions or cases, to the extent in which general international law or international agreements allow institute proceedings against a state before the courts of another state. These provisions also apply to service of documents, summoning of the aforesaid persons as witnesses, enforcement of decisions or other procedural acts. As regards exceptions from immunity in general, the PIL Act corresponds in principle to the Vienna Convention on the Diplomatic Relations of 1961 and to the UN Convention on Jurisdictional Immunities of States and Their Property of 2004, both conventions were ratified by the Czech Republic.

407. The concept of functional jurisdictional immunity of states has been introduced in 2012 with the adoption of the current PIL Act. Its predecessor, the PIL Act 1963, was based on the principle of the absolute immunity of states and their property, which was criticized by some Czech authors.[176] The decision of the Supreme Court of the Czech Republic of 2008 was important.[177] The Supreme Court held that neither the Brussels I Regulation, nor the Agreement on Legal Aid between the Czechoslovak Republic and the Republic of Poland, nor the Vienna Convention on Diplomatic Relations resolve the question of immunity of States and jurisdiction of civil courts of the Czech Republic in matters relating to an employment dispute of a Czech citizen against the Republic of Poland – Embassy of the Republic of Poland. This issue was to be resolved on the basis of a general rule on exclusion from the jurisdiction of Czech courts laid down in section 47 PIL Act 1963. The contents of immunity, in the past conceived as absolute, has developed towards the functional concept. If a foreign state acts as a legal entity in matters arising from individual employment relations, the rules of international law lead to the conclusion that the foreign state does not enjoy immunity and that Czech courts have jurisdiction in these matters. Undoubtedly, this decision of the Supreme Court represented a turning point in the practice of the Czech Republic.[178] Currently, Czech law clearly differentiates between *acta iure imperii* and *acta iure gestionis* of a state and its representatives, and thus belongs to jurisdictions that follow the concept of functional immunity.

408. Rules on both the exclusive and facultative jurisdiction of Czech courts, as well as on exclusion from the jurisdiction of Czech courts, can be contained in an

---

176. *See* V. Balaš & M. Pauknerová, *The Czechoslovak Approach to the Draft Convention on Jurisdictional Immunities of States and Their Property*, 12 Michigan J. Int. Law, 874–902 (1991).
177. *See* decision of the Supreme Court No. 21 Cdo 2215/2007 of 25 Jun. 2008.
178. For details *see* M. Pauknerová, *Jurisdictional Immunity of States and Brussels I Regulation – Recent Developments in the Czech Republic*, Eur. Legal Forum 241 (2009).

international treaty or convention which shall have precedence over Czech domestic law (*see* section 2 PIL Act and Article 10 of the Constitution).

§2. Choice of Forum Agreement

409. In Czech autonomous law, choice of forum agreements is permitted in property disputes only. Under section 85 PIL Act, jurisdiction of the Czech courts in matters of obligations and of other property rights may be established also by a written agreement of the parties. Nevertheless, the substantive (subject-matter) jurisdiction of the Czech courts shall not be altered by such an agreement.

410. In addition, jurisdiction of a foreign court in matters of obligations and of other property rights can be established by a written agreement of the parties. In matters of insurance and consumer contracts such an agreement shall be admissible only after a dispute arises or provided it enables only the policyholder, the insured, another beneficiary, the injured or the consumer to initiate proceedings in the courts of another state. If jurisdiction of a foreign court is determined, jurisdiction of the Czech courts shall thereby be excluded; a Czech court shall nevertheless hear the case provided (a) the parties unanimously declare they do not insist on the agreement, (b) a judgment given abroad would not be recognized in the Czech Republic, (c) a foreign court declined to hear the case, or (d) a jurisdiction agreement is contrary to the public policy (section 86 PIL Act).

411. Under EU law, in civil and commercial matters, choice of forum agreement is recognized under the Brussels I Recast Regulation (the so-called prorogation of jurisdiction). If the parties, regardless of their domicile, have agreed that a court or the courts of a Member State are to have jurisdiction to settle any disputes which have arisen or which may arise in connection with a particular legal relationship, that court or those courts shall have jurisdiction unless the agreement is null and void as to its substantive validity under the law of that Member State. Such jurisdiction shall be exclusive unless the parties have agreed otherwise. The agreement conferring jurisdiction shall be in writing or in a form which accords with practices which the parties have established between themselves (for details *see* Article 25 Brussels I Recast).

412. EU is also a contracting party to the Hague Convention of 2005 on Choice of Court Agreements. When signing the Convention, the EU declared under Article 30 of the Convention that it exercises competence over all the matters governed by the Convention. Consequently, the EU Member States shall be bound by the Convention by virtue of its approval by the EU. As for the conclusion of the jurisdiction agreement the Convention requires a stricter form of jurisdiction agreements (writing or other means of communication which renders information accessible (Article 3 of the Convention)). The relationship between the Convention and the Brussels I Recast is regulated by Article 26(6) of the Convention. This provision gives precedence to the rules of the EU (as a Regional Economic Integration Association) where both parties are resident in different Member States or where the recognition or enforcement of judgments between Member States of the EU is concerned.

413. A limited choice of court is admitted by the Maintenance Regulation. The parties may agree that the following court or courts of a Member State shall have jurisdiction to settle any disputes in matters relating to a maintenance obligation which have arisen or may arise between them: a court or the courts of a Member State in which one of the parties is habitually resident; a court or the courts of a Member State in which one of the parties has the nationality; in the case of maintenance obligations between spouses or former spouses: the court which has jurisdiction to settle their dispute in matrimonial matters; or a court or the courts of the Member State which was the Member State of the spouses' last common habitual residence for a period of at least one year. The choice of court agreement shall be in writing. These rules, however, shall not apply to a dispute relating to a maintenance obligation towards a child under the age of 18 (for details *see* Article 4 Maintenance Regulation).

414. Under the Succession Regulation, choice of court agreement is also permitted. Where the law chosen by the deceased to govern his succession is the law of a Member State, the parties concerned may agree that a court or the courts of that Member State are to have exclusive jurisdiction to rule on any succession matter. Such a choice of court agreement shall be expressed in writing, dated and signed by the parties concerned. Any communication by electronic means that provides a durable record of the agreement shall be deemed equivalent to writing (Article 5 of the Succession Regulation).

415. Choice of court in matters of matrimonial property and property consequences of registered partnership is permitted under Article 7 of the Regulation on Matrimonial Property Regimes, and under Article 7 of the Regulation on Registered Partnerships' Regimes. Such agreements shall be expressed in writing, dated and signed by the parties. Any communication by electronic means that provides a durable record of the agreement shall be deemed equivalent to writing.

§3. Procedural Requirements

416. Under Czech law of civil procedure, court hearings are direct, oral and, unless otherwise stated by the law, public. In civil proceedings, including proceedings with a foreign element, all parties have an equal status in claiming their rights (*see* section 18 CCP and section 8 PIL Act). During the hearing, the parties can be represented by a lawyer, but in civil proceedings the representation by a lawyer is not obligatory. Pursuant to section 26(2) CCP, the Office for International Legal Protection of Children may represent a participant in proceedings regarding maintenance when matters in relation to abroad are concerned. In employment matters and matters arising out of the Act on the residence of foreigners in the territory of the

Czech Republic, a foreigner, residing in the Czech territory with a visa for a seasonal employment, may be represented by a legal entity, the activities of which include protection of aliens' rights.

417. The parties are entitled to litigate in their own language before the court and may speak and submit documents in their native language, and the court is obliged to respond to them in their native language through an interpreter (*see* section 18 CCP). Section 9 PIL Act relates to the capacity of foreigners in Czech courts (*see supra* Part III Chapter 2). Foreigners and foreign legal entities shall be, under the same conditions as the citizens of the Czech Republic and the Czech legal entities, entitled to an exemption from court fees and deposits and to an appointment of a free-of-charge representative to protect their interests, provided reciprocity is guaranteed. The guarantee of reciprocity condition does not apply to the citizens of the EU Member States and other countries of the EEA (section 10 PIL Act). At the request of the defendant, the court could order a foreigner who is seeking a decision on a property claim to put up a security deposit for the payment of costs (with many exceptions, for details *see* section 11 PIL Act) unless they are citizens of the EU Member States and other countries of the EEA.

418. Legal assistance between the Czech Republic and foreign countries is regulated by sections 102–110 PIL Act; however, it is often preceded by EU law or international treaties or conventions, both multilateral and bilateral (*see infra* §4 and §5).

419. Under section 103 PIL Act, if requested, Czech judicial organs shall provide legal assistance to foreign judicial organs provided reciprocity exists. Legal assistance may only be refused if the requested act is not within the jurisdiction of the requested Czech judicial organ,[179] or if the requested act is contrary to Czech public order. Requested legal assistance shall be provided under Czech regulations; if so requested, a foreign procedural rule may be applied, provided that the requested procedure is not contrary to Czech public order (*see* section 104 PIL Act).

§4. International Service

420. Under Czech autonomous law, the service of documents upon request of foreign judicial organs is either formal or simple. A formal service shall be provided in conformity with Czech procedural rules on service in the CCP. The foreign document is to be accompanied by a certified Czech translation (section 105 PIL Act). If a foreign document is not accompanied by a certified translation into the Czech language, it shall be served to the recipient provided the recipient is willing to accept it; the recipient shall be informed about the legal consequences which may occur abroad should he or she refuse to accept the document (section 105 PIL Act). The foreign document may not contain a threat to use compulsory means at any

179. However, if such an act is within the jurisdiction of another judicial organ or within the jurisdiction of other Czech organs, the request shall be passed on for settlement to the proper organ (*see* s. 103 PIL Act).

point (the infliction of a fine, bringing before court, etc.) because such a threat would be contrary to Czech public policy and would be a reason for refusing legal assistance (section 103 b) PIL Act).

421. Pursuant to section 106 PIL Act, upon a request of a Czech court, Czech embassy shall perform (a) service to persons in the state of its jurisdiction, provided it is admissible under an international treaty or general international law or provided it is not precluded by laws of the state where the act is to be performed; (b) service to the Czech citizens in the state where the act is to be performed who enjoy diplomatic privileges and immunities there, as well as questioning of such citizens as witnesses, experts or parties to the proceedings; (c) questioning of witnesses, experts and parties to the proceedings as well as other procedural acts, should such persons come voluntarily and provided it is not precluded by provisions applicable in the state where the act is to be performed or provided it is not precluded by serious defences. Czech embassy shall proceed according to the rules that the requesting court would follow, *mutatis mutandis*, and the acts performed by the embassy shall have the same effect as if they were performed by the court itself.

422. Service effected upon a request of a Czech court by a foreign authority as well as evidence taken before it shall be effective even when not in accordance with the provisions of a foreign law provided they comply with the Czech legislation (section 107 PIL Act).

423. Within the EU, efficiency and speed in judicial procedures in civil matters require that judicial and extrajudicial documents be transmitted directly and by rapid means between local bodies designated by the Member States. International service is included in the Regulation on the Service in the Member States of Judicial and Extrajudicial Documents in Civil or Commercial Matters (Service of Documents). Speed in transmission warrants the use of all appropriate means, provided that certain conditions as to the legibility and reliability of the document received are observed. Security in transmission requires that the document to be transmitted be accompanied by a standard form, to be completed in the official language or one of the official languages of the place where service is to be effected, or in another language accepted by the Member State in question (the Czech Republic indicated English, German and Slovak). The service of a document should be effected as soon as possible and in any event within one month of receipt by the receiving agency.

424. Important role is played by international treaties: either bilateral treaties on providing legal assistance, or multilateral treaties, in particular the Hague Convention on the Service Abroad of Judicial and Extrajudicial Documents in Civil or Commercial Matters of 1965 and the European Agreement on the Transmission of Applications for Legal Aid of 1967.

§5. Rules of Evidence

425. The procedure law of Czech courts is the Continental type.[180] The burden of proof lies upon the respective parties. However, the court itself is obliged to ascertain the truth relating to the matter in dispute. Consequently, the court examines the evidence and in explicitly mentioned cases is entitled to order of its motion any evidence that it may deem necessary and that was not put forward by any party to litigation (section 120 CCP). The court takes all necessary measures to ascertain the provisions of a foreign law (*see* section 23 PIL Act).

426. Among Member States of the EU, the Regulation on Cooperation between the Courts of the EU Member States in the Taking of Evidence in Civil or Commercial Matters shall apply. The efficiency of judicial procedures in civil or commercial matters requires that the transmission and execution of requests for the performance of taking of evidence is to be made directly and by the most rapid means possible between Member States' courts. Speed in transmission of requests for the performance of taking of evidence warrants the use of all appropriate means, provided that certain conditions as to the legibility and reliability of the document received are observed. To ensure the utmost clarity and legal certainty the request for the performance of taking of evidence must be transmitted on a form to be completed in the language of the Member State of the requested court or in another language accepted by that State (the Czech Republic indicated English, German and Slovak). For the same reasons, forms should also be used as far as possible for further communication between the relevant courts. A request for the performance of the taking of evidence should be executed expeditiously. If it is not possible for the request to be executed within ninety days of receipt by the requested court, the latter should inform the requesting court accordingly, stating the reasons which prevent the request from being executed swiftly.

427. In addition, Czech Republic is a contracting state to the Hague Convention on the Taking of Evidence Abroad in Civil or Commercial Matters of 1970, as well as to the European Convention on Information on Foreign Law of 1968, as amended by the Strasbourg Additional Protocol of 1978.

428. Documents executed by a court, a notary or an authority in a foreign state, which are in the place of its origin deemed to be a public document,[181] or a public document executed by a diplomatic officer or consular agent working in the Czech Republic, shall be taken as a public document evidence also in the Czech Republic, provided it possesses the required legalization. Should the document executed abroad fail to possess the required legalization in accordance with international practice and should the relevant embassy of the Czech Republic have no doubts

180. For details *see* in particular L. Neustupná, *Czech Republic*, in *Transnational Litigation: A Practitioner's Guide* 40–59 (Oceana Publications, Inc., 1997).

181. The PIL Act does not mention anything other than public documents issued abroad, so that other such documents shall be evaluated by a court according to its free assessment as evidence in general, *see* Kučera, *Mezinárodní právo soukromé*, 2009, at 398.

about its authenticity, the embassy shall place a certificate on the document declaring that the embassy has no doubts about the authenticity of the document (section 12 PIL Act). Upon a request of a document's holder, the Ministry of Justice and consequently the Ministry of Foreign Affairs shall attach its superlegalization (authentication) to documents issued or legalized by courts or to documents prepared or legalized by a notary or a bailiff which are to be applied abroad. A superlegalization cannot be attached to a simple copy of the document (section 109 PIL Act).

429. The Czech Republic is a contracting state to the Hague Convention Abolishing the Requirement of Legalization for Foreign Public Documents of 1961 (the Apostille Convention), and to the European Convention on the Abolition of the Legalization of Documents Executed by Diplomatic Agents or Consular Officers of 1968; exceptions to the authentication requirements are also contained in treaties on legal assistance. Within the material scope of the Regulation No. 2016/1191 on promoting the free movement of citizens by simplifying the requirements for presenting certain public documents in the EU, apostille is no longer required.

§6. Temporary Relief

430. The emergency measures available to Czech courts are included in the CCP. Czech civil procedure law regulates two kinds of emergency measures that can be ordered by a court: interim measure (temporary relief) and provisional enforceability of decisions. Under section 74 CCP an interim measure may be ordered by the court before proceedings are initiated, if necessary, to provisionally modify the relation of participants, or if feared the enforcement of the judicial decision could be jeopardized. The participants in the proceedings are the plaintiff and those who would be participants if the matter itself were concerned. The court competent for ordering an interim measure shall be the court competent for the proceedings for the matter unless otherwise provided by law. Pursuant to section 75b CCP, to cover any compensation for damage or any other loss that would be caused by the interim measure, the plaintiff shall be obliged to provide a security, otherwise the court shall refuse the interim measure application (section 75b CCP).

431. An interim measure may impose on the participant, *inter alia*, to pay a financial amount or deposit an item with the court, not to dispose of some items or rights, or to perform, refrain from performing, or withstand. When an interim measure is ordered, the court shall impose the plaintiff to file a proceedings initiation proposal at the court in a time specified by the court. The court may limit the interim measure so that it only lasts for a specified time (section 76 CCP).

432. The interim measure expires when the plaintiff files an application for proceedings initiation; the application has not been granted; the application has been granted and fifteen days following the enforceability have expired; the specified time for which the interim measures were to last has expired. The court shall abolish the interim measure if reasons for which it had been ordered no longer exist or if the plaintiff has failed to pay the ordered supplement to security within the determined term (section 77 CCP).

433. Under the Code of Special Civil Procedure, if the proceedings may be initiated of its own motion, it is possible to order an interim measure of its own motion, too. A security for damage or any other loss that would be caused by the interim measure shall not be required in cases of interim measures that can be ordered of its own motion, in protection against domestic violence or in matters of maintenance (section 12 CCPSC).

434. The Insolvency Regulation applies to procedures which grant a temporary stay on enforcement actions brought by individual creditors where such actions could adversely affect negotiations and hamper the prospects of a restructuring of the debtor's business. Such procedures should not be detrimental to the general body of creditors and, if no agreement on a restructuring plan could be reached, should be preliminary to other procedures covered by this Regulation (*see* Recital 11 of the Preamble and Article 1.1.c) of the Insolvency Regulation).

435. The Brussels I Recast Regulation contains special provision on provisional, including protective, measures in Article 35. Application may be made to the courts of a Member State for such provisional, including protective, measures as may be available under the law of that Member State, even if the courts of another Member State have jurisdiction as to the substance of the matter. Similar provision is included in Article 14 of the Maintenance Regulation.

436. Provisional and protective measures are also admitted under the Brussels II*bis* Regulation, however, the conditions being stricter. In urgent cases, the provisions of this Regulation shall not prevent the courts of a Member State from taking such provisional, including protective, measures in respect of persons or assets in that State as may be available under the law of that Member State, even if, under this Regulation, the court of another Member State has jurisdiction as to the substance of the matter. These measures shall cease to apply when the court of the Member State having jurisdiction under this Regulation as to the substance of the matter has taken the measures it considers appropriate (Article 20 Brussels II*bis* Regulation).

437. Under the Succession Regulation, application may be made to the courts of a Member State for such provisional, including protective, measures as may be available under the law of that State, even if, under this Regulation, the courts of another Member State have jurisdiction as to the substance of the matter (Article 19 Succession Regulation).

438. Similar provisions on provisional measures are contained in Article 19 of the Matrimonial Property Regimes Regulation and in Article 19 of the Registered Partnerships' Regimes Regulation.

Chapter 5. Acceptability and Enforcement of Foreign Judgments

439. Under the Czech autonomous PIL, foreign judgments, that is, judgments of foreign courts and judgments of foreign authorities on rights and obligations which would be, based upon their private-law nature, decided by courts in the Czech Republic, as well as foreign court settlements and foreign notarial acts or other public documents on these matters, shall be effective in the Czech Republic provided a certificate of the foreign authority confirms the judgment has become final and provided it has been recognized by the Czech public authorities (section 14 PIL Act). The recognition and enforcement of foreign decisions in the Czech Republic is governed by the rules of the PIL Act, provided EU law or a binding international treaty does not provide otherwise.

440. Currently, the most important European instruments concerning recognition and enforcement of foreign judgments are several EU Regulations which contain a relatively simple procedure for recognition and enforcement of judgments given in another Member State. They are based on the principle of mutual trust in the administration of justice in the EU. These rules justify judgments given in a Member State being recognized automatically without the need for any special procedure, except in cases of dispute. The content of the European Regulations relating to the recognition and enforcement of foreign judgments issued by courts of Member States of the EU has been quite significant for the Czech Republic since the general rules contained in the Czech PIL Act are rather complicated (requiring reciprocity, *see infra*). However, Czech autonomous international civil procedure law does not include the *exequatur* proceedings, i.e., declaration of enforceability of foreign judgments, which is required by a number of EU Regulations and international conventions, e.g., Brussels II*bis* Regulation, Succession Regulation, Maintenance Regulation, Matrimonial Property Regimes Regulation, Registered Partnerships' Regulation or Lugano Convention.

441. After the Czech Republic became a Member State of the EU, special provisions on declaration of enforceability were implemented in the former PIL Act 1963 and similar rules are included in sections 17–19 of the new PIL Act (Part Two, Title IV, Special Provisions on Recognition and Enforcement of Certain Foreign Judgments). Under section 17 PIL Act, the provisions of this Title shall apply onto proceedings on recognition and enforcement of foreign judgments which are governed by the directly applicable provisions of the EU law or international treaties that require a declaration of enforceability. If a party requests, under a directly applicable provision of the EU law or international treaties, to have recognition decided upon in special proceedings, the court shall decide by means of a judgment on recognition. A hearing does not need to be ordered (section 18 PIL Act). Along with the application for a declaration of enforceability an application for a writ of execution may be submitted. In such a case, a court shall decide in a single judgment on both applications by separate reasoned statements. The judgment must be reasoned even when deciding only upon one of these applications. A writ of execution of a judgment shall not become final prior to the declaration of the judgment's enforceability (for details *see* section 19 PIL Act).

442. In civil and commercial matters, the recognition and enforcement of judgments given by a tribunal in the other EU Member States is based on Articles 36–57 of the Brussels I Recast Regulation. A judgment given in a Member State shall be recognized in the other Member States without any special procedure being required. A judgment shall not be recognized for explicitly stated reasons, in particular, if such recognition is manifestly contrary to public policy in the Member State in which recognition is sought; where it was given in default of appearance, if the defendant was not served with the document which instituted the proceedings or with an equivalent document in sufficient time and in such a way as to enable him to arrange for his defence; if it is irreconcilable with a judgment given in a dispute between the same parties in the Member State addressed; if it is irreconcilable with an earlier judgment given in another Member State or in a third State; or if it conflicts with special provisions on jurisdiction in matters of insurance, consumer or employment contracts, etc. (for details *see* Article 45 Brussels I Recast).

443. A judgment given in a Member State and enforceable in that State shall be enforceable in another Member State without any declaration of enforceability being required (Article 39 Brussels I Recast). On the application of the person against whom enforcement is sought, the enforcement of a judgment shall be refused where one of the grounds referred to in Article 45 is found to exist (Article 46 Brussels I Recast). These rights of defence of the person against whom the enforcement is sought should compensate the abolition of exequatur (*see also* Recital 29 of the Preamble to the Regulation).

444. Under no circumstances may a judgment given in a Member State be reviewed as to its substance in the Member State addressed (Article 52 Brussels I Recast).

445. Regulation creating a European Enforcement Order for Uncontested Claims permits, by laying down minimum standards, the free circulation of judgments throughout all Member States without any intermediate proceedings needing to be brought in the Member State of enforcement prior to recognition and enforcement. A judgment which has been certified as a European Enforcement Order in the Member State of origin shall be recognized and enforced in the other Member States without the need for a declaration of enforceability and without any possibility of opposing its recognition.

446. Regulation creating a European Order for Payment Procedure permits the free circulation of European orders for payment throughout the Member States by laying down minimum standards, compliance with which renders unnecessary any intermediate proceedings in the Member State of enforcement prior to recognition and enforcement. If within the stipulated time limit, taking into account an appropriate period of time to allow a statement to arrive, no statement of opposition has been lodged with the court of origin, the court of origin shall without delay declare the European order for payment enforceable using standard forms. A European order for payment which has become enforceable in the Member State of origin shall be recognized and enforced in the other Member States without the need for a declaration of enforceability and without any possibility of opposing its recognition.

447. Regulation establishing a European Small Claims Procedure simplifies litigation concerning small claims (where the value of a claim does not exceed EUR 5,000) in cross-border cases, and to reduce costs. This Regulation also eliminates the intermediate proceedings necessary to enable recognition and enforcement, in other Member States, of judgments given in one Member State in the European Small Claims Procedure. In principle, the European Small Claims Procedure is a written procedure using standard forms. A judgment given in a Member State in the European Small Claims Procedure shall be recognized and enforced in another Member State without the need for a declaration of enforceability and without any possibility of opposing its recognition.

448. In matrimonial matters and the matters of parental responsibility, the recognition and in some cases enforcement of judgments given in the other Member States shall be governed by the Brussels II*bis* Regulation. A judgment given in a Member State shall be recognized in the other Member States without any special procedure being required (*see* Article 21 Brussels II*bis*). A judgment relating to a divorce, legal separation or marriage annulment shall not be recognized: if such recognition is manifestly contrary to the public policy of the Member State in which recognition is sought; where it was given in default of appearance; if it is irreconcilable with a judgment given in proceedings between the same parties in the Member State in which recognition is sought; or if it is irreconcilable with an earlier judgment given in another Member State or in a non-Member State (for details *see* Article 22 Brussels II*bis*). Grounds of non-recognition for judgments relating to parental responsibility are, *inter alia*, that such recognition is manifestly contrary to the public policy of the Member State in which recognition is sought taking into account the best interests of the child; that it was given, except in case of urgency, without the child having been given an opportunity to be heard; where it was given in default of appearance; the request of any person claiming that the judgment infringes his or her parental responsibility if it was given without such person having been given an opportunity to be heard; that it is irreconcilable with a later judgment relating to parental responsibility given in the Member State in which recognition is sought; that it is irreconcilable with a later judgment relating to parental responsibility given in another Member State or in the non-Member State (under specified conditions, for details *see* Article 23 Brussels II*bis*). The jurisdiction of the court of the Member State of origin may not be reviewed. A judgment on the exercise of parental responsibility in respect of a child given in a Member State which is enforceable in that Member State and has been served shall be enforced in another Member State when, on the application of any interested party, it has been declared enforceable there. The rights of access granted in an enforceable judgment given in a Member State, similarly as the return of a child entailed by an enforceable judgment, shall be recognized and enforceable in another Member State without the need for a declaration of enforceability and without any possibility of opposing its recognition if the judgment has been certified in the Member State of origin (for details *see* Articles 28, 41 and 42 Brussels II*bis*).

449. In matters relating to maintenance obligations, the rules on recognition and enforcement of decisions given in the other Member States are contained in the Maintenance Regulation. The Maintenance Regulation differentiates between decisions given in a Member State bound by the 2007 Hague Protocol (*see supra* Part II, Chapter 5, §6) and those given in a Member State not bound by this Protocol. A decision given in a Member State bound by the 2007 Hague Protocol shall be recognized in another Member State without any special procedure being required and without any possibility of opposing its recognition. A decision given in a Member State bound by the 2007 Hague Protocol which is enforceable in that State shall be enforceable in another Member State without the need for a declaration of enforceability. For decisions on maintenance obligations given in a Member State not bound by the 2007 Hague Protocol, the Maintenance Regulation includes special provisions for a procedure for recognition and declaration of enforceability. That procedure is modelled on the procedure and the grounds for refusing recognition set out in the Brussels I Regulation (for details *see* Articles 23–38 of the Maintenance Regulation).

450. In succession matters, a decision given in a Member State shall be recognized in the other Member States without any special procedure being required (for details *see* Article 39 Succession Regulation). Under Article 40 Succession Regulation, a decision shall not be recognized: if such recognition is manifestly contrary to public policy (*ordre public*) in the Member State in which recognition is sought; where it was given in default of appearance if the defendant was not served with the document which instituted the proceedings or with an equivalent document in sufficient time and in such a way as to enable him to arrange for his defence, unless the defendant failed to commence proceedings to challenge the decision when it was possible for him to do so; if it is irreconcilable with a decision given in proceedings between the same parties in the Member State in which recognition is sought; if it is irreconcilable with an earlier decision given in another Member State or in a third State involving the same cause of action and between the same parties, provided that the earlier decision fulfils the conditions necessary for its recognition in the Member State in which recognition is sought. Decisions given in a Member State and enforceable in that State shall be enforceable in another Member State when, on the application of any interested party, they have been declared enforceable there (for details *see* Articles 43–58 Succession Regulation).

451. In matters of matrimonial property regimes, a decision given in a Member State shall be recognized in the other Member States without any special procedure being required (for details *see* Article 36 Matrimonial Property Regimes Regulation). A decision shall not be recognized: if such recognition is manifestly contrary to public policy (*ordre public*) in the Member State in which recognition is sought; where it was given in default of appearance if the defendant was not served with the document which instituted the proceedings or with an equivalent document in sufficient time and in such a way as to enable him to arrange for his defence, unless the defendant failed to commence proceedings to challenge the decision when it was possible for him to do so; if it is irreconcilable with a decision given in proceedings between the same parties in the Member State in which recognition is sought; if it is irreconcilable with an earlier decision given in another Member State or in a third State involving the same cause of action and between the same parties, provided that the earlier decision fulfils the conditions necessary for its recognition in the Member State in which recognition is sought (Article 37 of the Regulation). Decisions given in a Member State and enforceable in that State shall be enforceable in another Member State when, on the application of any interested party, they have been declared enforceable there (for details *see* Articles 42–57 Matrimonial Property Regimes Regulation).

452. Similarly, in matters of the property consequences of registered partnerships, a decision given in a Member State shall be recognized in the other Member States without any special procedure being required (for details *see* Article 36 Registered Partnerships' Regimes Regulation). The grounds for non-recognition of a decision given in another Member State, contained in Article 37 of the Registered Partnership Regulation, are identical with those included by Article 37 of the Matrimonial Property Regulation. The Regulation contains similar provisions on enforcement as those included by Articles 42–57 of the Matrimonial Property Regulation, with the same numbering.

453. The Regulation No. 655/2014 on establishing a European Account Preservation Order procedure to facilitate cross-border debt recovery in civil and commercial matters introduces a Union procedure enabling a creditor to obtain a European Account Preservation Order which prevents the subsequent enforcement of the creditor's claim from being jeopardized through the transfer or withdrawal of funds up to the amount specified in the Order which are held by the debtor or on his behalf in a bank account maintained in a Member State.

454. The Czech Republic is a contracting party to a number of bilateral treaties on legal assistance and also a contracting party to some special conventions on the recognition and enforcement of foreign decisions. In addition, questions concerning the recognition and enforcement of foreign decisions are contained in some multilateral conventions, for example the New York Convention on the Enforcement of Maintenance Obligations Abroad of 1956, or the Hague Convention on the Recognition and Enforcement of Decisions Relating to Maintenance Obligations in Respect of Children of 1958, etc., not leaving aside the Lugano Convention.

455. Provision concerning relations of EU Regulations with international conventions concluded by the EU Member States are contained in all EU regulations, giving in principle (with some exceptions) precedence to international conventions.

456. In Czech autonomous law, the general conditions for the recognition and enforcement of foreign judgments are contained in section 14 PIL Act, under which foreign judgments shall be effective in the Czech Republic provided a certificate of the foreign authority confirms the judgment has become final and provided it has been recognized by the Czech public authorities. Under section 15 PIL Act a final foreign judgment shall not be recognized if (a) the matter falls into an exclusive jurisdiction of the Czech courts or if the proceedings could not be implemented by any authority of a foreign state, should the provisions on jurisdiction of the Czech courts apply to assess the jurisdiction of a foreign authority, unless the party to the proceedings against which the foreign judgment is focused voluntarily submits to the jurisdiction of a foreign authority; (b) proceedings involving the same legal relation are brought in the courts of the Czech Republic and the Czech court was seized prior to the foreign court which rendered a judgment the recognition of which is being applied for; (c) a Czech court has rendered a final judgment on the same legal relation or if a foreign final judgment rendered by a third state's authority has already been recognized in the Czech Republic; (d) the party against which the judgment is to be recognized has been disabled by a foreign authority's action to properly participate in the proceedings, in particular the party has not been served with the summons to appear or with the document which instituted the proceedings; (e) the recognition would be manifestly contrary to the public policy, or (f) reciprocity is not guaranteed; reciprocity shall not be required provided the foreign judgment is not aimed against a national of the Czech Republic or a Czech legal entity. The defence referred to under letter (d) shall be taken into consideration only if requested by the party against which the foreign judgment is to be recognized. This shall also apply to the defences referred to under letters (b) and (c), unless the authority deciding upon recognition is otherwise aware of their existence.

457. These provisions are rather strict compared to EU legislation. They are applicable to foreign judgments rendered by courts of third states with respect to which no treaty or convention exists and also to foreign judgments rendered by courts of EU Member States in matters where no uniform rules were adopted. As to the requirement of reciprocity, a decision of a court is in fact enforceable abroad (and *vice versa*) only if the states in question have concluded a respective convention or a bilateral treaty, or if reciprocity on the part of another State exists. Upon request, the Ministry of Justice shall provide the court with information about reciprocity with another state (section 13 PIL Act). Such information, however, is not binding upon the court.[182]

458. Special rule on recognition of decisions in property matters and property rights on the one hand, and for non-property matters on the other, is contained in section 16 PIL Act. Recognition of a foreign judgment in property matters shall not be rendered in a separate judgment. A foreign judgment shall be recognized by the fact that a Czech public authority considers it as if it was a judgment of a Czech public authority. Foreign decisions in other matters shall be recognized on the basis of a special decision should the PIL Act not stipulate that foreign decisions shall be

182. This is an important change compared to the old PIL Act, under which the declaration of reciprocity of the Ministry of Justice on the part of another State, issued in consultation with the Ministry of Foreign Affairs and other Ministries concerned, was binding for the courts and other agencies of the Czech State (*see* s. 54 PIL Act 1963).

recognized without further proceedings. Even in case foreign decisions are recognized without further proceedings, they can be recognized upon application by means of a special decision. Final foreign decisions in matters of divorce, legal separation, annulment of marriage and declaring whether a marriage exists or not provided at least one of the parties was a citizen of the Czech Republic, shall be recognized only on the basis of a separate decision. To declare that such a decision shall be recognized falls into the jurisdiction of the Supreme Court. An application may be filed by the parties as well as by any person who shall prove a legitimate interest (section 51 PIL Act; this provision only applies unless EU law or international conventions provide otherwise).

459. Pursuant to section 16(2) PIL Act, unless otherwise stipulated by law, the District Court which is the general court of the party claiming recognition, otherwise the District Court in the district of which a fact (event) occurred or may occur for which the recognition is of importance, shall have local jurisdiction (venue) on recognition. The court shall decide upon recognition by judgment; a hearing does not need to be ordered.

460. On the basis of a foreign decision on property matters which fulfils the conditions for recognition under the PIL Act, an enforcement of such a decision may be ordered by a reasoned decision of a Czech court (section 16(3) PIL Act).

Chapter 6. International Insolvency Law

461. Czech autonomous law on insolvency is contained in the InsA.[183] The former Act on bankruptcy and composition[184] contained provisions on international insolvency law in relation to EU and also to non-EU countries. Currently, there is a dual system of international insolvency law in the Czech Republic. International insolvency, provided that the centre of main interests (COMI) is located in the EU, is governed by the EU Insolvency Regulation (Regulation No. 2015/848) and the InsA. International insolvency provided that the COMI is located in a third country is governed by the PIL Act. Czech Republic did not adopt the UNCITRAL Model Law for cases of international insolvency in relation to non-EU countries. There is no international treaty binding for the Czech Republic containing regulation of international insolvency law.[185]

462. The concept of insolvency, which is the key concept of national insolvency law, is defined in section 3 InsA. Insolvency proceedings may be instituted only with respect to a debtor already insolvent or facing imminent insolvency. Section 3 InsA distinguishes two basic types of insolvency: equity (or cash-flow) insolvency and balance-sheet insolvency. The InsA provides for several methods of solving insolvency. Under section 4 of the InsA, the following methods of solving insolvency or imminent insolvency are listed: bankruptcy, reorganization, discharge, and special types stipulated by the InsA for particular types of persons and particular types of cases.

463. Sections 426–430 InsA govern international insolvency with a European element, i.e., in relation to the EU Member States. Section 426 defines these insolvency proceedings as proceedings where the COMI is in an EU Member State (except for Denmark), and, at the same time, at least one creditor or a portion of the property estate are located in another EU Member State (except for Denmark). Such insolvency proceedings are to be governed by the Insolvency Regulation.

464. The Insolvency Regulation applies to public collective proceedings, including interim proceedings, which are based on laws relating to insolvency and in which, for the purpose of rescue, adjustment of debt, reorganization or liquidation: (a) a debtor is totally or partially divested of its assets and an insolvency practitioner is appointed; (b) the assets and affairs of a debtor are subject to control or supervision by a court; or (c) a temporary stay of individual enforcement proceedings is granted by a court or by operation of law, in order to allow for negotiations between the debtor and its creditors, provided that the proceedings in which the stay is granted provide for suitable measures to protect the general body of creditors, and, where no agreement is reached, are preliminary to one of the proceedings referred

183. Act No. 182/2006 Coll., the Insolvency Act (InsA).
184. Act No. 328/1991 Coll., on Bankruptcy and Composition.
185. *See* in particular J. Brodec; M. Pauknerová & M. Pfeiffer, *International Insolvency Law in the Czech Legal System*, in *European and National Perspectives on the Application of the European Insolvency Regulation* 257–272 (I. Queirolo & S. Dominelli ed., Aracne 1st ed. 2017).

to in point (a) or (b) (*see* Article 1 Insolvency Regulation). The courts of the Member State within the territory of which the centre of the debtor's main interests (COMI) is situated shall have jurisdiction to open insolvency proceedings. The centre of main interests shall be the place where the debtor conducts the administration of its interests on a regular basis, and which is ascertainable by third parties (for details *see* Article 3 Insolvency Regulation).

465. Pursuant to Article 7, the law applicable to insolvency proceedings and their effects shall be that of the Member State within the territory of which such proceedings are opened, save as otherwise provided in the Insolvency Regulation.[186]

466. Any decision opening insolvency proceedings handed down by a court of a Member State which has jurisdiction pursuant to Article 3 shall be recognized in all other Member States from the moment that it becomes effective in the State of the opening of proceedings. This rule shall also apply where, on account of a debtor's capacity, insolvency proceedings cannot be brought against that debtor in other Member States (*see* Article 19 Insolvency Regulation). Where main insolvency proceedings have been opened by a court of a Member State and recognized in another Member State, a court of that other Member State which has jurisdiction pursuant to Article 3(2) may open secondary insolvency proceedings (for details *see* Article 34 Insolvency Regulation).

467. As mentioned above, international insolvency where the COMI is located in a third country is governed by the PIL Act. Under section 111 PIL Act, should the Czech courts have jurisdiction to open insolvency proceedings under the Insolvency Regulation, the proceedings shall extend also to the debtor's assets in a foreign state other than a Member State of the EU provided the foreign state attributes effects to the proceedings in its territory; the extension is effective to the extent of the attributed effects. An insolvency liquidator shall exercise his or her powers also in the territory of a foreign state provided the law of the foreign state allows it and only within the limits of such law. The Czech courts may open and conduct insolvency proceedings if the debtor has an establishment in the Czech Republic provided it is requested by the creditor with habitual residence or seat in the Czech Republic or the creditor's claim arose in connection with the establishment's activities. The effects of the proceedings shall be in such a case limited to the assets in the Czech Republic.

468. The conflict of law provisions of the Insolvency Regulation may apply to cases outside the scope of this Regulation *mutatis mutandis* (*see* section 111(3) PIL Act). If a judgment on insolvency of a participant of a payment system with settlement finality, of a foreign payment system with settlement finality, of a settlement system with settlement finality or of a foreign settlement system with settlement finality was given, or if another judgment against that party was issued or other

186. For details *see* J. Brodec, *Determination of Applicable Law in International Insolvency Proceedings*, in I. Queirolo & S. Dominelli, *European and National Perspectives on the Application of the European Insolvency Regulation*, *supra*, 83–103.

action with similar effects undertaken by a public authority, the rights and obligations of the participant arising from the participation in the system shall be governed by the same law which governs a legal relation between the system participants during settlement. The choice of another law is excluded (section 111(4) PIL Act).

469. A foreign decision in the insolvency proceedings matters shall be recognized under the condition of reciprocity provided in a foreign state in which it was given the debtor has a centre of main interests and provided the debtor's assets in the Czech Republic are not a subject of pending proceedings. In these cases and also otherwise, unless the property which became a subject of insolvency proceedings abroad is a subject of initiated insolvency proceedings before a Czech court, the debtor's movable properties located in the Czech Republic shall be given out to a foreign court at its request, provided a court of a state which maintains reciprocity is concerned. Nevertheless, the debtor's assets may be given out abroad only when the rights to exclude properties from the estate have been satisfied as well as the rights of secured creditors acquired before the request of a foreign court or other competent authority was received (section 111(5) PIL Act).

470. Special provisions concern insolvency of financial institutions and insolvency of insurance undertakings (sections 112–116 PIL Act). These provisions implement the EU Directive No. 2001/24/EC of 4 April 2001 on the reorganization and winding up of credit institutions and the Directive No. 2009/138/EC of 25 November 2009 on access to insurance and reinsurance activities and pursuit (Solvency II).

Chapter 7. International Arbitration

471. In the Czech Republic, arbitration, both international and national, is a common form of dispute settlement in the area of private, especially commercial, law. Legal sources are the Act Relating to Arbitration and to the Enforcement of Arbitration Awards (Arbitration Act, hereinafter AA)[187] and the PIL Act, which governs arbitration with respect to foreign countries: it includes the former provisions of Part Five AA 'Relations to foreign countries' which were transferred from the AA to the new PIL Act.

472. Czech Republic is a contracting state to a series of multilateral international conventions concerning arbitration proceedings, and in particular the recognition and enforcement of foreign arbitral awards, that is, arbitral awards issued abroad. The most important of multilateral treaties are the Protocol on Arbitrators Clauses of 1923, the Convention on Enforceability of Foreign Arbitral Awards of 1927, the NY Convention on Recognition and Execution of Foreign Arbitral Awards of 1958, and the European Convention on International Commercial Arbitration of 1961. Apart from multilateral conventions, bilateral treaties, especially treaties on legal assistance, are of importance in this respect as well.

473. The Arbitration Act makes it possible to decide disputes through arbitration proceedings regarding property disputes by independent and impartial arbitrators. Parties may agree to submit to one or more arbitrators or to a permanent arbitration court property disputes between themselves, except for disputes arising out of contracts between consumers and entrepreneurs, disputes which have arisen in connection with the execution of decisions, and further, except for incidental disputes. Additional conditions for a valid arbitration agreement are that a court of law would otherwise be empowered to deal with and make a decision in the dispute, or a special act provides so. An arbitration agreement may be validly entered into if the parties are free to conclude settlements in respect of the subject matter of the dispute (*see* sections 1 and 2 AA and section 99 CCP). The arbitration agreement must be concluded in writing; otherwise, it is invalid (for details *see* section 3 AA). Arbitration proceedings are thus allowed for a relatively wide range of legal property relations between Czech persons as well as in relationships with an international element. In the latter, PIL Act applies.

474. Under section 117 PIL Act, an admissibility of an arbitration agreement shall be governed by Czech law. Other constituents of the arbitration agreement shall be governed by the law of the state in which an arbitral award is to be issued. A form of the arbitration agreement shall be governed by the law applicable to other constituents of the arbitration agreement; nevertheless, it shall be sufficient if a law of the place or places where the intent was manifested is to apply. If the Czech law

187. Act No. 216/1994 Coll, Relating to Arbitration and to Enforcement of Arbitration Awards (Arbitration Act).

is the *lex arbitri* (the law of the country where arbitration proceedings are conducted), the admissibility of the arbitration agreement will be assessed under the provisions on arbitrability contained in section 2 AA (*see supra* the preceding paragraph).

475. As for the law applicable to the merits, either it is chosen by the parties or it is determined by the arbitrators in accordance with the provisions of the PIL Act. The conflict of law provisions of the applicable law shall be taken into consideration only provided it follows from the choice of law made by the parties (generally, *renvoi* is not admitted). Should the parties expressly mandate the arbitrators thereto, the arbitrators may decide the dispute in accordance with the principles of justice.

476. Arbitral awards issued in a foreign state shall be recognized and enforced in the Czech Republic as Czech arbitral awards, provided reciprocity is guaranteed. Reciprocity shall be considered as guaranteed also in the case that one state generally declares foreign arbitral awards enforceable under the condition of reciprocity. Recognition or enforcement of a foreign arbitral award shall be refused if the foreign arbitral award (a) is not final or enforceable under the law of the state where it was made, (b) was set aside in a state in which or under the law of which it was made, (c) is vitiated by an error which is the reason for setting aside of the Czech arbitral award by a court, or (d) is contrary to the public policy (sections 120 and 121 PIL Act). These grounds correspond in principle to the New York Convention on Recognition and Execution of Foreign Arbitral Awards of 1958, which was ratified by the Czech Republic, and when applicable takes precedence over the national rules.

477. Recognition of a foreign arbitral award shall not be rendered in a separate decision. A foreign arbitral award shall be recognized automatically as if it was a Czech arbitral award. Enforcement of a foreign arbitral award shall be ordered by a reasoned decision of a Czech court (section 12s PIL Act).

Selected Bibliography

Till 2001

Monographs

Bystrický, R. *Mezinárodní právo soukromé* [*Private International Law*, in Czech]. Prague: Orbis, 1958.

Kalenský, P. *Trends of Private International Law*. Prague: Academia, 1971. Cited as: Kalenský, *Trends of Private International Law*.

Knapp, V. *Velké právní systémy, Úvod do srovnávací právní vědy* [*Great Legal Systems, Introduction to Comparative Law*, in Czech]. 1st ed. Prague: Beck 1996.

Krčmář, J. *Úvod do mezinárodního práva soukromého* [*Introduction to Private International Law*, in Czech]. Prague: Bursík&Kohout, 1906.

Kučera, Z. *Mezinárodní právo soukromé* [*Private International Law*, in Czech]. 5th ed. Brno: Doplněk, 2001.

Kučera, Z. *Suretyship in Private International Law*. Prague: AUC Iuridica, 1967.

Kučera, Z. & L. Tichý. *Zákon o mezinárodním právu soukromém a procesním. Komentář* [*Act on Private International Law and Rules of Procedure Relating Thereto, Commentary*, in Czech]. Prague: Panorama, 1989. Cited as: Kučera & Tichý. *Komentář*.

Neustupná L. 'Czech Republic'. In *Transnational Litigation: A Practitioner's Guide*. New York: Oceana Publications, Inc., 1997.

Pauknerová, M. (ed.). *Doing Business in the Czech Republic*. New York: Juris Publishing, Inc., 1999.

Pauknerová, M. *Společnosti v mezinárodním právu soukromém* [*Companies in Private International Law*, in Czech with English summary]. Prague: Karolinum, 1998. Cited as: Pauknerová. *Společnosti v mezinárodním právu soukromém* [*Companies in Private International Law*)].

Zimmermann, M.A. *Mezinárodní právo soukromé* [*Private International Law*, in Czech]. Brno: Čs. A.S. Právník, 1933.

Articles

Balaš, V. & M. Pauknerová. 'The Czechoslovak Approach to the Draft Convention on Jurisdictional Immunities of States and their Property'. *Michigan Journal of International Law* 12, no. 4 (Summer 1991): 874.

Bystrický, R. 'The New Czechoslovak Act Concerning Private International Law and the Rules of Procedure Relating Thereto'. *Bulletin of Czechoslovak Law* no. 4 (1963): 213.

Kanda, A. 'Caractéristiques et tendances de la réglementation juridique des relations commerciales internationales'. (in Czech with French summary). In *Studie z mezinárodního práva* [*Studies in International Law*]. no. 20 Prague: Academia, 1986, 204.

Kučera, Z. 'Private International Law in Czechoslovakia'. *Bulletin of Czechoslovak Law* 24, nos 1–2 (1985): Prague, 1.

Kučera, Z. 'The Problem of Classification'. In *Miscellany of Papers in International Law* AUB, vol. 92. Brno: Masarykova univerzita, 1991, 99.

Pauknerová, M. 'Tzv. nutně použitelné normy před Rozhodčím soudem při HK Č R a AK ČR' ['The So-Called Rules of Immediate Application Before the Arbitration Court Attached to the Economic Chamber of the Czech Republic and Agricultural Chamber of the Czech Republic', in Czech]. *Právní praxe v podnikání* [*Legal Practice in Business*] nos 7–8 (1996): 16.

Pauknerová, M. 'Gründungs- und Sitztheorie im tschechischen Gesellschaftsrecht'. In *Der Eintritt der Tschechischen Republik in die Europäische Wirtschafts – und Währungsunion – Ausgewählte Fragen* (in German). Tübingen: Prag, 2002.

2002–2010

Monographs

Bělohlávek, A. *Evropské a mezinárodní insolvenční právo*: *komentář* [*European and International Insolvency Law: Commentary*, in Czech]. Prague: C.H. Beck, 2007.

Bělohlávek, A. *Římská úmluva a Nařízení Řím I: komentář* [*Rome Convention and Regulation Rome I: Commentary*, in Czech]. Prague: C.H. Beck, 2009.

Kučera, Z. *Mezinárodní právo soukromé* [*Private International Law*, in Czech]. 7th ed. Brno – Pilsen: Doplněk a Čeněk, 2009. Cited as: Z. Kučera. *Mezinárodní právo soukromé (2009)*.

Kučera, Z., et al. *Právo mezinárodního obchodu* [*Law of International Commerce*, in Czech]. Pilsen: Čeněk, 2008.

Pauknerová, M. 'Brussels II bis: Its Impact and Application in the Czech Republic'. In *Brussels IIbis: Its Impact and Application in the Member States*, *European Family Law Series*, edited by K. Boele-Woelki & C. Gonzáles-Beilfuss. Antverpen – Oxford: Intersentia, 2007, 69.

Pauknerová, M. 'Codification of Czech Private Law in the Middle and on the Outskirts of Europe'. In *Liber Amicorum Valentinas Mikelenas*. Vilnius: Justitia, 2008, 239.

Pauknerová, M. 'Conflict of Laws Conventions and Their Reception – Czech Republic'. In *The Impact of Uniform Law in National Law. Limits and Possibilities*, edited by Jorge Sánchez Cordero. México: Instítuto de Investigaciones jurídicas, 2010, 299.

Pauknerová, M. 'Einflüsse des Europarechts auf das internationale Privatrecht in der Tschechischen Republik'. In *Rett og toleranse Festskrift til Helge Johan Thue*. Oslo, 2007, 390.

Pauknerová, M. 'Eingriffsnormen im tschechischen Internationalen Privatrecht'. In *Festschrift für Hans Jürgen Sonnenberger.* München: Verlag Beck, 2004, 575.

Pauknerová, M. *Evropské mezinárodní právo soukromé* [*European Private International Law*, in Czech]. Prague: C.H. Beck, 2008.

Pauknerová, M. 'International Conventions and Community Law: Harmony and Conflicts'. In *Nuovi strumenti del diritto internazionale privato* [*New Instruments of Private International Law – Liber Fausto Pocar*]. Milano: Giuffrè Editore, 2009, 793.

Pauknerová, M. 'Presumptions, Escape Clauses and International Carriage of Goods Contracts'. In *Convergence and Divergence in Private International Law*, edited by K. Boele-Woelki et al., The Hague: Eleven International Publishing Schulthess, 2010, 482.

Pauknerová, M. 'The *Contrat Sans Loi* in Czech and European Private International Law'. In *Vers nouveaux équilibres entre ordres juridiques, Mélanges Hélène Gaudemet-Tallon*. Paris: Dalloz 2008, 775.

Pauknerová, M. & K. Růžička. 'Arbitration in the Czech Republic'. In *Arbitration in Central Europe*, edited by P. Oberhammer et al., Wien: Manz Verlag, 2005, 253.

Rozehnalová, N. *Právo mezinárodního obchodu* [*Law of International Commerce*, in Czech]. Prague: ASPI-Wolters Kluwer, 2006.

Rozehnalová, N. *Rozhodčí řízení v mezinárodním i vnitrostátním obchodním styku* [*Arbitration in International and National Commercial Relations*, in Czech]. Prague: ASPI-Wolters Kluwer, 2008.

Tomášek, M. et al., *Czech Law Between Europeanization and Globalization*. Prague: Charles University, 2010

Vaške, V. *Uznání a výkon cizích rozhodnutí v České republice* [*Recognition and Enforcement of Foreign Judgments in the Czech Republic*, in Czech]. Prague: C.H. Beck, 2007.

Articles

Bělohlávek, A. 'Law Applicable to the Merits of International Arbitration and Current Developments in European Private International Laws: Conflict-of-laws Rules and the Applicability of the Rome Convention, Rome I Regulation and Other EU Law Standards in International Arbitration'. *Czech Yearbook of International Law* (2010): 25.

Brodec, J. 'Surmounting the Wall of Legal Entity and Some Aspects of International Private Law in International Insolvency Proceedings'. *Czech Yearbook of International Law* (2010): 95–109.

Dobiáš, P. 'Principles of European Insurance Contract Law in Comparison with Czech Law on Insurance Contracts'. *Czech Yearbook of International Law* (2010): 111.

Kučera, Z. 'K rekodifikaci mezinárodního práva soukromého' ['On Recodification of International Private Law', in Czech]. *AUC* no. 1–2 (2003): 167.

Pauknerová, M. 'Einige Bemerkungen zum heutigen Stand und der künftigen Rekodifikation des Privatrechts in der Tschechischen Republik unter besonderer Berücksichtigung des europäischen Verbraucherprivatrechts'. *Grundfragen des europäischen Verbraucherprivatrechts*. IFEC (2006): 29.

Pauknerová, M. 'Entwicklungen im tschechischen internationalen Gesellschaftsrecht'. *IPRax* no. 2 (2007): 162.

Pauknerová, M. 'Czech Republic, Jurisdiction over Consumer Contracts under Article 15(1) of the Brussels I Regulation and the Definition of the Consumer's Domicile'. *Yb PIL* IX (2007): Sellier, 495.

Pauknerová, M. 'Private International Law in the Czech Republic: Tradition, New Experience and Prohibition of Discrimination on Grounds of Nationality'. *Journal of Private International Law* 4, no. 1 (2008): 83.

Pauknerová, M. 'Law Applicable to Obligations in the European Union – Some Questions on the Borderline (Procedural and Unilateral Undertakings)'. *Revue hellénique de droit international*. Anniversary issue (2009): 531.

Pauknerová, M. 'Jurisdictional Immunity of States and Brussels I Regulation – Recent Developments in the Czech Republic'. *The European Legal Forum* no. 5/6 (2009): 241.

Pauknerová, M. 'Mandatory Rules and Public Policy in International Contract Law'. *ERA Forum* no. 11 (2010): 29.

Pauknerová, M. 'Overriding Mandatory Rules and Czech Law'. *Czech Yearbook of International Law* (2010): 81.

Rozehnalová, N. & J. Valdhans. 'A Few Observations on Choice of Law'. *Czech Yearbook of International Law* (2010): 3.

Týč, V. & N. Rozehnalová. 'Kolizní smluvní právo, výhrada veřejného pořádku a mezinárodně kogentní normy' ['Law Applicable to Contracts, Public Order and Overriding Mandatory Rules', in Czech]. *Právník* [*Lawyer*] no. 6 (2002): 634.

2011–2018

Monographs

Bělohlávek, A. *Arbitration Law of Czech Republic: Practise and Procedure*. Huntington, New York: JurisNet LLC, 2013.

Bělohlávek, A. *Zákon o rozhodčím řízení a o výkonu rozhodčích nálezů. Komentář.* (Law on Arbitration and on Enforcement of Arbitral Awards. Commentary). 2nd ed. Praha: C. H. Beck, 2012.

Bělohlávek, A. & N. Rozehnalová (eds.) *CYArb – Czech (& Central European) Yearbook of Arbitration: Party Autonomy versus Autonomy of Arbitrators*. Huntington, New York: Juris Publishing Inc., 2012.

Bělohlávek, A. & N. Rozehnalová (eds.) *CYIL Public Policy and Ordre Public*. Huntington, New York: JurisPublishing Inc., 2012.

Bělohlávek, A., N. Rozehnalová & F. Černý (eds.) *CYArb – Czech (& Central European) Yearbook of Arbitration: Borders of Procedural and Substantive Law in Arbitral Proceedings (Civil versus Common Law Perspectives)*. Huntington, New York: JurisPublishing Inc., 2013.

Bříza, P. *Volba práva a voba soudu v mezinárodním obchodě* [*Choice of Law and Choice of Court in International Trade*]. 1st ed. Praha: C. H. Beck, 2012.

Bříza, P. et al., *Zákon o mezinárodním právu soukromém. Komentář* [*Act on the Private International Law. Commentary*]. Praha: C. H. Beck, 2014.

Dobiáš, P., et al. *Zákon o mezinárodním právu soukromém. Komentář* [*Act on the Private International Law: Commentary*]. 1st ed. Praha: Leges, 2013.

Drličková, K. *Vliv legis arbitri na uznání a výkon cizího rozhodčího nálezu* [*The

Influence of lex arbitri on the Recognition and Enforcement of the Foreign Arbitration Award]. 1st ed. Brno: Masarykova univerzita, 2013.

Drličková, K. & Z. Nový *Role veřejného zájmu v mezinárodní obchodní a investiční arbitráži* [*The Role of the Public Interest in the International Commercial and Investment Arbitration*]. Praha: C. H. Beck, 2017.

Kadlecová, *Evropské mezinárodní právo soukromé v kontextu pracovního práva* [*European Private International Law in the Context of Employment Law*, in Czech]. Prague: Wolters Kluwer, 2013, 212 p.

Kučera, Z. et al., *Mezinárodní právo soukromé* [*Private International Law*]. 8th ed. Plzeň: Aleš Čeněk a Doplněk, 2015.

Kučera, Z. & J. Gaňo *Zákon o mezinárodním právu soukromém, Komentované vydání* [*Act on Private International Law, Commented Edition*]. Plzeň: Aleš Čeněk a Doplněk, 2014.

Kyselovská T. & N. Rozehnalová *Rozhodování Soudního dvora EU ve věcech příslušnosti (analýza rozhodnutí dle Nařízení Brusel Ibis)* [*Decision Making of the European Court of Justice in the Matters of Jurisdiction (Analysis of the Decisions According to the Brussel Ibis Regulation)*]. 1st ed. Brno: Masarykova univerzita, 2014.

Pauknerová, M. *Evropské mezinárodní právo soukromé* [*European Private International Law*]. 2nd ed. Praha: C.H. Beck, 2013.

Pauknerová, M. et al., *Zákon o mezinárodním právu soukromém: komentář* [*Act on the Private International Law: Commentary*]. Praha: Wolters Kluwer, 2013.

Pfeiffer, M. *Dědický statut – právo rozhodné pro přeshraniční dědické poměry* [*Succession Statute – The Law Applicable to the Cross-Border Succession Matters*]. 1st ed. Praha: Wolters Kluwer, 2017.

Pfeiffer, M. *Kritérium obvyklého pobytu v mezinárodním právu soukromém* [*The Criterion of Habitual Residence in Private International Law*]. 1st ed. Praha: Leges, 2013.

Rozehnalová, N. et al., *Czech Private International Law*. Brno: Masarykova univerzita, 2015.

Rozehnalová, N. *Rozhodčí řízení v mezinárodním a vnitrostátním obchodním styku* [*Arbitration Proceedings in International and National Business Relations*]. 3rd ed. Praha: Wolters Kluwer, 2013.

Rozehnalová, N. et al., *Nový občanský zákoník pohledem mezinárodních obchodních transakcí* [*The New Civil Code from the Perspective of the International Business Transactions*]. Brno: Masarykova univerzita, 2014.

Rozehnalová, N. & T. Kyselovská *K některým vývojovým otázkám mezinárodního práva soukromého* [*To Some Developmental Questions of the Private International Law*]. 1st ed. Brno: Masarykova univerzita, 2013.

Rozehnalová, N. et al., *Mezinárodní právo soukromé Evropské unie (Nařízení Řím I, Nařízení Řím II, Nařízení Brusel I)* [*Private international law of the European Union (Regulation Rome I, Regulation Rome II, Regulation Brussels I)*]. 1st ed. Praha: Wolters Kluwer.

Rozehnalová, N. *Instituty českého mezinárodního práva soukromého* [*Institutions of the Czech Private International Law*, in Czech]. Prague: Wolters Kluwer 2016, 272 p.

Valdhans, J. & K. Drličková, a kol. *Rozhodování Soudního dvora EU ve věcech uznání a výkonu cizího soudního rozhodnutí (Analýza rozhodnutí dle Nařízení Brusel Ibis)* [*Decision Making of the European Court of Justice in the Matters of Recognition and Enforcement of Judgments (Analysis of the Decisions According to the Brussel Ibis Regulation)*]. Brno: Masarykova univerzita, 2015.

Articles, chapters in monographs and collections of papers

Bělohlávek, A. 'Importance of the Seat of Arbitration in International Arbitration: Delocalization and Denationalization of Arbitration As an Outdated Myth'. *ASA Bulletin*, 31, 42 (2013): 262–292.

Bělohlávek, A. 'Public Policy and Public Interest in International Law and EU Law'. In *CYIL – Czech Yearbook of International Law,* Vol. III. Huntington, New York: JurisPublishing Inc., 2012, 117–147.

Bělohlávek, A. 'Recognition and Enforcement of Foreign Arbitral Awards: The Application of The New York Convention by National Courts – Czech Republic'. *The Lawyer Quarterly,* Praha no. 2 (2014): 91–107.

Bělohlávek, A. 'The Law Applicable to the Arbitration Agreement and the Arbitrability of a Dispute'. In *Yearbook on International Arbitration,* edited by M. Roth & M. Geistlinger, Vol. III. Antverpen/Zurich/Wien: Intersentia 2013, 27–57.

Brodec, J. 'Determination of Applicable law in International Insolvency Proceedings'. In *European and National Perspectives on the Application of the European Insolvency Regulation*, edited by I. Queirolo & S. Dominelli. Aracne, Scritti di diritto privato europeo e internazionale, ISBN: 978-88-255-0906-9, 83–103.

Brodec, Jan, Monika Pauknerová & Magdalena Pfeiffer 'International Insolvency Law in the Czech Legal System'. In *European and National Perspectives on the Application of the European Insolvency Regulation*, edited by Ilaria Queirolo & Stefano Dominelli. 1st ed. Aracne, 2017, 257–272.

Drličková, K. & I. Rohová 'Habitual Residence as a Single Connecting Factor under the Succession Regulation'. In *Scientific Cooperations. Scientific Cooperations Workshops on Social Sciences*. Ankara: Scientific Cooperations, 2015, 371–381.

Drličková, K. *Cofola International 2015: Current Challenges to Resolution of International (Cross-border) Disputes: Conference Proceedings*. Brno: Masaryk University, 2015. ISBN 978-80-210-8020-1.

Drličková, K. 'Confidentiality of the Materials Used in the Course of Arbitral Proceedings'. In *Czech (and Central European) Yearbook of Arbitration: Conduct of Arbitration*, edited by Alexander J. Bělohlávek & Naděžda Rozehnalová. The Hague: LexLata, 2017, 45–66.

Drličková, K. 'Deletion of the Arbitration Exception in the Regulation Brussels I – The Way Towards the European Regulation of Arbitration?' In *Harmonization and Unification of Law in the European Context*. Bratislava: Comenius University in Bratislava, Faculty of Law, 2011, 247–258.

Drličková, K. 'Interpretation of the CISG'. In *COFOLA International,* edited by Klára Drličková, Tereza Kyselovská & David Sehnálek. Brno: Masarykova univerzita, 2014, 85–106.

Drličková, K. 'Law Applicable to Arbitration Agreement – "Lex Arbitri" or "Lex Causae" of the Principal Contract?' In *Czech (& Central European Yearbook of Arbitration),* edited by Černý Bělohlávek & Rozehnalová, Vol. III. New York: JurisNet, LLC, 2013, 71–87.

Drličková, K. 'Legal Basis of Parties' Duty to Maintain Confidentiality in International Commercial Arbitration'. In *COFOLA International 2016: Conference Proceedings*, edited by K. Drličková & T. Kyselovská. Brno: Masarykova univerzita, 2016, 21–37.

Drličková, K. 'Multiple Places of Performance in Cross-Border Commercial Contracts: Problems with International Jurisdiction'. In *Evolution of Private Law*, edited by E. Zielińska & P. Pinior. Katowice: Wydawnictwo Uniwersytetu Ślaskiego, 2014, 19–32.

Drličková, K. 'Prorogation under the New Brussels I Regulation'. In *Cross-border Civil Proceedings in the EU*, edited by V. Rijavec & T. Ivanc. Maribor: Univerza v Mariboru, Pravna fakulteta, 2012, 97–110.

Drličková, K. 'Experience with the Application of Article 5(1) of Brussels I Regulation before Czech Courts'. In *Proceedings of the 2nd International Conference on European Integration 2014*, edited by I. Honová et al., Ostrava: VŠB – Technical University of Ostrava, 2014, 102–109.

Elischer, D., O. Frinta & M. Pauknerová 'Recodification of Private Law in the Czech Republic'. In *The Scope and Structure of Civil Codes*, edited by J.C. Rivera. Dordrecht: Springer, 2013, 105–132.

Elischer, D., O. Frinta & M. Pauknerová 'Private Law'. *The Lawyer Quarterly* 2 no. 2. (2012): 69–107.

Feigerlová, M. & M. Pauknerová 'Private International Law for Corporate Social Responsibility'. *The Lawyer Quarterly*. č. 4 (2018): 379–399.

Kozárek, T. 'Refusal of Recognition of Judgements in Civil and Commercial Matters Based on Public Order in European Judicial Area – Can We Define European Public Order?' *Humanities and Social Science Review* [online] 7, no. 1 (2017): 351–355. [cit. 2017]. ISSN 2165-6258. Available at: http://www.universitypublications.net/hssr/0701/html/S7Y154.xml.

Kyselovská, T. 'Arbitrability of Intellectual Property Rights Disputes'. In *Czech (& Central European) Yearbook of Arbitration*, edited by Alexander J. Belohlávek. Huntington, NY: JurisNet, LLC, 2016.

Kyselovská, T. 'Interaction of Intellectual Property Rights and Private International Law: Need for a Common Approach and Solutions'. *Law and Forensics Science* no. 11 (2016): 129–137.

Kyselovská, T. 'Online Cross-Border (Consumer) Contracts from the Point of View of the Case-law of the Court of Justice of the EU'. In *COFOLA International 2017. Resolution of International Disputes (Conference Proceedings)*, edited by K. Drličková & T. Kyselovská. Brno: Masaryk University, 2017, 78–92.

Kyselovská, T. 'Recognition and Enforcement of Judgments under the Brussels I Regulation in the Czech Republic'. In *2nd International Conference on European Integration 2014*. Ostrava: VŠB – Technical University of Ostrava, 2014.

Pauknerová, M. 'EU Regulations and International Conventions – Shifts in Time'. In *Between Brussels and The Hague. Essays on the International and Regional Unification of Private International Law*. Barcelona, 2013, 671–684.

Pauknerová, M. 'Czech Republic – Treatment of Foreign Law in the Czech Republic'. In *Treatment of Foreign law – Dynamics Towards Convergence?* edited by Y. Nishitani. Springer Verlag, 2017, 113–129.

Pauknerová, M. 'Czech Republic'. In *Encyclopedia of Private International Law*, edited by Jürgen Basedow et al., 1st ed. 1–4. Cheltenham: Edward Elgar Publishing Limited, 2017, 2008–2019.

Pauknerová, M. 'Defendants with Unknown Address. In *Essays in Honour of Michael Bogdan*, edited by Patrik Lindskoug, 1st ed. Lund: Författarna och Juristförlaget i Lund, 2013, 411–424.

Pauknerová, M. 'Escape Clauses and Legal Certainty in Private International Law'. *Yearbook of Private International Law*, 2018, 61–82.

Pauknerová, M. 'La nueva Ley de Derecho ìnternacional privado de la República Checa. Observaciones introductorias'. *Revista Española de Derecho Internacional* 66, no. 2 (2014): 348–393.

Pauknerová, M. 'Private International Law As a Necessary Component of Private Law in a Modern Society'. In *Rule of Law and Mechanism of its Protection*, edited by L. Pítrová, 1st ed. Waldkirchen: rw&w Science & New Media Passau-Berlin-Prague, 2015, 167–180.

Pauknerová, M. 'Proof of and Information About Foreign Law'. *The Lawyer Quarterly* 5, no. 4 (2015): 246–260.

Pauknerová, M. 'Some Remarks on the Treatment of Foreign Law in Arbitration'. In *Rozprawy z prawa prywatnego: Ksega jubileuszowa dedykowana Profesorowi Wojciechowi Popiolkowi*. 1st ed. Warsaw: Wolters Kluwer Polska, 2017, 961–972.

Pauknerová, M. 'UNIDROIT Principles and Czech Law'. In *Eppur si muove: The Age of Uniform Law: Essays in Honour of Michael Joachim Bonell to Celebrate His 70th birthday*, Vol 2. 1st ed. Rome: UNIDROIT, 2016, 1583–1592.

Pauknerová, M. 'Unilateral Juridical Acts and Uniform Conflict of Law Rules'. *The Journal of Comparative Law* 6, no. 1 (2011): 115–126.

Pauknerová, M. 'International Jurisdiction of a Court and the Law Applicable to a Share Transfer Agreement'. In *Europa als Rechts- und Lebensraum, Liber Amicorum für Christian Kohler*, edited by B. Hess, E. Jayme & H.-P. Mansel. Bielefeld: Gieseking Verlag, 2018, 385–392.

Pauknerová, M. & J. Brodec 'Czech Republic and Slovakia'. In *Application of Foreign Law*, edited by Carlos Esplugues, 1st ed. Munich: Sellier, 2011, 173–183.

Pauknerová, M., J. Brodec & M. Pfeiffer 'Czech Republic'. In *Civil and Commercial Mediation in Europe, vol. I National Mediation Rules and Procedures*, edited by José Luis Iglesias Buhigues & Guillermo Palao Moreno, 1st ed. Mortsel (Antwerpen): Intersentia, 2012, 97–130.

Pauknerová, M. & M. Pfeiffer 'Czech Republic'. In *International Surrogacy Arrangements: Legal Regulation at the International Level*, edited by Paul Beaumont & Trimmings. Oxford: Katarina Hart Publishing, 2013, 105–117.

Pauknerová, M. & M. Pfeiffer 'Act on Mediation – Significant Step on a Long Way to Make Mediation Work in the Czech Republic'. In *New Developments in Civil and Commercial Mediation: Global Comparative Perspective*, edited by Carlos Esplugues & Louis Marquis, 1st ed. Springer, 2015, 225–244.

Pauknerová, M. & M. Pfeiffer 'International Aspects of Mediation (from a Czech Law Perspective)'. *Essays in honour of Spyridon Vl. Vrellis*, 1st ed. Athene: Nomiki Bibliothiki, 2014, 763–775.

Pauknerová, M. & M. Pfeiffer 'Mediation, More Particularly Cross-Border and Judicial Mediation'. *The Lawyer Quarterly* 5, no. 2 (2015): 116–132.

Pauknerová, M. & M. Pfeiffer 'The New Act on Private International Law in the Czech Republic: Starting Points and Perspectives within the European Union'. *Journal of Private International Law* 10, no. 2 (2014): 205–226.

Pauknerová, M., M. Pfeiffer & J. Brodec 'Czech Republic'. In *Civil and Commercial Mediation in Europe, vol. II Cross-Border Mediation,* edited by Carlos Esplugues Mota, 1st ed. Cambridge: Intersentia, 2014, 125–138.

Pauknerová, M. & H. Skalská 'Enforcement and Effectiveness of Consumer Law in the Czech Republic'. *The Lawyer Quarterly* 7 no. 4 (2017): 243–254.

Pauknerová, M., M. Zavadilová & J. Grygar 'Czech Republic'. In *Cross-Border Litigation in Europe*, edited by P. Beaumont et al., 1st ed. Oxford: Hart Publishing, 2017, 285–294.

Pauknerová, M. & H. Skalská 'Enforcement and Effectiveness of Consumer Law in the Czech Republic'. In *Enforcement and Effectiveness of Consumer Law*, edited by H.W. Micklitz & G. Saumier. Springer Verlag, 2018, 227–248.

Pauknerová, M. & M. Pfeiffer 'Use of UNIDROIT Principles of International Commercial Contracts to Interpret or Supplement Czech Contract Law'. *The Lawyer Quarterly*. č. 4 (2018): 452–468.

Pauknerová, M. 'Réflexions sur la Convention de Bruxelles du point de vue tchèque – Reflections on the Brussels Convention from the Czech perspective'. *Revue critique de droit international privé*, 3 (2018): 529–540.

Pauknerová, M. & J. Brodec 'Czech Republic'. In *Private International Law of Companies in Europe*, edited by C. Gerner-Beuerle et al., Munich: C.H.Beck 2019, 340–365.

Pfeiffer, M. 'Choice of Law in International Family and Succession Law'. *The Lawyer Quarterly* 2, no. 1 (2012): 291–305.

Pfeiffer, M. 'Czech Republic'. In *The Evidentiary Effects of Authentic Acts in the Member States of the European Union, in the Context of Successions*: *Study for the JURI Committee*, edited by Paul Beaumont, Jonathan Fitchen & Jayne Holliday, 1st ed. Brussels: European Parliament. Directorate-General for Internal Policies, 2016, 90–97.

Pfeiffer, M. 'La solución salomónica en las normas de conflicto de leyes aplicables para la cuestión previa en el derecho internacional privado checo'. *Anuario Español de Derecho Internacional Privado* 2016, no. 16 (2016): 565–588.

Rozehnalová, N. & J. Valdhans 'Overriding Mandatory Rules, Rules of Safety, Protective Mandatory Rules and Other Limits on Application of Law Determined by Conflict-of-Law Rules under the Rome I and Rome II Regulations'. In *Free Movement of Goods and Persons Across the Polish – Czech – Slovak Borders*. 2012. Katowice: Oficina Wydawnicza, 2012, 49–63.

Uhlířová, P. 'New Private International Law in the Czech Republic'. *Yearbook of Private International Law* 16 (2014/2015): 469–510.

Valdhans, J. et al., 'Civil Law Consequences of Corruption in International Commercial Contracts'. *The Lawyer Quarterly* 4, no. 2 (2014): 155–168.

Valdhans, J. & T. Kyselovská 'Selected Issues of Recognition and Enforcement of Foreign Judgments from the Perspective of EU Member'. In *24th Conference*

Selected Bibliography

Corporate Entities at the Market and European Dimensions, 19th, 20th and 21st May 2016, Faculty of Law University of Maribor and Institute Of Business Law Maribor, Portorož, Slovenija, 2016, edited by V. Rijavec. Maribor: University of Maribor Press, 2016, 157–172.

Zavadilová, L. 'Adaptation of Rights in Rem According to the EU Regulation on Matrimonial Property Regimes'. In *Studia Juridica Et Politica Jaurinensis*. Győr, Hungary: Deák Ferenc Faculty of Law, Széchenyi István University 4, no. 2 (2017): 55–68.

Principal EC/EU Regulations in the field of Private International Law

Regulation No. 1346/2000 on Insolvency Proceedings, OJ 2000 L 160, p. 1 (Insolvency Regulation).

Regulation No. 44/2001 on Jurisdiction and the Recognition and Enforcement of Judgments in Civil and Commercial Matters, OJ 2001 L 12, p. 1 (Regulation Brussels I).

Regulation No. 1206/2001 on Cooperation Between the Courts of the Member States in the Taking of Evidence in Civil or Commercial Matters, OJ 2001 L 174, p. 1.

Regulation No. 2201/2003 Concerning Jurisdiction and the Recognition and Enforcement of Judgments in Matrimonial Matters and the Matters of Parental Responsibility, OJ 2003 L 338, p. 1 (Regulation Brussels II*bis*).

Regulation No. 805/2004 Creating a European Enforcement Order for Uncontested Claims, OJ 2004 L 143, p. 15.

Regulation No. 1896/2006 Creating a European Order for Payment Procedure, OJ 2006 L 399, p. 1.

Regulation No. 861/2007 Establishing a European Small Claims Procedure, OJ 2007 L 199, p. 1.

Regulation No. 864/2007 on the Law Applicable to Non-contractual Obligations, OJ 2007 L 199, p. 40 (Regulation Rome II).

Regulation No. 1393/2007 on the Service in the Member States of Judicial and Extrajudicial Documents in Civil and Commercial Matters (Service of Documents), and Repealing Council Regulation No. 1348/2000, OJ 2007 L 324, p. 79.

Regulation No. 593/2008 on the Law Applicable to Contractual Obligations, OJ 2008 L 177, p. 6 (Regulation Rome I).

Regulation No. 4/2009 on Jurisdiction, Applicable Law, Recognition and Enforcement of Decisions and Cooperation in Matters relating to Maintenance Obligations, OJ 2009 L 7, p. 1 (Maintenance Regulation).

Regulation No. 650/2012 on Jurisdiction, Applicable Law, Recognition and Enforcement of Decisions and Acceptance and Enforcement of Authentic Instruments in Matters of Succession and on the Creation of a European Certificate of Succession, OJ 2012 L 201, p. 107 (Succession Regulation).

Regulation No. 1215/2012 on Jurisdiction and the Recognition and Enforcement of Judgments in Civil and Commercial Matters (recast), OJ 2012 L 351, p. 1 (Brussels I Recast).

Principal EC/EU Regulations in the field of Private International Law

Regulation No. 655/2014 Establishing a European Account Preservation Order Procedure to Facilitate Cross-Border Debt Recovery in Civil and Commercial Matters, OJ 2014 L 189, p. 59.

Regulation No. 2015/848 on Insolvency Proceedings (Recast), OJ 2015 L 141, p. 19 (Insolvency Regulation Recast).

Regulation No. 2015/2421 Amending Regulation (EC) No. 861/2007 Establishing a European Small Claims Procedure and Regulation (EC) No. 1896/2006 Creating a European Order for Payment Procedure, OJ 2015 L 341, p. 1.

Regulation No. 2016/1103 Implementing Enhanced Cooperation in the Area of Jurisdiction, Applicable Law and the Recognition and Enforcement of Decisions in Matters of Matrimonial Property Regimes, OJ 2016 L 183, p. 1 (Matrimonial Property Regimes Regulation).

Regulation No. 2016/1104 Implementing Enhanced Cooperation in the Area of Jurisdiction, Applicable Law and the Recognition and Enforcement of Decisions in Matters of the Property Consequences of Registered Partnerships, OJ 2016 L 183, p. 30 (Registered Partnerships Property Regulation).

Regulation No. 2016/1191 on Promoting the Free Movement of Citizens by Simplifying the Requirements for Presenting Certain Public Documents in the European Union and Amending Regulation (EU) No. 1024/2012, OJ 2016 L 200, p. 1 (Public Documents Regulation).

Index

The numbers here refer to paragraph numbers.

Index

Index

Made in the USA
Monee, IL
18 October 2026

66041392R10111